DATE

fun with the family

Colorado

Praise for the *Fun with the Family* series

"Enables parents to turn family travel into an exploration."
—Alexandra Kennedy, Editor, *Family Fun*

"Bound to lead you and your kids to fun-filled days, those times that help compose the
memories of childhood."
—Dorothy Jordon, *Family Travel Times*

Help Us Keep This Guide Up to Date

We would love to hear from you concerning your experiences with this guide and how you feel it could be improved and kept up to date. Please send your comments and suggestions to:

editorial@GlobePequot.com

Thanks for your input, and happy travels!

fun with the family
Colorado

hundreds of ideas for day trips with the kids

Seventh Edition

Doris Kennedy

gpp®

travel

Guilford, Connecticut

All the information in this guidebook is subject to change. We recommend that you call ahead to obtain current information before traveling.

Copyright © 2010 Morris Book Publishing, LLC

Editor: Amy Lyons
Project Editor: Lynn Zelem
Layout: Joanna Beyer
Text Design: Nancy Freeborn and Linda R. Loiewski
Maps: Rusty Nelson © Morris Book Publishing, LLC
Spot photography throughout © Photodisc and © RubberBall Productions

ISSN 1543-1231
ISBN 978-0-7627-5710-7

Printed in the United States of America
10 9 8 7 6 5 4 3 2 1

Contents

Dedication

This book is dedicated to my husband, best friend, and fellow traveler, professional photographer Gary Kennedy, who patiently encouraged and consoled me through research and deadlines; to my wonderful dad, James Clark, who blessed me with sensitivity, honesty, and an endless love for animals; and to my forever friends whose steadfast support I can never repay.

About the Author

Doris Kennedy has fifteen travel guidebooks to her credit and is co-author of five others. She and her professional photographer husband, Gary Kennedy, travel throughout the world in search of stories and photographs for publication in regional and national magazines and in the travel sections of major newspapers. Her weekly travel column appeared in the travel section of the *Denver Post* (circulation 800,000) for ten years. Her work earned a first prize award for *Fun with the Family Colorado* from Colorado's most prestigious writers' organization, the Colorado Authors' League. She is a member of the Society of American Travel Writers, the American Society of Journalists and Authors, and the Colorado Authors' League. Doris and her family have traveled the state extensively. She still lives and writes in Colorado and teaches English as a Second Language in the Denver area.

Introduction

I have lived in Colorado for more than forty years and have traveled extensively throughout the state. After visiting nearly every city, town, resort, attraction, park, and nook and cranny, I am delighted to share my finds with you. In this book you will discover where to dig for dinosaur bones, ski on sand dunes, walk through ancient cliff dwellings, fish in Gold Medal waters (the designation given to only the highest quality trout habitats), find Buffalo Bill's grave, slide down snow-covered mountains on custom-made tubes, go dog sledding, ski downhill and cross-country, and visit Santa's North Pole almost any day of the year. You will find family-friendly lodging and eateries, encounter an alligator farm, and explore a gold mine, underground caves, and a bug museum. I hope you enjoy *Fun with the Family Colorado*. It was written with you and your family in mind.

HOW TO USE THIS BOOK

A tremendous amount of travel, research, and thought have gone into the writing of this book, making it comprehensive but by no means all-inclusive. New activities, attractions, accommodations, and eateries continually sprout up; therefore, you will find some pleasant surprises along your journey. If you discover something of interest that I have missed and you think other families would appreciate knowing about, please let me know by writing to the publisher. Also, proprietors will change their days and hours of operation according to how good business is or how much snowfall there has been. It is imperative that you phone in advance of your travels to ensure that items of interest to you as stated in this book are still available.

For your ease the state has been divided into five sections: Metropolitan Denver and Suburbs, Northeastern, Southeastern, Northwestern, and Southwestern. You will find a map at the beginning of each chapter pinpointing the towns mentioned in that chapter, plus lists of the best attractions and festivals for that part of the state. At the back of the book is an alphabetical index of all places and attractions.

In many areas within the state of Colorado, callers must dial ten digits (the area code plus the regular number) when making local phone calls. All numbers with a 303 or 720 prefix are in this category. The 970-prefix communities of Berthoud, Dillon, Estes Park, Frisco, Greeley, La Salle, Mead, Platteville, and Wiggins also require ten-digit dialing for local calls. Regions with a 719 area code are not affected by this new system.

I have listed lodging and dining recommendations that I feel are appropriate for families. Please keep in mind, however, that in most locations there are many additional options.

COLORADO

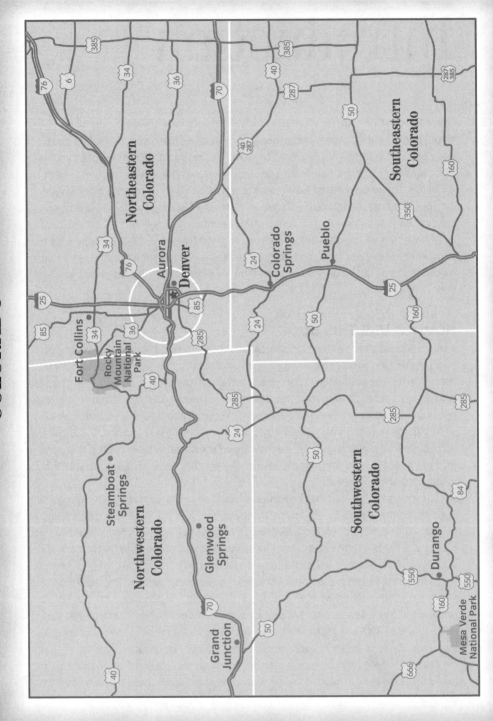

Rather than give dollar amounts for the cost of attractions, activities, lodging, and dining, I have used the following guide:

Rates for Accommodations

(one-night stay for two adults)

$	up to $75
$$	from $75.01 to $125
$$$	from $125.01 to $175
$$$$	more than $175

Rates for Restaurants

(one complete adult meal)

$	up to $10
$$	from $10.01 to $15
$$$	from $15.01 to $20
$$$$	most more than $20

Attractions and Activities

(per adult; fees for children are often less)

$	up to $7
$$	from $7.01 to $12
$$$	from $12.01 to $20
$$$$	more than $20
Free	if there is no charge

WILDLIFE AND YOUR FAMILY

First let me say that Colorado wildlife rarely attack humans unless threatened, surprised, or bothered in some way. That said, it's important to know that when you are hiking or picnicking in the high country, or even in semi residential urban areas, there is a chance of meeting up with dangerous animals.

Coloradans and visitors to Colorado spend a good deal of their time outdoors. For that reason, it is important to know what to do if you encounter a mountain lion, bear, fox, or coyote. All of Colorado is considered mountain lion country. To lessen the hazard of meeting up with a mountain lion when hiking, especially at dawn or dusk, always make a lot of noise. Talk loudly, shout once in a while, or even carry and ring a "bear bell," available at most large sporting-goods stores.

I know it is frightening to think about but mountain lions are attracted to children because of their size. Keep your children close to you when in the wilderness and don't let them wander off the trail.

Here are some suggestions from the Colorado Division of Wildlife for your serious consideration:

Do not turn your back on or run from a mountain lion. Make yourself appear as large as possible by putting a small child on your shoulders, raising your hands into the air, or lifting your coat above your head. This will tend to intimidate the lion and it will retreat. If it does attack, fight it off with anything you can get hold of, including your fists. This has worked successfully.

You are unlikely to encounter a black bear because it will become aware of you and run off before you see it. If you should meet up with a bear, however, stop and slowly back away. Again, try to appear as large as possible by opening up your jacket and spreading

Colorado
FastFacts

Colorado: A Spanish word meaning red.

Population: Approximately 5 million.

Nickname: Centennial State (admitted to the Union in 1876).

Highest Point: Mt. Elbert at 14,433 feet.

State Flower: The lavender-and-white Rocky Mountain columbine, adopted in 1899.

State Bird: Lark bunting, designated in 1931.

State Song: "Where the Columbines Grow" by A. J. Flynn, adopted in 1915.

State Animal: Rocky Mountain bighorn sheep, designated in 1961.

State Tree: Colorado blue spruce, adopted in 1939.

State Fossil: Stegosaurus, designated in 1982.

State Insect: Colorado hair streak butterfly, adopted in 1996.

it above your head. What to do if it attacks is controversial. Some say to lie down, do not move, and pretend to be dead. Others say to fight back. The best idea is to make as much noise as possible when you enter their environment in order to frighten them away.

Coyotes and fox, although usually cautious around humans, do attack small pets and have been known to attack children. Advice from the Colorado Division of Wildlife: "Carry a walking stick or staff with you. You can convert it to a weapon if necessary. Always be aggressive if you come across a coyote or fox. Throw things at it, rocks, your water bottle, anything other than food."

Please don't let these warnings discourage you from enjoying Colorado's mountain country and wilderness. My husband and I, like thousands of others, have hiked alone in the Colorado wilderness and have never seen a mountain lion, bear, fox, or coyote. It just makes good sense, however, to remember that your best defense against dangerous wildlife is to be informed and to be consistently aware of your surroundings.

Neither the author nor the publisher will be held responsible for injury or harm resulting from any activity described in this book. Care should be taken and rules followed when traveling in the backcountry or engaging in recreational activities. When traveling to high-altitude areas, it is advisable to gradually (over a period of several days) ascend to your destination. For instance, plan to stay a day or two in Denver, at a 5,280-foot altitude, before continuing on to an altitude of 8,000 or more feet so that your body can adjust to the higher elevation.

Attractions Key

The following is a key to the icons found throughout the text.

SWIMMING		FOOD	
BOATING/BOAT TOUR		LODGING	
HISTORIC SITE		CAMPING	
HIKING/WALKING		MUSEUM	
FISHING		PERFORMING ARTS	
BIKING		SPORTS/ATHLETICS	
AMUSEMENT PARK		PICNICKING	
HORSEBACK RIDING		PLAYGROUND	
SKIING/WINTER SPORTS		SHOPPING	
PARK		PLANTS/GARDENS/NATURE TRAILS	
ANIMAL VIEWING		FARM	

Metropolitan Denver and Suburbs

The Denver area is often mistakenly considered to be in the mountains when, actually, it is against the foothills, along the front range of the Rocky Mountains. The climate is also often misunderstood. To be sure, the region is blanketed with a heavy snow now and then throughout the winter, but it lies just east of a high mountain barrier and far distant from any moisture source, resulting in a mild and arid climate. Annual precipitation ranges between 8 and 15 inches (about the same as Los Angeles), and Denver area residents bask in approximately 300 days of sunshine a year—more annual hours of sun than received by residents of San Diego, Honolulu, or Miami Beach. When snow does fall, it usually melts within a few days.

TopPicks in Denver and the Suburbs

- **Butterfly Pavilion and Insect Center**, Westminster
- **Children's Museum of Denver**
- **Denver Firefighters Museum**, Denver
- **Denver Museum of Nature and Science**, Denver
- **Denver Zoo**, Denver
- **Elitch Gardens Amusement Park**, Denver
- **Four Mile Historic Park**, Denver
- **Littleton Historical Museum**, Littleton
- **The Wildlife Experience**, Parker
- **Wings Over the Rockies Air & Space Museum**, Denver

METROPOLITAN DENVER AND SUBURBS

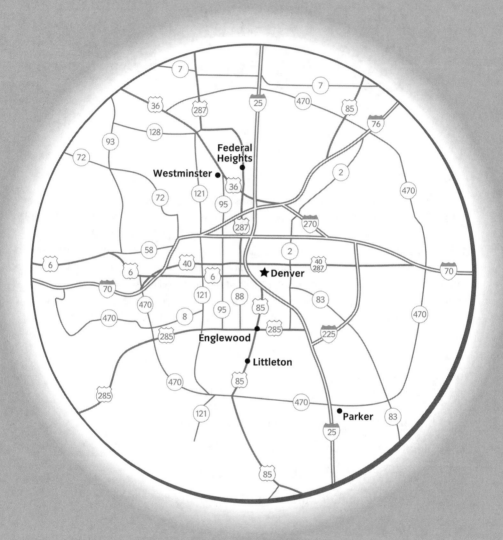

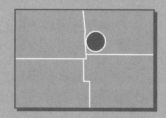

Denver

Home to a world-class amusement park and a 50,000-seat baseball stadium in the center of the city, Denver boasts more than 200 parks and four major-league sports teams: the NHL Stanley Cup-winning Avalanche, NFL Super Bowl champions the Denver Broncos, the NBA Nuggets, and the National League Colorado Rockies. The Denver International Airport is deemed to be the safest, most high-tech air facility in the world.

Colorado State Capitol Building (ages 5 and up)

1475 Sherman St.; (303) 866-2604 or (303) 866-4747; www.colorado.gov/dpa/doit/archives/ cap/contents.htm. Tours available year-round. Sept through May, Mon through Fri, 9:15 a.m. to 2:30 p.m.; June through Aug, Mon through Fri, 9 a.m. to 2:30 p.m. Tours take about 45 minutes. Dome tours are given every hour from 9 a.m. to 2 p.m. Mon through Fri. Reservations are recommended. Call (303) 866-3834. Free.

Elegance prevails at Colorado's State Capitol Building, where priceless wainscoting of rose-onyx marble sheaths the walls; bronze work glistens on stairway balusters and at the base of floor-to-ceiling pillars; rich woods glow under glittering chandeliers; and striking, hand-painted murals tell the history of Colorado in picture and verse.

Construction began in 1886 and took twenty-two years to complete. The dome was originally covered in copper, but when citizens complained that copper was not a primary metal in the state, Colorado miners contributed a total of 200 ounces of pure gold to cover its surface.

Amazing
Denver Facts

Due to its elevation of 5,280 feet, Denver is known as the "Mile High City." Consequently, visitors to the state capitol often photograph the step on the west side of the building, which is marked as being one mile above sea level. In 1969, however, students from the engineering school at Colorado State University found the measurement to be incorrect. As a result of their finding, a geodetic survey plug was placed three steps above the original marker and now serves as the accurate "mile high" designation.

The Colorado rose-onyx marble wainscoting, located throughout the capitol building, contains more than a thousand designs that resemble animals, objects, and faces of famous people. Among those easily recognized are George Washington, Molly Brown (Denver socialite and *Titanic* heroine), and Franklin Delano Roosevelt.

Getting around **Denver**

Two standouts in Denver's public transportation system can make getting around town easy—and fun! Regional Transportation District (RTD) information, (303) 299-6000; www.rtd-denver.com.

Light Rail

Light rail began service in 1994. The Central Corridor line runs right through downtown. On Denver's south side, a large Park-n-Ride at I-25 and Broadway makes it easy for riders to leave their cars (**free** parking). Purchase train tickets from vending machines at the station. The tracks are ground level, and trains come every ten minutes midday, every six minutes during rush hour. Consider riding it with your children just to let them experience another form of transportation.

16th Street Mall Shuttle

It's **free**—and frequent! The shuttle runs along the otherwise free-of-traffic pedestrian mall, from the Civic Center to LoDo (lower downtown). The electric buses are scheduled so closely that there's usually one in sight. So if the kids start to whine about too much walking as you sightsee along the mall, just hop on the shuttle.

Although preschool children may not be thrilled with touring the State Capitol Building, those ages 5 and above usually are impressed by the splendor. They are sure to enjoy the challenge of climbing the ninety-three stairs, beginning on the third floor, to the gleaming gold dome rising 272 feet above the ground. From here they will get a wonderful bird's-eye view of the entire city and the Rocky Mountains beyond.

The elevator, which serves all levels except the dome, is located in the east wing behind the rotunda. There are a cafeteria and souvenir shop in the basement. The stairway to the basement is behind the grand staircase in the center rotunda.

Free forty-five-minute tours begin at the tour desk near the north entrance (Colfax Avenue) on the first floor. Or ask for a Visitor's Guide at the desk and explore on your own.

Colorado History Museum (ages 6 and up)

Long a popular stop for Coloradans and out-of-state visitors, the Colorado History Museum will be closed until the summer of 2012, at which time it will reopen in a stunning new structure at the corner of 12th Street and Broadway Avenue, a few blocks south of its former location. Museum patrons can look forward to outstanding exhibits, realistically detailed dioramas, historic photographs, fascinating artifacts, and family-oriented special events.

Denver Public Library (all ages)

10 West 14th Ave. Parkway and Broadway; (702) 865-1111; www.denverlibrary.org. Open Mon and Tues 10 a.m. to 8 p.m., Wed through Fri 10 a.m. to 6 p.m., Sat 9 a.m. to 5 p.m., Sun 1 to 5 p.m. Free.

Designed to reflect the shapes and colors of other buildings around Civic Center Park, the seven-story Denver Public Library houses 1.5 million books on 47 miles of shelves and includes a world-class western history and art collection. Once a day, a free one-hour tour gives visitors an overview of the facility. An orientation video runs continuously near the east entry.

The children's section of the library has a self-guided tour laid out as an adventure game. Ask the librarian for a map to follow. Check the library's Web site for a schedule of "Super Saturdays" family events, such as Stuart the Balloony Magician, musical programs, and Fairy Tale Theatre productions.

Denver Art Museum (all ages)

100 West 14th Ave. Parkway; (720) 865-5000; www.denverartmuseum.org. Open Tues through Thurs 10 a.m. to 5 p.m., Fri 10 a.m. to 10 p.m., Sat 10 a.m. to 5 p.m., Sun noon to 5 p.m. $.

Easy to spot, this building has been described as an Italian castle wrapped in aluminum foil. Two seven-story towers, plus a $1.1 million spectacular addition, display the largest

Home Cookin' **Down on the Farm**

White Fence Farm, 6263 West Jewell Ave., Lakewood (between Sheridan and Wadsworth Boulevards, just twenty minutes from downtown Denver); (303) 935-5945; www.whitefencefarm.com. Open Tues through Sat 4:30 to 8:30 p.m. and Sun 11:30 a.m. to 8 p.m. Closed Mon and the month of Jan.

The motto of the White Fence Farm restaurant in Lakewood, a western suburb of Denver, is "The best food in town is down on the farm." And so is one of the nicest dining experiences. Come early, give your name to the hostess, and then stroll the beautifully landscaped grounds. Let your children climb the ladder to a handsome Bavarian-style tree house with shutters, flower boxes, and shake roof. Walk through the trellised rose arbors, sit a spell in the gazebo, or borrow a croquet set for a game before dinner. Then take your children to the OK Corral to see the chickens, goats, horse, cow, and woolly sheep. Step into the Country Cottage for a memento or two. And when you are called to dinner, sit down to a family-style meal of delicious fried chicken, salads, mashed potatoes and gravy, and homemade pies like only Grandma could make. This is like Sunday dinner used to be, but you don't have to do the dishes.

The Persistent **Penny**

Although the one-cent coin is often looked upon as a nuisance, there was a time when a kid with a penny in his pocket would excitedly run to the corner grocery store seeking the glass display case filled with more than a dozen tempting varieties of "penny candy." While the grocery clerk waited, it could take five to ten minutes for the child to make a choice.

True, the penny sucker and penny root beer barrel have gone the way of the penny postcard and the penny postage stamp, but the small, copper coin continues to endure.

When the United States Mint was created in 1792, one of the first coins made was the one-cent piece depicting a woman with wind-blown hair who symbolized liberty and freedom. Larger than today's penny, it was made of 100 percent copper.

In 1857, the penny was redesigned to reveal a flying eagle on the obverse (front) and an olive wreath on the reverse (back).

A smaller one-cent coin featuring the profile of an American Indian on the front and an olive wreath on the back was released in 1864, followed by the first Lincoln Head penny in 1909. Designed to commemorate the 100th anniversary of President Abraham Lincoln's birth, a profile of Lincoln was on the obverse and wheat sheaves were on the reverse.

Fifty years later, in 1959, a replica of the Lincoln Memorial in Washington, D.C. replaced the reverse wheat sheaves, while the Lincoln profile on the obverse remained the same.

During 2009, in honor of the bicentennial of Lincoln's birth, the United States Mints in Denver, Colorado, and Philadelphia, Pennsylvania, issued a total of four different penny coins. All four retained the same Lincoln profile on the obverse while each one revealed a different segment of Lincoln's life on the reverse.

One of the four coins portrayed Lincoln's early childhood spent in Kentucky. The second displayed Lincoln as a frontier farm boy living in Indiana. The third version of the series revealed Lincoln's professional years when he lived in Illinois, and the fourth represented his presidency years in Washington, D.C. These distinctly different Lincoln Pennies were produced only during the year 2009.

The current Lincoln Penny was designed in 2010. The obverse portrait of Lincoln remains the same as in previous years, and the reverse commemorates President Abraham Lincoln's dedication to the restoration and preservation of the United States of America as one united country.

Perhaps the little one-cent piece no longer purchases much, even at the candy counter, but it does have a lengthy history and it is the longest running coin series.

The coin-producing United States Mint in Denver and the one in Philadelphia are each capable of striking 1,040 pennies per second and 30 million pennies per day, with each coin expected to remain in circulation for approximately 30 years. The number of pennies in circulation at any one time is estimated to be 150 billion and, although it looks as though the penny will remain with us for many years to come, it's probably not likely that any one of those 150 billion pennies will ever again be held as tightly and with as much anticipation as the one in the pocket of a small child on his way to the corner grocery store so many years ago.

art collection between Kansas City and the West Coast. This family-friendly museum offers an amazing array of **free** activities for children. On the second Wed of each month, children ages 3 to 5 can drop in to create an art project, listen to story time, and go on a scavenger hunt. **Free** family activities are located in every gallery and on every floor. Watch for Seymour, the Family Programs mascot who likes to lead the way to kid-friendly places within the museum. More **free** things especially for kids include the Just for Fun Family Center, the Kids Corner, Family Backpacks, Art Tubes, and Hotspots. Call (720) 913-0048 for the "Family Information Line" to listen to friendly invitations to all the current events. Check out the museum's family Web site at www.wackykids.org for art projects your children can print out and do at home.

For dining, try the museum's Palettes Express cafe for tasty salads, sandwiches, desserts, and beverages.

Denver Mint (ages 4 and up)

320 West Colfax Ave. (between Cherokee and Delaware Streets); (303) 405-4761; www.us mint.gov. Open year-round, Mon through Fri. The visitors' entrance is on Cherokee Street. Open 8 a.m. to 2 p.m. Security is tight, and many regulations apply since Sept 11. Visitors are strongly advised to make reservations in advance by going to www.usmint.gov. Without reservations, there is no guarantee that you will be admitted (usually only if there has been a cancellation). Reservations can be made up to two months in advance. The mint is usually closed for yearly inventory the last week of June and the first week of July. Free. The Mint Gift Shop (303-572-9500), located directly adjacent to the tour entry on Cherokee Street, is open Mon through Fri, 8 a.m. to 3:30 p.m. It offers money-related items for the entire family, from numismatic collectibles to toys, games, and clothing.

If you want to prove to your kids that money doesn't grow on trees, take them for a tour of the Denver Mint. Here they will see the various steps in minting coins. While soundproofing cubicles around each stamping machine diminish the view, you still see shiny copper-clad pennies tumbling into carts. Looking down on an estimated half-million dollars' worth of coinage, adults and kids gape into the weighing and bagging area. Using handheld sewing machines, workers close cloth bags of coins and neatly stack them onto pallets. From here all the coins are shipped to Federal Reserve Banks.

The final stop on the tour, the salesroom, provides an opportunity to purchase souvenir coin sets, commemorative coins, and other numismatic treasures. For a quarter, mint personnel place a blank in an old press, and you push the button to strike a souvenir medal. Every child in your family will want one.

Denver Firefighters Museum (ages 2 and up)

1326 Tremont Place (across from the Denver Mint); (303) 892-1436 or (888) 632-7085; www .denverfirefightersmuseum.org. Open year-round, Mon through Sat, except on holidays, from 10 a.m. to 4 p.m. $.

What kid, big or little, wouldn't love the opportunity to climb aboard a gleaming white fire truck, ring the bell, take hold of the steering wheel, and pretend to race the vehicle to a raging fire? Kids can do this and a whole lot more at Old Firehouse No. 1, a Denver landmark with a listing on the National Register of Historic Places. Youngsters are invited to try on firefighters' coats, hats, and boots; listen as the tour guide relates harrowing stories about blazes of long ago; and watch a video about fire safety featuring Jiminy Cricket and Donald Duck. Among the fire-fighting apparatus you will see are hand-drawn hook-and-ladder carts, buckets once used for bucket brigades, horse-drawn pumpers, and wonderful old fire trucks. Be sure to take a peek upstairs to see the former sleeping area and the "fire laddies'" old metal cots. A pair of boots sits on the floor beside each bed. One wall is covered with the names of firefighters who responded to the 9/11 tragedy and lost their lives that day. Throughout the year, besides hosting special events and birthday parties, the museum offers several **free** days with planned activities for children. Phone for dates.

16th Street Mall (all ages)

The 16th Street Mall, a mile-long, outdoor pedestrian promenade, runs through the heart of Denver, connecting the Civic Center to LoDo.

Free shuttle buses run continuously. Hop on and off as often as you please for easy access to shopping, restaurants, and attractions.

Denver Pavilions (all ages)

Mid-downtown Denver, along the 16th Street Mall; (303) 260-6000; www.denverpavilions .com.

The Denver Pavilions complex—offering entertainment facilities, restaurants, and retail shops—covers two entire midtown city blocks. At this polestar of energy and activity, you can browse the dozens of specialty shops and, if your children have earned the privilege of embarking on a memorable dining experience, treat them to dinner at Maggianos Little Italy, where outstanding meals are served family-style.

Pedal **Pleasures**

Bicycling magazine named Denver one of the top-ten best cities in the nation for bicycling. And it's no wonder—there are more than 450 miles of biking trails in the Denver metro area. Maps (including descriptions of the routes and rankings from easy to difficult) are **free** at the Denver Metro Convention and Visitors Bureau. Commercial pamphlets and books are available at metro Denver bookstores.

A good place to start is at Confluence Park in downtown Denver. You can follow the creek all the way to Cherry Creek Reservoir (16⁴⁄₁₀ miles one way) or just traverse the distance that works best for all members of your family. This is a gentle ride, avoiding traffic via bike underpasses. Or perhaps you'd like to cycle through City Park. A 3½-mile jaunt will take you leisurely past Duck Lake, City Park Lake, tennis courts, playing fields, the Museum of Nature and Science, and the southwest side of the zoo. Pause beside the zoo to listen for the cries of the peacocks and other assorted animals. This is an easy ride, with lots of opportunities for stopping to rest along the way.

Denver Performing Arts Complex (ages 4 and up)

1245 Champa St. (in mid-downtown Denver). The box office is located at Speer and Arapahoe in the Helen Bonfils Theater Complex, (303) 893-4100 or (800) 641-1222; www.arts complex.com. Open Mon through Sat 10 a.m. to 6 p.m. $$$–$$$$.

The Denver Performing Arts Complex (DPAC), with ten theaters that cover four square blocks, is the second-largest complex of its kind in the nation, surpassed only by New York City's Lincoln Center. "The Plex," as it is known locally, features music, opera, theater, and ballet. Always popular with families, *The Nutcracker Suite* ballet is an annual event.

Operating within the DPAC is the Denver Center Theatre Company (DCTC), a nurturing ground for new plays, a national training school for actors, and the site of some of the most dynamic live theater in the Rocky Mountain West. The largest resident professional theater company between Chicago and the West Coast, the DCTC includes four theaters plus the Denver Center Theatre Academy, with classes in acting, voice, creative dramatics, playwriting, and stage taught by working professionals. For information phone (303) 446-4892.

Coors Field (all ages)

20th and Blake Streets; (303) 762-5437 or (800) 388-7625; www.coloradorockies.com. Game tickets $–$$$$, depending on seating location; tours $7 for adults, $5 for children age 5 to 12, and $6 for seniors age 55 and older. Children age 4 and under free. Times for tours vary greatly due to game schedules. It's best to phone for times.

Built in the classic style of Fenway Park and Wrigley Field, Coors Field is an old-fashioned ballpark almost in the center of town. The red-brick exterior, live organist, and "muscle board" (scoreboard changed by hand) hark back to the good old days. The wide, tree-lined perimeter of this park edges LoDo, Denver's hottest place to be. Art galleries, boutiques, bistros, and sports bars attract crowds along the surrounding streets, day and night.

The Rockies encourage families to come on out to the ball games. Youngsters merit special attention on the Buckaroo's concourse. Here, a fast-food stand with lower counters offers them smaller portions at smaller prices. For those under 4 feet tall, there's a playground where Dinger, the Rockies mascot, often visits. In designated family-seating sections, no alcohol is allowed.

Even if the Rockies are on the road or it's winter, Coors Field is a great stop. A one-hour tour will take you into the visitors' locker room, a luxury box, the press box, and out to the home team's dugout. Call ahead for dates and times for ballpark tours.

Be sure to examine *Evolution of the Ball,* just outside the park. It's a tongue-in-cheek sculptured arch paying homage to the ball—including gumball, eyeball, and Lucille Ball.

Denver Skatepark (ages 10 and up)
2205 19th St. (between Platte and Little Raven Streets); www.denverskatepark.com. Open daily 5 a.m. to 11 p.m. Free.

Beautifully designed and landscaped, this skatepark is a work of art. It is so popular during the middle of the day that kids are willing to get out of bed at sunrise in order to take advantage of the small and large bowls, staircases, ledges, rails, and gaps. They can bring their skateboards, in-line skates, bikes without pegs, and nonmotorized scooters but they will have to leave their cones and other obstacles at home. As would be expected, the usual protective gear—helmets; wrist, elbow, and knee pads; and more (according to the sport)—are required.

Day-Tripper: **Downtown Adventure**

Explore the Mile High City's downtown area without worrying about driving and parking. Leave your chariot in the **free** Broadway Park-n-Ride at I-25 and Broadway. Board the light rail for a short ride into the city. Watch for the 16th Street Mall stop.

The outdoor pedestrian mall is lined with shops and restaurants—something for everyone. Walk west until the mall ends at Market Street, or jump on the **free** shuttle that runs up and down the mall.

A short walk along Market Street brings you to Coors Field, home of the Colorado Rockies, where you can take the one-hour ballpark tour. When you finish exploring, take the light rail back to the Broadway station to retrieve your car.

Baseball on a **Budget**

To make a major-league ballgame an affordable family adventure, purchase seats in the Rockpile and pack a picnic. Many games at Coors Field are sold out; however, an allotment of Rockpile (straightaway centerfield) seats goes on sale two and a half hours before game time. Cost for Rockpile seats is $4 for adults, $1 for children 12 and younger and seniors 55 and older. A lenient food-and-beverage policy throughout the park allows fans to bring their own treats, but no glass or aluminum containers are allowed.

Central Platte Valley (all ages)
Along the South Platte River from Colfax Avenue north to 23rd Street.

In 1858 a prospector spotted flakes of gold near the confluence of Cherry Creek and the South Platte River, and the rush was on.

Once the location of Denver's first crude buildings and gold-rush-incited tent city, the Central Platte Valley today attracts those seeking sports and entertainment. Paved paths along both the river and creek bring in-line skaters, cyclists, joggers, and parents pushing strollers to Confluence Park. Six Flags Elitch Gardens amusement park; playgrounds; the Children's Museum; and the Pepsi Center, Denver's newest arena for professional hockey and basketball, draw visitors of all ages. Just to the west stands Invesco Field at Mile High, home to the Denver Broncos.

Elitch Gardens (ages 2 and up)
In Denver's Platte Valley, near I-25 and Speer Boulevard; (303) 595-4386; www.elitchgardens .com. Open May through Oct, weather permitting, varying days and hours. Water park open Memorial Day through Labor Day, 10 a.m. to 7 p.m. Admission includes entry to both the amusement park and the water park. $$$–$$$$, depending on age. Admission is free for ages 3 and younger or 70 and older.

In 1890 John and Mary Elitch turned their small vegetable farm and apple orchards into picnic areas and ball fields and opened them to the public. Over the years a theater that hosted such luminaries as Sarah Bernhardt, Edward G. Robinson, and Grace Kelly was added, along with amusement rides, extensive gardens, and a dance pavilion. In 1995, after continual operation for more than 104 years, the park was relocated near the center of the city.

People swarm to Elitch Gardens for its thrill rides, little thrills for little tykes, and extreme thrills for big kids and adults. The park features seemingly endless major attractions, including the Tower of Doom, a controlled free fall from twenty-two stories in the sky; and Disaster Canyon, where riders experience the excitement of white-water rafting while they whirl through churning, surging rapids.

Still more attractions include the 100-foot-high Ferris wheel and the spinning teacups. A 1905 carousel, fully restored in 1995, features sixty-seven exquisitely hand-carved animals and chariots—a park highlight for visitors of every age.

Ice-Cream **Breaks**

There's nothing like an ice-cream cone to lift the spirits. Squelch that back-seat squabbling or refresh tired sightseers with a simple treat. No matter what end of town you're in, you're not far from a delicious delight.

Bonnie Brae Ice Cream, 799 South University Blvd.; (303) 777-0808.

Cold Stone Creamery, 14233 West Colfax Ave., Lakewood; (303) 215-9364.

How Sweet It Is, 2217 East Mississippi Ave.; (303) 777-0414.

Lik's Ice Cream Parlor, 2039 East 13th Ave.; (303) 321-2370.

Maggie Moo's Ice Cream and Treatery, 8225 South Chester St., Centennial; (303) 221-6244.

Coaster aficionados find three choices for their ultimate thrill. Twister II, a wooden coaster in the classic style, reaches nearly 100 feet at its highest point. A steel coaster, Sidewinder, blasts passengers twice through a giant loop, forward and in reverse. On Mind Eraser riders hang suspended, feet dangling, from the looping, iron-clad track soaring ten stories skyward before plummeting at 60 miles per hour.

The park has approximately 84,000 square feet of garden space and extensive landscaping that includes acres of lawn and flowerbeds and nearly 3,000 trees. Of special note are the topiary carousel horses and other figures placed throughout the grounds.

Included in your admission to Elitch Gardens is Island Kingdom, an expansive tropical paradise packed with water adventures for the whole family. Here you will find dozens of twisting and turning water slides; a five-story water-play structure with more than seventy-five interactive features; a huge tree house anchored in the center of Hook's Lagoon; a meandering, peaceful river to float down; soaking pools; and sunning spaces.

Children's Museum of Denver (all ages)

2121 Children's Museum Dr. (at I-25 and 23rd Street, exit 211); (303) 433-7444; www .mychildsmuseum.org. The teal-and-raspberry building is easy to spot. Open Mon, Tues, Thurs, and Fri 9 a.m. to 4 p.m., Wed 9 a.m. to 7:30 p.m., Sat and Sun 10 a.m. to 5 p.m. Closed Thanksgiving, Christmas, New Year's Day, and Easter Sun. $–$$.

For kids who love to touch—and what kid doesn't? This hands-on facility has been a favorite with Denver kids for close to thirty years, celebrating curiosity and creativity. The Children's Museum, a nonprofit facility, provides stimulating ideas and learning experiences for children and their families. With innovative, hands-on exhibits, theater performances, educational programs, and special events, the museum encourages youngsters to create, explore, discover, imagine, and just plain have fun. The museum is designed for newborns to kids 8 years old, but older siblings are welcome to tag along.

Be sure to check out Arts a la Carte where your little ones will find a playscape featuring whimsical puppet shows, noodle art, finger-painting, princess and cowboy dress-up clothes, and mirrors for practicing dance steps, When you're ready for a break, the museum's Eat Street Café is perfect for a snack stop.

Black American West Museum and Heritage Center
(ages 5 and up)

3091 California St.; (303) 482-224; www.blackamericanwestmuseum.com. Open June through Aug, Tues through Sat, 10 a.m. to 5 p.m.; Sept through May, Tues through Sat, 10 a.m. to 2 p.m.; $, children age 4 and younger free.

The former home of Dr. Justina Ford, the first African-American female doctor in the state of Colorado, is now a museum. Housing a remarkable collection of memorabilia and artifacts, this is one of the most comprehensive sources of historic materials representing African-American western pioneers.

The assemblage began as a personal hobby of Paul Stewart, an African American who was forced as a child to always take the role of the Indian when playing cowboys and Indians with his white friends, because his chums insisted that there had never been a "black cowboy." Imagine his surprise when, as an adult, he met exactly that—a black cowboy who had led many a cattle drive at the turn of the 20th century. That was all Stewart needed. He became a self-taught historian and curator, determined to search out and make known the African-American influence on the settlement of the West.

Paul Stewart's personal collection became the nucleus for today's museum, opened in 1971. He unearthed letters, photographs, documents, and oral histories proving that nearly a third of the cowboys who helped settle the West were black. It may not be recorded in history books, but documents on display at the museum reveal that black families came west in covered wagons and established all-black towns, filling the necessary positions of merchant, blacksmith, doctor, teacher, and banker. African Americans were among the West's earliest millionaires, owning vast amounts of real

Saved by a **Bucket of Berries**

Cassie's Sweet Berry Pie by Karen Winnick is a story about a young girl in the South who uses huckleberries and a little imagination to keep Union soldiers from ransacking her home during the Civil War. Based on a factual historical anecdote, the story is unusual because it relates the events from a Southern perspective. That was the author's goal—to show children that there are good people on both sides of a conflict, and that they can overcome life's obstacles by relying on their own ingenuity. Her point is clearly made and can be applied to many situations, including the history of hostile encounters between the Native Americans and European settlers. I highly recommend this beautifully written and illustrated book for children ages 6 to 10.

Toddler's **Morning Out**

Want to spend some special time with the toddler in your life? One stop offers a morning of activities. The Children's Museum of Denver has a special Toddler Time every Mon and Wed from 10 a.m. to 11 a.m. Afterward hop aboard the Platte Valley Trolley (303-458-6255) and watch for wildlife along the river. Bring a snack or lunch to enjoy while romping at the Gates Crescent Park playground, especially toddler-friendly with soft landing surfaces. It will be nap time before you realize it.

estate and prominent businesses. At the museum you can see saddles, spurs, rifles, and vintage photographs—hundreds of items pertaining to the black influence on the Old West.

This museum also includes an exhibit depicting the story of the Buffalo Soldiers, black military units that played a huge, but little known, part in the settling of the West. Yet another exhibit showcases the contributions of the all-black Tuskegee Airmen Military Units during World War II.

Hammond's Candies Since 1920 (all ages)
5735 North Washington St.; (303) 333-5588; www.hammondscandies.com. Tours every 30 minutes Mon through Fri 9 a.m. to 3 p.m., Sat from 10 a.m. to 3 p.m. Free.

This is one special place your kids will want to visit more than once. Who could resist the opportunity to tour an old-fashioned candy factory to see how Hammond's Candies makes candy from the same recipes and in the same way today as they did in 1920—in small batches, hand-pulled, and hand-twisted. This candy company and their handmade candy canes, lollipops, ribbon candy, traditional hard candies, and delicious chocolates have been featured on national TV and in numerous magazines. Free samples.

Museum of Miniatures, Dolls and Toys (ages 4–12)
1880 Gaylord St.; (303) 322-1053; www.dmmdt.org. Open Wed through Sat 10 a.m. to 4 p.m. and Sun 1 to 4 p.m. $.

Although the Museum of Miniatures, Dolls and Toys is for the most part a no-touch museum, children, especially little girls, love wandering through its eight galleries. Permanent and changing exhibits include scale-model dollhouses, a teddy bear closet, and a wonderful collection of Steiff stuffed animals.

Located in the 1899 Dutch Colonial Revival-style Pearce–McAllister Cottage, the museum showcases more than 10,000 miniatures, toys, and dolls. The house is listed on the National Register of Historic Places and contains one room filled with the priceless antique furnishings of the former owners, Phebe and Henry McAllister.

One entire gallery of the museum, the fourth largest of its kind in the United States, is devoted to Southwestern miniatures. A nine-room adobe dollhouse features hand-woven wool Native American rugs, authentic Santa Clara Pueblo pottery, hand-woven Papago baskets from Arizona, hand-carved furniture, kiva fireplaces, and hanging ristras (decorative swags) of tiny red chilies.

Holding court in another chamber, the Kingscote Dollhouse is an exact replica of a ca. 1839 Carpenter Gothic mansion that still stands in Newport, Rhode Island. The three-story, 1-inch-scale house is 6½ feet long, weighs 250 pounds, and boasts sixteen rooms. The floors are oak, teak, cherry, and Brazilian rosewood parquet. The Chippendale dining-room furniture, made of lustrous cherry wood, was imported from England. The dining-room table is set with eighteen-karat-gold flatware, hand-painted porcelain dishes, and handsome crystal stemware rimmed in fourteen-karat gold. A sterling-silver candelabra serves as the centerpiece.

Of special note are the 19th-century Dutch and German "cabinet houses" in a cupboardlike enclosure. These are the forerunners of today's dollhouses and once belonged to extremely wealthy women of the period.

Denver City Park (all ages)

North of 17th Avenue, between Colorado Boulevard and York Street. Free.

City Park is home to the Denver Zoo and the Museum of Nature and Science. But it's also a large park with three lakes, a formal rose garden, athletic fields, and a public golf course. There are two playgrounds, paddleboats for rent, and lots of picnic areas. Be sure to stop at the playground just outside the zoo's west entrance. Your kids' eyes will light up when they see the massive community-built layout. An appealing gorilla sculpture, carved from a tree trunk, overlooks the area.

Raindrops Keep Falling **on My Head**

Denver, a city that boasts 300 days of sunshine a year, still gets a little rain. Even on the sunniest summer days, the clouds often roll in during the afternoon, delivering a brief thunderstorm. So where can you take your kids until our perfect weather returns?

The Denver Museum of Nature and Science is not the stuffy, dead-bones sort of museum you may remember from childhood. DMNS is loaded with dinosaurs, glow-in-the-dark rocks and minerals, an interactive Hall of Life, and an IMAX Theater. There's decent food in an informal setting, and the gift store has quality, yet affordable, souvenirs.

The zoo is usually a sunny-day destination, but the Denver Zoo also has many indoor exhibits. Wandering through climate-controlled Tropical Discovery or Bird World, you'll forget the rain. The Hungry Elephant provides indoor dining, right next door to the gift shop.

Where **Are They?**

Elves, Yoda, and Galileo can be found by eagle-eyed observers in the Denver Museum of Nature and Science's dioramas, paintings, and murals. Spotting the elves painted into the Kent Pendelton backgrounds is a favorite activity for Denver children. Places to search include Edge of the Wild, Explore Colorado, and Prehistoric Journey. If you want help, Guest Services will provide a "Museum Secrets" guide sheet. In the IMAX lobby check out the large Tom Buchannon painting for hidden *Star Wars* images. The search will make detectives out of all of you.

Denver Museum of Nature and Science (all ages)

2001 Colorado Blvd. (in City Park); (303) 322-7009 or (800) 925-2250; www.dmns.org. Open daily 9 a.m. to 5 p.m., except Christmas. IMAX additional fee; combination tickets available. $$–$$$.

"Entertain your brain" is its motto, and it's well deserved. From the moment a giant tyrannosaurus greets you at the main entrance, you'll be hooked. Try on mule deer ears (not real!) to see how they funnel sound. Push the button to smell what attracts a doe to a buck. Feel the fuzz on antlers. The Edge of the Wild is just one of many interactive exhibits that fascinate children (and grown-ups) with the wonders of the natural world. From the hoof prints in the floor to the recorded animal sounds, you'll be immersed in this western habitat.

In Coors Mineral Hall visit Tom's Baby, Colorado's largest gold specimen, which is displayed in a safe. Glow-in-the-dark rocks, birthstones, and diamonds intrigue kids here.

Of particular interest to children is the permanent Prehistoric Journey exhibit, where they can experience prehistoric times through an extraordinary display of fossils, interactive technology, videos, touchable specimens, and time stations. Designed to stimulate, excite, and satisfy the curiosity of children and adults, the $7.7-million, 17,000-square-foot display encompasses a working fossil laboratory with public viewing areas, more than 500 real fossil specimens, and a total of twelve dinosaur skeletons, seven dinosaur skulls, and two fleshed-out dinosaurs enhanced by innovative lighting and astonishing sound effects.

You begin your journey with a time-travel theater production where you are taken back 4.5 billion years to the origins of Earth and then brought up to 3.5 billion years ago, when the first forms of life are said to have appeared. Next you move from the theater into the sights and sounds of ancient worlds. You pass by natural habitat scenes and walk through "enviroramas."

When you arrive at the Nebraska Woodland Envirorama, you witness Nebraska as it was twenty million years ago. A giant dinohyus appears on a distant ridge in pursuit of a herd of small camels, and a salivating, vicious-looking carnivore resembling a giant wild boar (nicknamed the "Terminator Pig") grunts menacingly. From the distance is heard the sound of rumbling thunder.

Space Odyssey is the museum's most ambitious project in its one-hundred-year history. It establishes the Denver Museum of Nature and Science as the leading space-science resource in the Rocky Mountain region. State-of-the-art technology and participatory experiences provide visitors with the feeling that they are traveling across the universe without ever leaving the ground.

The amazing, incredible you. That's what Expedition Health is all about. Learn how the choices you make affect your body through highly personalized activities, enjoy a theater experience designed to engage your senses, participate in live demonstrations and programs, and examine microscopic cells from your own body.

The IMAX Theater is not your typical neighborhood movie house. The screen is nearly five stories high, the surround sound is state-of-the-art, and the film subjects are spectacular. You can call ahead to reserve tickets for specific show times.

Denver Zoo (all ages)

On 23rd Avenue, between Colorado Boulevard and York Street (in City Park); (303) 376-4800; www.denverzoo.org. Open daily year-round; Mar through Oct, 9 a.m. to 5 p.m.; Nov through Feb, 10 a.m. to 4 p.m. It's important to note that admission gates close one hour before the zoo closes, Bird World and Tropical Discovery close at 4 p.m., and snack stands sometimes close early also, so don't wait too long to take care of the hungries. Push chairs, little red wagons, and strollers are available for rent. $–$$, depending on age; children 2 or younger free. Check for free days during the off-season.

Founded in 1896, the Denver Zoo features more than 3,500 animals representing 642 species. An accredited member of the American Zoo and Aquarium Association, it draws visitors from coast to coast. It gained worldwide attention by successfully hand-raising two polar bear cubs.

Its Predator Ridge, a new eight-acre area, is a prime example of what accredited zoos nationwide are trying to achieve—larger, more naturalistic, and educational exhibits. Designed to re-create a portion of the Samburo National Reserve in Kenya, it reveals

Wildlights

Each Dec the Denver Zoo turns into a spectacular winter wonderland when thousands of sparkling lights in animal shapes enhance the pathways and animal enclosures for the nightly Wildlights extravaganza. Bundle the kids up in scarves, mittens, and caps, and participate in this festive tradition. Here's an opportunity to view the animals at night, when many nocturnal species are more active. Music, caroling by local choirs, and roasting chestnuts add to the holiday atmosphere. In the Northern Shores area Santa listens to wish lists. Visitors are encouraged to bring along a nonperishable food item to be distributed to the less fortunate. Call the zoo for Wildlights exact times (303-376-4800). $–$$; no charge for children 2 or younger.

spectacular views of lions, African wild dogs, and hyenas. Besides providing up-close encounters with the occupants, it encompasses an off-exhibit, outdoor yard built for the sole purpose of providing the animals with a degree of privacy.

Primate Panorama, a seven-acre, $14-million facility, houses more than twenty-five species of primates, from tiny squirrel monkeys to 400-pound gorillas, all in environments that resemble their natural habitats. Visitors enter the area through an African village setting with bamboo and thatch-roofed structures and view the primates from special blinds that allow them to stand as close as 15 feet from a gorilla with seemingly nothing in between. Thick vegetation, outdoor streams, and waterfalls simulate a tropical setting.

Artists, biologists, curators, veterinarians, architects, and horticulturists helped design and construct this fascinating facility, which contains one of the country's largest outdoor habitats dedicated to the endangered lowland gorilla. Primate Panorama replicates primate habitats to such a degree that normal social groups are established, thus increasing breeding potential. Its mission is to care for the animals' needs and encourage normal social behaviors by creating spacious, naturalistic habitats.

The zoo's Bird World, with spacious indoor and outdoor habitats, contains more than 500 birds, including threatened and endangered species from around the world. The endangered African black-footed penguin, the Bali mynah, and the black palm cockatoo, along with numerous other species, are involved in the zoo's highly specialized breeding programs. A colony of six endangered Humboldt penguins resides in a replica of a Chilean intertidal coastline, complete with rocky cliffs for nesting. Chilly water and faux sea kelp make this area seem like home to the penguins.

Another not-to-miss attraction is Tropical Discovery, a 45-foot-tall glass pyramid where you can view more than 1,200 animals in a rain-forest environment. You'll see venomous and nonvenomous snakes, vampire bats, alligators, and a capybara, the world's largest rodent.

Be sure to check out the Pachyderm Habitats, the indoor-outdoor Giraffe House, and Bear Mountain. Northern Shores houses sea lions, polar bears, and other Arctic wildlife. Don't forget to stop by the nursery to check for new babies to observe. Wildlife Theater, with animal shows, and a Komodo dragon exhibit are both popular attractions.

For a nominal fee hop aboard the open-air Zoo Liner; a narrated spin around the park can help you plan your visit. Or take a lift when legs are beginning to tire and little feet have taken too many steps. Ride with your youngsters on the zoo's Pioneer Train, the first natural gas-powered train ride in the country.

Molly Brown House (ages 6 and up)

1340 Pennsylvania St.; (303) 832-4092; www.mollybrown.org. Open Tues through Sat 10 a.m. to 3:30 p.m. and Sun noon to 3:30 p.m. Closed on all major holidays. Tours run daily starting every half hour. They last 45 minutes, and the last tour departs at 3:30 p.m. $–$$, children 5 and younger free.

If your children's history lessons have included the voyage and sinking of the *Titanic*, they may be interested in seeing the former home of the "Unsinkable Molly Brown." Molly

Brown is credited with taking command of one of the *Titanic*'s lifeboats and suppressing a panic.

Located in Denver's historic Capitol Hill District, the three-story home is filled with priceless antiques, many of which were once owned by the spirited Molly. Political activist, philanthropist, and suffragist, Molly received her "Unsinkable" moniker as the result of her remark following the *Titanic* incident. According to Molly, her survival was "typical Brown luck. We're unsinkable."

Tours of the museum, lasting approximately forty-five minutes, are led by costumed guides who entertainingly reveal Molly's rags-to-riches story, her remarkable bravery during the *Titanic* disaster, and the house's resident ghosts.

Denver Botanic Gardens (all ages)

1005 York St.; (720) 865-3500; www.botanicgardens.org. Open daily 9 a.m. to 5 p.m.; open until 8 p.m. during summer months, Sat through Tues. $$.

Vegetable Garden, Scripture Garden, Romantic Garden, Windsong Garden, or Monet Garden, to name just a few—the Denver Botanic Gardens presents plants in their special environments. Whether you stop in for a relaxing stroll or come to learn about xeriscaping or endangered plants, you'll appreciate this spot of greenery in Denver.

All ages enjoy the Tropical Conservatory. Look for fossils embedded in the walls. Ride the glass elevator into the treetops for a bird's-eye view.

In summer, sip a cool drink and enjoy a salad at the Monet Deck Cafe, adjacent to the Monet Garden. It is open from 9 a.m. until the garden closes. Or dine at Offshoots at the Gardens, open during garden hours. Menu ranges from breakfast burritos to paninis, soups, salads, and sandwiches. Family Guides, available at the Information Desk, are **free** with admission and provide fun activities and kid-friendly information about the gardens.

Cheesman Park borders the Botanic Gardens on the west side. It's one of Denver's most attractive urban parks and has a playground.

Blossoms of **Light**

The Denver Botanic Gardens also celebrates the holiday season with a blaze of lights. Join the visitors strolling through the outdoor gardens, oohing and aahing over festive light displays. There's hot chocolate and cider for sale inside, and the indoor gardens are also decorated.

The Denver Zoo and the Botanic Gardens encourage you to see both light displays. When you purchase tickets at one stop, you receive a discount coupon ($2 off) for tickets at the other.

Day-Tripper: **City Park Adventure**

Pack a picnic lunch and head to City Park. Here the Denver Zoo and the Museum of Nature and Science offer hours of family fun. Choose one or do both. The park itself has lots of areas to run and play games, and you can rent paddleboats during summer months. The community-built playground, just outside the zoo's west entrance, is exceptional; picnic tables are close by.

Cherry Creek Shopping Center (all ages)

3000 East 1st Ave.; (303) 388-3900; www.shopcherrycreek.com. Open Mon through Sat 10 a.m. to 9 p.m. and Sun 11 a.m. to 6 p.m. Some store and restaurant hours may vary.

Denver is the shopping capital of the Rocky Mountain West, and the Cherry Creek Shopping Center is top of the line. Neiman Marcus, Saks Fifth Avenue, and Tiffany—this center is lined with luxury shopping. Sculptures, skylights, and plenty of open space make shopping here a pleasant experience. Comfy seating areas entice shoppers to rest tired feet and regroup.

You'll have no trouble finding Kids' Kourt, the playground area with a breakfast theme. Just follow the kids. There are not many places where you're allowed to play in a giant bowl of shredded wheat, slide down a piece of bacon, or stomp on a waffle, so don't miss this opportunity.

Even if your children don't recognize the status of Neiman Marcus, they won't soon forget their visit to Build-A-Bear (303-320-9888; www.buildabear.com), where they can choose an animal priced between $10 and $30, stuff it, give it a heart, dress it, name it, and make a birth certificate for it. The shop also carries already-stuffed animals, accessories, and a selection of fashions for your child's pet animal that celebrate the various holidays throughout the year.

Hungry? Johnny Rockets ($) is a favorite lunch stop for families, where you will find super-thick milk shakes (consider sharing one between two kids), hamburgers, chili dogs, American fries, cheese fries, chili fries, chicken tenders, and sandwiches.

Tattered Cover Book Store (all ages)

Three locations: 1) 2526 East Colfax Ave., (303) 322-7727; open Mon through Fri, 7 a.m. to 9 p.m.; Sat, 9 a.m. to 9 p.m., Sun, 10 a.m. to 6 p.m. 2) 1628 16th St., (303) 436-1070; open Mon through Fri, 6:30 a.m. to 9 p.m.; Sat, 9 a.m. to 9 p.m.; Sun, 10 a.m. to 6 p.m. 3) 9315 Dorchester St., (303) 470-7050; open Mon through Sat, 9 a.m. to 9 p.m., Sun 10 a.m. to 6 p.m. www.tatteredcover.com.

The Tattered Cover Book Store began as a small, intimate bookshop in 1974. The cozy atmosphere, attention to customer needs, and an eclectic selection of books soon attracted a faithful following of book-lovers. Alas, bookshelves hold only so many volumes, so owner Joyce Meskis had to expand to a second location and then a third.

Miraculously, by designing cozy nooks with reading lamps and large, overstuffed couches and chairs, plus providing the hospitality and customer service that was always available at her original shop, she has maintained the same warm, welcoming ambience created decades ago. That's quite an accomplishment when you consider the fact that the three stores now contain more than 150,000 titles and 750,000 volumes.

Children are encouraged to indulge in the wonderful assortment of books in the kids' area. Here parents sit on the floor, youngsters in laps, and read aloud. Or often the reverse happens, as children read to their parents. Overheard in the children's section: "I love it here. Our whole family loves this bookstore. It's our favorite place to spend an afternoon."

Storytimes for young children occur Tues at 10:30 a.m. at both the East Colfax Avenue and the Dorchester Street stores, and Sat at 10:30 a.m. at the Dorchester Street store only.

Four Mile Historic Park (all ages)
715 South Forest St.; (720) 865-0800; www.fourmilepark.org. Open Apr through Sept, Wed through Fri noon to 4 p.m., Sat and Sun 10 a.m. to 4 p.m.; Oct through Mar, Wed through Sun noon to 4 p.m. Hours and days vary some, best to phone. Also phone to inquire about summer day camps and year-round special events. $, children age 5 and younger free. Horse-drawn rides $1.

This twelve-acre living-history museum is located 4 miles southeast of downtown Denver, hence its name. Spanning a period between 1859 and 1883, the farm park consists of the Four Mile House, a former tavern and wayside inn that once welcomed travelers on the Cherokee Trail, plus a reconstructed bee house where former owner Millie Booth kept her beekeeping equipment, three barns and a corral housing chickens and draft horses, a summer kitchen, and a privy.

Docents in period clothing lead visitors through the Four Mile House and are stationed around the grounds demonstrating 19th-century farm life. Children like the horse-drawn rides—stagecoach, hayride, or sleigh ride. You are welcome to visit the fragrant rose garden, check on the crops in the vegetable garden, and spread a blanket under a shade tree for a family picnic. There's a small gift shop in the bee house. Sunday is special-events day designed with the family in mind. Call for the latest schedule, which includes seasonal and holiday celebrations along with western heritage events.

A Lark in the **Park**

Washington Park is a local favorite in a neighborhood by the same name. Restricted traffic and the choice of several paths through the park make it easy to share this space with walkers, joggers, skaters, and dogs. Two ponds attract anglers, ducks, and geese. The excellent playground makes a good rest stop.

Shopping **"Only in Denver"**

You can shop at national chain stores just about anywhere but, like most cities, Denver has its hometown favorites, those few standouts that you will find only in the Mile High City.

Kazoo & Company, 2930 East Second Ave. (in Cherry Creek North); (303) 322-0973 or (800) 257-0008; www.kazootoys.com. Open Mon through Fri 10 a.m. to 8 p.m., Sat 10 a.m. to 5:30 p.m., and Sun noon to 5 p.m. "Toys That Play with the Imagination" is the theme here—two floors invitingly full of quality items. Stop in the Travel Section for something new to do when on the road. Toddlers to 12-year-olds will find puzzles, books, art supplies, and games.

There is a large section for your wee ones and a Dress-up Section (glittering shoes, pink tutus, magic wands) sure to enchant your little girls.

If you're going to be in town long-term, ask for a schedule of Kazoo Kid-Shops (art, crafts, science workshops for 2- to 12-year-olds). Be forewarned: It's really hard to get kids out of Kazoo!

The Bookies, 4315 East Mississippi, Glendale (2 blocks east of Colorado Boulevard); (303) 759-1117. Open Mon through Sat 10 a.m. to 6 p.m. and Sun noon to 5 p.m. A favorite haunt for parents and teachers, The Bookies features an amazing collection of books (fiction and nonfiction, picture books, learn-to-read), animals (cute, fuzzy characters from stories to rubbery, scientifically accurate invertebrates), games, puzzles, and art supplies for kids. Curriculum guides, workbooks, and an assortment of teaching aids draw educators and parents.

This store is overflowing, but the inventory is well organized, and the atmosphere is casual and friendly. There's always a bowl of pretzels to munch. The staff really know their stuff!

Caboose Hobbies, 500 South Broadway; (303) 777-6766; www.caboosehobbies .com. Open Mon through Fri 10 a.m. to 6 p.m., Sat 9 a.m. to 5 p.m., and Sun noon to 5 p.m. The family-owned Caboose Hobbies train store was established in 1938 and remains the world's largest model-railroad hobby shop. The 18,000-square-foot store contains 300,000 train-related items, including the largest selection of N scale items in the United States. The book department claims to have more than 1,000 titles and 300 different videos. Children will be fascinated by the displays of moving trains plunging in and out of tunnels, speeding through the countryside, and chugging past towns and villages. They also will be pleased to find toy locomotives, striped engineer caps, and train stickers and books.

Wings Over the Rockies Air & Space Museum (ages 2 and up)

7711 East Academy Blvd.; (303) 360-5360; www.wingsmuseum.org. Open Mon through Sat 10 a.m. to 5 p.m. and Sun noon to 5 p.m. $$, children age 4 and younger free.

Thanks to the enthusiasm of dedicated volunteers and the foresight of Russell Tarvin, a retired Army Air Corps colonel, this museum has an outstanding collection of irreplaceable aviation artifacts and lore. Beginning in 1982, Tarvin and like-minded followers used their military clout to save a score of outdated airplanes and other aviation items from the scrap heap. Civic leaders, recognizing the importance of preserving Tarvin's collection, won approval from the U.S. Department of Defense for the acquisition of two gigantic hangars located on the former Lowry Air Force Base to serve as a home for the museum.

A visit to the museum is a wonderful opportunity to get close to some mighty impressive aircraft, such as a rare B-18A Bolo; a *Star Wars* X-Wing Fighter; an RF84 Thunderflash Parasite; a ca. 1930 B-18 Bomber; and a T-33, America's first jet fighter plane. Especially popular with kids is the giant H-21 Helicopter, known as the "Flying Banana." Other prize aircraft include a Fokker D7, one of several German fighters from World War I; an Eagle Rock biplane from the 1920s; and a one-person glider used in the 1920s by the Germans after the Versailles Treaty banned them from the use of powered flight. Housed in former Air Force classrooms are exhibits including the Science of Flight, the History of Avionics, the Flying Tigers, and the Colorado Aviation Historical Society Heritage Hall.

Other exhibits of note include the Frederic Howard collection of model aircraft with wingspans of 2 feet or more and controls that respond to the maneuvering of the control stick, photographs and artifacts from the China–Burma–India theater of World War II, and an extraordinary display of World War I fighter-pilot uniforms placed on mannequins. Your kids can pick out inexpensive aviation pins and patches and attractive T-shirts in the small gift shop.

One day every other month, visitors are allowed into the cockpits of an Fl-ll, F4, B-57, and a helicopter. The aircraft are inside the hangar, so be sure to bring a flash unit for your camera to get a shot your child will cherish. Call for exact dates.

This place is a dream come true for aviation buffs. Visitors return time after time, usually bringing friends back with them to share in the experience. Watch for the huge B-52 Stratofortress, which is parked outside the hangar. It's too large to store inside the five-acre hangar and makes an ideal landmark.

Denver Suburbs

Lakeside Amusement Park (ages 2 and up)

4601 North Sheridan Blvd.; (303) 477-1621; www.lakesideamusementpark.com. Open daily June through Labor Day. The main park hours are Mon through Fri 6 to 11 p.m.; Sat, Sun, and holidays noon to 11 p.m. (Hours subject to change; best to phone.) Kiddies Playland open daily 1 to 10 p.m. It's best to arrive early with little ones, when the atmosphere is most suited to families with young children. Free parking. $$–$$$.

This old-fashioned, ca. 1908 amusement park appears somewhat like a movie set. The park's bell tower, currently housing refreshment booths and arcade games, is a Denver landmark.

The carousel, with its hand-carved wooden animals, is original to the park. Serious coaster-lovers come from far and wide to ride Cyclone, ranked as one of the top classic wooden roller coasters in the world. Built in 1940, the Art Deco station and cars are a throwback to another era.

Also of special interest are Puffing Billy and Whistling Tom, two miniature, coal-burning, steam-engine trains acquired from the 1904 St. Louis World's Fair and are original to the park. Both trains, among the last in the country that burn coal for power, are still in operation today. A diesel streamliner also shares the scenic 1¼-mile track that leads around the amusement park and skirts Lake Rhoda.

With the addition of the Mini Skater, the Kiddies Playland now comprises sixteen rides sure to please the preschoolers in your family, and the Cyclone Roller Coaster will no doubt thrill your teenagers.

Butterfly Pavilion and Insect Center (ages 3 and up)
6252 West 104th Ave., Westminster; (303) 469-5441; www.butterflies.org. Open daily 9 a.m. to 5 p.m. Closed Thanksgiving and Christmas. $–$$, children 1 year old and younger free. Maximum of two free child admissions per paid adult.

This fascinating, 16,000-square-foot facility has a 7,800-square-foot glass conservatory housing a tropical forest with free-flying butterflies. Here you can walk among butterflies of every color from all over the world. Beautiful flowers and foliage, a goldfish pond, and a rippling stream create a desirable environment for as many as 1,200 butterflies. A special viewing area reveals how the adults eventually emerge from the chrysalis.

One section of the center features tarantulas, crayfish, giant centipedes, huge cockroaches, and all sorts of other creepy-crawlers that your kids will absolutely love. Volunteers are on hand to remove an insect or two from their enclosures so that youngsters can carefully stroke and pet them. You can actually hold Rosie, the Chilean Rose Hair tarantula. The volunteers are well versed in the habits and habitats of insects and are excellent with children.

Cussler Museum (ages 8 and up)
14959 West 69th Ave., Arvada; (303) 420-2795; www.cusslermuseum.com. Open May through Sept, Mon and Tues only, from 10 a.m. to 7 p.m. $.

Dedicated to the preservation of rare and vintage automobiles from around the world, the Cussler Museum is the realized boyhood dream of Clive Cussler, renowned *New York Times* best-selling author of more than 100 titles, including the famous Dirk Pitt series. His books have been published in more than 40 languages in over 100 countries. He also is an internationally recognized authority on locating shipwrecks. Cussler's writing success and shipwreck expertise have made it possible for him to acquire over 100 exotic automobiles, ranging from a 1906 Stanley Steamer to a 1918 Cadillac V8 touring Car, a 1921 Rolls Royce Silver Ghost, a 1929 Packard Roadster 640, and a 1965 Corvette Stingray.

If there are any Hot Wheels or Match Box car collectors in your family, this is one museum they are sure to fall in love with. Restored to perfection, Cussler's gleaming masterpieces reside in a warehouse showroom in the northwest Denver suburb of Arvada. One side of the structure holds the classics and the other side displays convertibles from the 1950s. Merchandise for sale online includes T-shirts, caps, calendars, and posters with classic car motifs.

Hyland Hills Water World (ages 2 and up)

1800 West 89th St., Federal Heights; (303) 427-7873; www.waterworldcolorado.com. Open daily Memorial Day until late Aug, 10 a.m. to 6 p.m. $$$–$$$$, children 3 and younger free.

Located only twenty minutes from downtown Denver, this sixty-acre park has more than three dozen aquatic attractions. Ride the white-water rapids of River Country. Or pile into a five-person raft to float past the lair of a sea monster and through the earthquake cavern for an up-close encounter with the giant T-Rex, king of the underground on the Voyage to the Center of the Earth. The Lost River of the Pharaohs will take you on a wild ride into an ancient Egyptian pyramid. Wally World, a miniature water park, is just the right size for toddlers. Older children and their parents will love the 4-foot-high waves of Thunder Bay. Many of the rides are family oriented and can accommodate the entire family on the same craft.

Although food, from blueberry funnel cakes and chocolate chip cookies to pepperoni pizzas, is readily available, you are allowed to bring in your own picnic lunches (no glass bottles or jars, please). It's wise to bring along some sort of bathing footwear because the cement pathways can be hot and slippery.

Belleview Park (all ages)

On West Belleview Road between Broadway and Windemere, Englewood; www.engle woodgov.org. Children's Farm and Train open Memorial Day through Labor Day, Tues through Sat 10 a.m. to 4 p.m. and Sun 11 a.m. to 4 p.m. $.

Picnic tables under shady old cottonwoods, lots of grass, a stream, and a playground make this a good stop for all families. But those with younger children will think this place

When Thunderclouds **Appear**

During summer in Colorado, white, puffy thunderclouds often turn dark and threatening. This usually occurs in the afternoon, sometimes forcing water and amusement parks to close. For this reason it is always best to arrive in the morning hours in order to give your children plenty of time to experience all the rides and attractions.

is too good to be true: There's also a Children's Farm and a miniature train. The Lions Club International operates the train. Tracks loop through the park, crossing a trestle over Big Dry Creek. At the Children's Farm, you'll find a changing selection of animals, on loan from area farmers. It's all refreshingly low-key.

The Wildlife Experience (ages 5 and up)

10035 South Peoria St., Parker; (720) 488-3300; www.wildlifeexperience.org. Open Tues through Sun, 9 a.m. to 5 p.m. Normally closed on Mon except for Martin Luther King Jr. Day, President's Day, Memorial Day, and Labor Day. $–$$$, children under age 2 are free.

This interactive museum helps your child connect with wildlife and their habitats, and teaches children how to have a positive effect on the environment through dynamic natural history exhibits, artwork, video games, and large-format movies. Stroll through the Fine Arts, Africa, Children's, and Conservation Galleries; check out the hands-on, interactive exhibits; and view a movie in the spectacular iWERKS Extreme Screen Theater. Then rest weary little legs while enjoying a treat or lunch in the cafe. Don't try to leave without letting the kids graze the gift shop, though. It's just not going to happen.

Littleton Historical Museum (all ages)

6028 South Gallup St., Littleton; (303) 795-3950; www.littletongov.org/museum/events. Open Tues through Fri 8 a.m. to 5 p.m., Sat 10 a.m. to 5 p.m., and Sun 1 to 5 p.m. Free.

Take your family back, way back, to the early days of Littleton. The 1860s homestead farm and the 1890s farm are two separate living-history museums on this property. Interpreters work the farm sites, run the blacksmith shop, and teach in the school (Littleton's first one-room schoolhouse).

Cows, sheep, horses, pigs, chickens, ducks, and geese ensure that your kids will like this place. Those too young to understand the history can work on math or language skills. What does the sheep say? How many pigs are wallowing in the mud? Take a moment to try out the old wooden swing hanging from the willow. Have a picnic on the front lawn under the old cottonwoods. A rooster or pheasant may join you.

The main building of this museum houses three galleries with changing exhibits. Ask about year-round special events ranging from evening concerts during the summer to a pioneer Christmas celebration.

Where to Eat

Blue Bonnet Cafe, 457 South Broadway; (303) 778-0147; www.bluebonnetrestaurant .com. Open Mon through Thurs 11 a.m. to 10 p.m., Fri and Sat 11 a.m. to 11 p.m., and Sun 11 a.m. to 9 p.m. Unbelievably popular, Blue Bonnet wows Denverites with award-winning Mexican food. It's family owned and has been at this location for more than thirty years. Affordable prices and fast service make this a good family stop. $

Bonnie Brae Tavern, 740 South University Blvd.; (303) 777-2262; www.bonniebrae tavern.com. Open Tues through Thurs 10:30

a.m. to 9 p.m., Fri through Sun 10:30 to 9:30 p.m. The Dire family has been serving pizza on this spot for more than sixty years. Considered a neighborhood treasure, Bonnie Brae is usually filled with a mix of singles, young families, and older folks. Televisions keep patrons tuned to the latest sports events. It's noisy and crowded but friendly and unpretentious. Their menu includes nightly specials, but try their award-winning pizza. $–$$

Casa Bonita, 6715 West Colfax Ave., Lakewood; (303) 232-5115; www.casabonita denver.com. Open daily for lunch and dinner. Folks don't come to the Casa Bonita restaurant for quiet, sophisticated dining, and the food is definitely only "so so." On the other hand, it is sure to become one of your kids' favorite eateries. While cliff divers plunge 30 feet from the top of a waterfall into a pool of water, and the sheriff engages bad guy Black Bart in a shoot-'em-up, youngsters can indulge in a Piñata Plate of cheese enchiladas, tacos, refried beans, rice, and a sopapilla from the "Little Amigos" menu. This is a lively, fun place, with serenading mariachis, puppet shows, magicians, and fire jugglers. Kids delight in exploring the dark passages of Black Bart's mysterious, secret hideout. **Free** chips, chili con queso, salsa, and homemade sopapillas come with each dinner. $–$$

The Cherry Tomato, 4645 East 23rd Ave. (near City Park); (303) 377-1914; www.cherry tomatodenver.com. Open for dinner 5 p.m. Tues through Sun. Head to this delightful Italian cafe in Denver's Park Hill neighborhood. It was started by four couples in a former drug store. You still walk on the original black-and-white tile floor. The relaxed atmosphere will keep the kids happy. Great food will keep you happy. $$

Dozens Restaurant, 236 West 13th Ave.; (303) 572-0066. Open 6:30 a.m. to 2 p.m. every day except Christmas and Thanksgiving. Located in a beautifully restored historic home in Denver's Golden Triangle Museum District, only a few steps from the Denver Art

Museum, Dozens is an excellent choice for a reasonably priced breakfast or lunch. Meals made from quality ingredients are tasty and nicely presented. $

Where to Stay

Hotel Monaco, 1717 Champa St. at 17th Ave.; (303) 296-1717 or (800) 990-1303; www .monaco-denver.com. "Please send up an extra set of towels and a goldfish." If the kids miss the animals left at home, they can borrow a pet goldfish, complete with name and bowl, during their stay at Hotel Monaco. Or you can bring the family dog or cat to this hotel. Weekend rates are especially family friendly for a great "city escape" with the kids. Hotel Monaco's spacious suites, quality food, and convenient location make it an excellent choice. $$$–$$$$

Inverness Hotel & Conference Center, I-25 south at exit 192, 200 Inverness Dr. West, Englewood; (800) 832-9053; www.inverness hotel.com. This is "Denver's only Resort Hotel." Inverness is a AAA Four-Diamond hotel on its own championship golf course. State-of-the-art business facilities meet the needs of those families combining business and vacation. Your kids will definitely enjoy the attractive outdoor pool during the summer. Extravagant evening buffets and Sun brunch are popular with locals as well as guests. Nearby Park Meadows Mall offers upscale shopping. $$$$

Loews Denver Hotel, 4150 East Mississippi Ave. (just off Colorado Boulevard, southeast of the Cherry Creek area); (303) 782-9300 or (800) 345-9172; www.loewshotels.com. Looking for a convenient location away from downtown? Known to locals as the Darth Vader building, this black-glass luxurious hotel offers exceptional consideration for parents traveling with children. Fisher-Price welcome gifts, games, children's menus, Kids-Camp, supervised recreational programs, and "kidbanas" by the pool are just some of the

Star Bright, **Star Light . . .**

It was Christmas Eve 1914, and on a quiet city street in downtown Denver, a young boy lay in his upstairs bedroom too ill to be carried downstairs to join family members around the Christmas tree. The lad's grandfather, D. D. Sturgeon, one of Denver's pioneer electricians, could not bear to see his grandson completely miss out on the festivities. Wanting to brighten the small boy's holidays, he took some ordinary light bulbs, dipped them in red and green paint, connected them to electrical wire, and proceeded to string the glowing baubles onto the branches of a pine tree outside his grandson's bedroom window within easy view of the boy's appreciative gaze. Thus a Denver tradition began.

From early Dec to late Jan, Denver's annual World's Largest Christmas Lighting Display adorns the neoclassical City and County Building with as many as 40,000 bulbs, innumerable floodlights, 17 miles of electrical wiring, and tons of evergreen boughs. Nightly, thousands of folks drive past to catch a glimpse of the glowing masterpiece. Thousands more brave the cold winter evenings to stroll Civic Center Park; pause before Santa, sleigh, and reindeer; and admire Mary, Joseph, and the Christ child in the nativity scene.

This extraordinary exhibit of Christmas lighting seems a fitting tribute to a little boy who, but for the ingenuity of his grandfather, would never have known the splendor of colored electric lights on a glistening outdoor pine tree. The display is lighted nightly from 6 to 10 p.m. during the Christmas season and then again during the National Western Stock Show, from early to mid-Jan. **Free.** For information call (303) 892-1112.

kid-friendly amenities provided at this fine hotel. $$$–$$$$

Marriott Courtyard, on the 16th Street Mall at Curtis, downtown; (303) 571-1114 or (888) 249-1810. While this is a newer choice in downtown lodging, it's actually a historic landmark—the old Joslin's department store, built in 1886. Many rooms front the lively 16th Street Mall with large Chicago-style windows. All rooms have dataports in case you haven't left your work at home. King suite rooms provide a sofa sleeper for the kids in the living area. Staff members welcome families. They have games for your youngsters and can

arrange babysitting if you wish. Starbucks and Rialto Cafe, a metropolitan bistro, are in the hotel. $$$$ weeknights; $$$ weekends.

The Westin Tabor Center, 1672 Lawrence St., downtown; (303) 572-9100; www.westin taborcenterdenver.com. If you request in advance, cribs and highchairs will be ready and waiting in your room upon arrival. Youngsters receive their own registration packets and either a sports bottle or sippy cup (depending upon the age of the child). The fourth floor beckons with an indoor/outdoor pool and health club. Referrals for licensed babysitting services are available through the concierge, and special children's menus offer such favorites as pizza, chicken fingers, and macaroni and cheese. Inquire about other kid-friendly features. $$$

For More Information

Denver Metro Convention and Visitors Bureau, 1555 California St., Denver, CO 80202; (303) 892-1112, (303) 892-1505, or (800) 233-6837; www.denver.org. Visitor Guide available.

Annual Events

Ethnic, cultural, historic, culinary, or just for laughs—the Denver metropolitan area loves to celebrate. Almost every weekend year-round, you'll find a festival or special event suitable for the family. For exact dates and times, call (303) 892-1112 unless otherwise noted. Following is a sampling of yearly offerings.

JANUARY

National Western Stock Show, early to mid-Jan; www.nationalwestern.com. This three-week-long Old West experience, said to be the "world's premier stock show and one of the nation's largest," consists of rodeo performances, livestock competitions, auctions, a children's petting area, name entertainers, and food and western merchandise booths. This is your chance to rub elbows with cowboys, ranch hands, and farm kids with their 4-H exhibits. The rodeos are often sellouts, so make reservations early. $–$$

MARCH

St. Patrick's Day Parade, mid-Mar. On the Sat preceding St. Patrick's Day, Denver celebrates the "wearin' of the green" with its annual parade winding through the downtown streets. This is an especially festive occasion for all who are Irish, if only for one day. **Free.**

March Powwow, mid-Mar; www.denver marchpowwow.org. More than seventy tribes of Native Americans take part in this annual gathering. Arts and crafts booths, drumming competitions, and more than 700 musicians and dancers add to the excitement. Children age 6 and under **free.** $$

APRIL

Heather Gardens Craft Fairs, Community Center, 2888 South Heather Gardens Way, Aurora. Come see how talented and creative our neighbors are. Two fairs, one in early Apr, the other in mid-Oct. Phone for exact dates, (303) 745-0018. **Free.**

MAY

Cinco de Mayo, early May. This is the state's largest event honoring those of Hispanic heritage. The main festival takes place in Denver's Civic Center. Booths offer crafts, art, and wonderful Mexican food; female dancers twirl in billowing red, orange, blue, and yellow dresses; and male performers in sleek black suits stamp their feet in time to lively mariachi music. Celebrating Mexico's victory over the invading French in 1862, Cinco de Mayo is now a national holiday in Mexico. **Free** admission.

JUNE

Capitol Hill People's Fair, early June. What began as a neighborhood block party expanded over the years to become a street fair. Now, more than twenty years later, it has become the largest annual arts and crafts fair in Colorado. Food booths, craft tables, strolling entertainers, and live music on several stages spread across the width and breadth of Denver's Civic Center. More than 700 volunteers work the fair, and the proceeds are divided among neighborhood nonprofit groups. **Free.**

JULY

Fourth of July Family Picnic, July 4. Four Mile Historic Park hosts a good old-fashioned picnic. Bring your picnic hamper and blanket to celebrate in the style of the mid-1800s.

Authentic live music by Denver's own 4th U.S. Artillery Regimental Band. $

Black Arts Festival, July; www.denbaf.org. This celebration extols African-American art, music, dance, food, and culture. You will find a replica of a traditional Nigerian village, a marketplace, and entertainment from around the world. **Free.**

OCTOBER
Harvest Festival, early Oct, (303) 795-3950. This annual celebration, held at Littleton Historical Museum, features interpreters in period clothing, hayrides, music, and the sale of honey from the museum's beehives. Pumpkins may be picked and purchased from the patch. Tasty treats include hot cider and pumpkin pie. **Free,** $ for pumpkins

The Great Pumpkin Harvest Festival, early Oct, (720) 865-0800. At this festive fall celebration, held at Four Mile Historic Park, your family can choose just the right pumpkin to become this year's Halloween jack-o'-lantern, watch pumpkin-carving demonstrations, and, for a small fee, fashion their own scarecrow. There's live music, cider tasting, and warm cookies baked on an outdoor woodstove. Or how about a hayrack ride? **Free.**

Boo at the Zoo, Denver. Kids are encouraged to wear their Halloween costumes, weather permitting. Phone for exact dates and times, (303) 376-4800; www.denver/zoo .org.

DECEMBER
Parade of Lights, early Dec, (303) 892-1112. This is an annual must for many families. Bring plenty of blankets, sit on the curb, and watch as hot-air balloons in the shapes of animals and cartoon characters, costumed figures representing favorite personalities from kids' TV shows, and clowns, clowns, and more clowns march by. Thousands of twinkling lights adorn floats. Santa's is the grand finale. **Free.**

World's Largest Christmas Lighting Display, early Dec to New Year's Day and then again during the National Western Stock Show from early to mid-Jan, (303) 892-1112. More than 40,000 colored lights adorn Denver's City and County Building. Christmas carols and animated displays add to the festivities. **Free.**

Wildlights, the month of Dec, (303) 892-1112. There's something special about taking your kids to the zoo on a brisk winter night when many of the animals are sound asleep and the quiet menagerie comes alive with thousands of lights in the form of huge animals and beautiful Christmas trees. Make sure the entire family wears their warmest woollies, and plan to make several trips to the concession stand for hot cider. $

Blossoms of Light, the month of Dec, (720) 865-3500; www.botanicgardens.org/content/ blossoms-light. Stroll through the Botanic Gardens amid twinkling lights in the form of giant flowers and leaping frogs. With Christmas carols floating across the frosty evening air, the outdoor gardens become a favorite holiday wonderland. Hot cider is available in the main building, so take your little ones inside occasionally to warm their tummies and toes. $–$$

Northeastern Colorado

The northeastern quadrant of the state is referred to as "Colorado's Final Frontier." Here you will find handcrafted hospitality provided by people who seem to have the time to listen and the heart to care. Besides a north-south ribbon of small cities, most of the countryside is made up of western-style towns, farms, cattle ranches, river valleys, and wide-open plains. Antelope, deer, prairie dogs, coyotes, raccoons, red foxes, and rabbits roam the prairie lands.

TopPicks in Northeastern Colorado

- **Colorado Railroad Museum,** Golden
- **Denver Botanic Gardens at Chatfield,** Littleton
- **Greeley Independence Stampede,** Greeley
- **Heritage Square,** Golden
- **Historic Centennial Village,** Greeley
- **KidSpree,** Aurora
- **Rocky Mountain National Park,** Estes Park
- **Rocky Mountain Pumpkin Ranch,** Longmont
- **Sunflower Farm,** Longmont
- **Wild Animal Sanctuary,** Keeneburg

NORTHEASTERN COLORADO

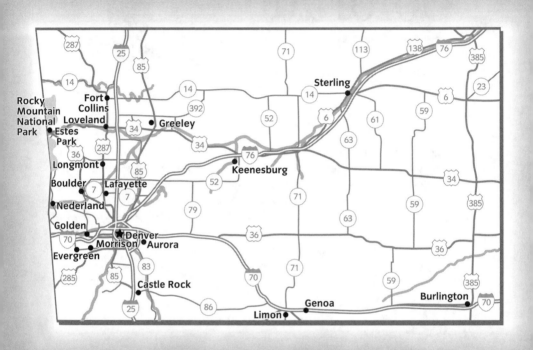

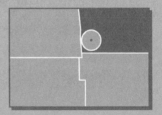

Aurora

With a population of nearly 310,000 residents, Aurora is the state's third-largest city. Located adjacent to Denver's city limits to the west, it stretches north, south, and far out east onto the high plains, covering an area of 151 square miles.

Aurora is listed as one of the top ten best cities in the United States in *50 Fabulous Places to Raise Your Family,* by Lee and Saralee Rosenberg, and *Sports Illustrated* magazine designated it as the best "Sportstown" in the state of Colorado. No doubt these honors are partially due to the numerous family-oriented outdoor activities available within the city's 8,000 acres of open space (including improved parks, reservoirs, golf courses, and unimproved natural grasslands). Families can indulge in hiking and biking on miles of urban trails; fishing, boating, and swimming at sandy-beached reservoirs; golfing on seven award-winning municipal golf courses; and playing and picnicking in more than 120 parks. And with at least 300 days of sunshine each year and a consistently low level of humidity, outdoors is the place to be when in Aurora.

Although the city's motto is, "We look to the future," it's intriguing to take a quick look at Aurora's past. As far back as A.D. 673, the Plains–Woodland Indians camped in the area, followed by the Kiowa, Apache, Comanche, Cheyenne, and Arapaho who all either spent time here or passed through. The Cheyenne and the Arapaho were the last to leave these lands.

The first Europeans to occupy the area were traders and trappers. Then came ranchers, farmers, miners, and merchants. When the Union Pacific Railroad came to Denver in 1870, it bought up most of the land that is now Aurora and the community developed much like other small towns along the railroad lines that crossed the Great Plains.

Aurora History Museum (ages 5 and up)

15051 East Alameda Parkway (on the northwest corner of East Alameda Avenue and Chambers Road between the Justice Center and City Hall on the Aurora Municipal Center Campus; (303) 739-6666 or (303) 739-6660; www.aurora-museum.org. Open year-round, Tues through Fri 9 a.m. to 4 p.m., Sat and Sun 11 a.m. to 4 p.m. Closed on Mon and all major holidays. Small fee for special programs. Normally free.

Aurora's first history museum opened in 1979 in a house with two small rooms used as galleries, an even smaller office and a handful of objects donated by local citizens.

Today, located in a handsome building, the museum features three galleries, two with changing exhibits and one dedicated to a permanent collection of numerous artifacts reflecting the history of Aurora. It's interesting to note, though, how only a few items, such as a tiny baby bonnet, a child's tea set, a woman's dress, and an old-fashioned iron, can say so much about the past.

The facility also has a community room, a small classroom, an enticing gift alcove, and storage space for more than 19,000 photographs and 21,000 collection pieces. Kids head for the hands-on, "Okay to Touch" room set up especially for them.

Throughout the year, the museum offers educational programs, workshops, lectures, tours, and family events for all ages. The "Outreach Program" has enlightened and entertained millions of school children.

Bluff Lake Nature Center (ages 4 and up)

9861 East Colfax Ave., Suite 100, (office location); (303) 344-1836; www.blufflakenaturecenter .org. Open daily, sunrise to sunset. Directions: Finding Bluff Lake Nature Center the first time can be a little difficult. There is no postal address for the site. It's best to go to the Web site and print out the satellite map and driving directions. Or, begin at the corner of East Colfax Avenue and Moline Street. Moline Street is east of Havana Street and west of Peoria Street. From East Colfax Avenue and Moline Street, proceed north on Moline Street until you reach the curve in the road. Follow the curve as it turns left (west). The Bluff Lake Nature Center entrance is on the right (north) side of the road. Small fee for some programs. Entry to park free.

Who would ever suspect that smack dab in the middle of a well-established residential neighborhood, not far from an industrial park, golf course, and a former international airport, there would exist a 123-acre wildlife refuge and a 9-acre lake alive with birdsong, chirps, chatter, squeaks, squeals. and howls? In this special place live cottontail rabbits, beavers, badgers, raccoons, red eared slider turtles, striped skunks, prairie coyotes, red fox, mule deer, and at least 20 species of waterfowl and birds, including the great horned owl.

Before pioneers settled in this area, Native Americans lived on the surrounding plains while depending upon the land for survival. They hunted bison and deer on the bluffs, and the Bluff Lake area sustained them well.

Then, the landscape changed. Farms and ranches emerged and an airport was built. The Bluff Lake land was bought by the Denver Aviation Department as an emergency "crash zone" required by the Federal Aviation Administration to exist at the end of all runways to protect the neighboring landowners. For the next 50 years, surrounded by barbed wire, the lake and bluff area was seemingly forgotten by all, except for the wildlife that found it to be a safe sanctuary.

Time passed, the airport closed, the region became residential and Bluff Lake was rediscovered. Dedicated environmental organizations worked together for years to ensure an ongoing stewardship of the property. In 2008, Denver's Department of Aviation transferred ownership to the Bluff Lake Nature Center, making it possible for them to continue to care for the site and provide quality environmental education for future generations.

Today, groomed trails lead into the wooded areas and around the lake, with wooden walkways permitting visitors to venture out into the wetlands. Amenities include a parking lot, restrooms, numerous trails (some that are handicapped accessible), interpretive signage, a xeriscaped garden, a trellised overlook with benches, and a small amphitheater. But, perhaps, the greatest amenity of all is the opportunity to walk the paths, absorb the quiet, watch for wildlife, and enjoy a bit of wilderness in the middle of the city.

The Center is in the planning stage of constructing a 5,000-square-foot Environmental Education Center overlooking the lake and wetlands. When completed, classrooms and the Center's office will be located in the structure.

One of Bluff Lake Nature Center's major goals is to get kids outside and help them gain an appreciation for the outdoors, nature, and wildlife. Children age 5 to 12 are welcome to join the Outdoor Adventure Club and attend half-day and weeklong camps during the summer months. (There is a charge for the camps.) Parents are especially encouraged to bring their children with them to the Fireside Chats. Regularly scheduled, highly successful programs, presented by the Center, include family oriented entertainment and guest speakers who preside over a variety of subjects. While the sun slowly sinks behind the mountains, guests listen, enjoy the campfire and a marshmallow roast, and watch as nocturnal animals awaken and poke their noses out of the underbrush to see what is going on.

A recent Fireside Chat, "History Comes Alive," centered on the "Homesteader Trunk," borrowed from the Aurora History Museum. The presentation focused on the early settlers who came to the Aurora and Denver areas. Still another Chat, held on a lovely autumn evening, featured a Native American flutist and storyteller. These are the types of activities you can expect at the Bluff Lake Nature Center. A schedule of events is published on their Web site.

Cherry Creek State Park (all ages)

4201 South Parker Rd. (located 1 mile south of I-225); (303) 690-1166 (information), (303) 470-1144 or (800) 678-2267 (campsite reservations), (303) 779-6144 (marina); http://parks .state.co.us. Open daily year-round (hours vary greatly according to season, best to phone). Park facilities (marina, concessions, etc.) are open Memorial Day through Labor Day. Park passes, $$; campsites, $$.

This suburban oasis contains more than one hundred campsites and as many picnic sites. The 3,915-acre recreational area boasts full-service camping, stables for renting horses, guided nature walks, an extensive trail system for biking and horseback riding, and a paved model airplane field. An 880-acre reservoir attracts water enthusiasts for boating, water-skiing, Jet-skiing, windsurfing, and fishing. Boat rentals are available at the marina on the west side of the lake. The swim beach provides a sandy, roped-off area for swimmers, plus a bathhouse, food concessions, and a first-aid station. Campsites fill quickly on summer weekends, so advance reservations are a must.

Aurora Reservoir (all ages)

5800 South Powhaton Rd. (enter at intersection of Quincy Avenue and Powhaton Road, 2½ miles east of E470); (303) 690-1286; www.auroragov.org. Park open daily, dawn to dusk, year-round; office open 9 a.m. to 5 p.m. Both closed Thanksgiving, Christmas, and New Year's Day. Parking fee $$. Free use of trail.

There is so much to do at this 2,500-acre recreation mecca, (the reservoir itself has a surface area of over 800 acres) it's best to plan to spend the day. You will find fishing, sailing, windsurfing, boating, ice skating, boat rentals, offshore moorings, dry storage, a wheelchair-accessible dock, a scuba area, an archery range, a playground, picnic shelters, and an 8½-mile multi-use, paved trail. The newest addition here is a U.S. Track and Field-certified 5K training course.

Aurora Wheel Park (ages 10 and up)

2500 South Wheel Park Circle (access from Iliff Avenue, ¼ mile east of Chambers Road); (303) 739-7160; www.auroragov.org. Open daily year-round (depending on weather conditions), 8 a.m. to dusk. Closed when city-sponsored events are scheduled. An event schedule is available by phoning (303) 326-8700. Free.

The fact that this facility has 150 parking spaces is a good indication of just how popular it is. The park features an 18,200-square-foot skateboard bowl with 60 x 120-foot bicycle freestyle ramps, two 6-foot quarter pipes, an 8-foot quarter pipe, a spine, two grind rails, a fun box, a jump box, and a 6-foot-radius wedge. Also awaiting kids with energy to spare are an over 1,000-foot BMX dirt racetrack, three in-line hockey rinks, and an 80 x 120-foot remote-control car track. This is a "use at your own risk" facility. Participants are required to follow an extensive list of rules and to wear helmets; knee, shin, and elbow pads; mouth guards; long pants; long-sleeved shirts; and gloves at all times. Additional safety gear may be needed. Be advised that the use of this park can result in serious injury. Be sure your kids take the safety rules seriously, then stand by to be certain they follow them.

Aurora Sports Park (all ages)

18601 East Sports Park Dr.; (303) 326-8401; www.auroragov.org/recreation. Open dawn to dusk; hours may change for a particular event. Best to phone. Cost varies depending on event. Some events free.

Located south of Colfax Avenue and east of Tower Road, the Aurora Sports Park is a sports-minded city's dream come true! The 220-acre complex was designed to fulfill a need to accommodate a variety of national and regional events, including ongoing league use for both youth and adults. It opened in the fall of 2002 to a series of soccer competitions and welcomed both softball and baseball the following spring. The largest multi-use athletic field conglomerate in the Rocky Mountain region, it contains twenty-two full-size soccer fields and one lighted championship soccer field; twelve youth baseball/full-size softball fields and one lighted championship baseball field (all softball and baseball fields have spectator seating); a small softball/T-ball area; parking for 2,200 vehicles, and numerous support structures (concessions, shelters, dugouts, and restrooms). Artfully landscaped around a natural creek that runs diagonally through the property, the park features lawns and native turf, more than 2,000 trees, picnic areas, and a trailhead to Sand Creek Regional Greenway. Future additions include batting cages and a winding trail corridor.

Hoops Park (ages 6 and up)

16300 East 6th Ave.; (303) 739-7160; www.auroragov.org. Open daily year-round, 8 a.m. to sunset. Free.

After the city of Aurora built the Aurora Sports Park and the Aurora Wheel Park, the pressure was on from those devoted to basketball. City officials reported that the Parks & Open Space Department received numerous requests from residents for a "hoops" version of the other two facilities. Hoops Park boasts three full-sized, outdoor courts and twenty-three parking spaces. Now those who want to work off stress or just play the game, can indulge in H-O-R-S-E or one-on-one, and shoot, dribble, and dunk on courts constructed of post-tension concrete with backboards made of clear polycarbonate.

Plains Conservation Center (ages 2 and up)
21901 East Hampden Ave.; (303) 693-3621; www.plains-center.org. Inquire about dates for special events ($) that are open to the public. Open Sat year-round. Free.

Bring your children here to see how the native population and pioneers once lived on Colorado's High Plains. Stand inside one of four authentically reproduced tepees and hear nothing but the sound of the wind sweeping over the prairie. Walk the trail for about ½ mile to "Wells' Garden," a ca. 1887 rural outpost featuring two "soddie" homesteads, a schoolhouse, a blacksmith's shop, a chicken coop, and an heirloom garden. Please keep in mind that this is a work in progress that depends primarily on volunteers. It is, however, well worth bringing along a picnic lunch and spending a few peaceful hours surrounded by 1,100 acres populated only by prairie dogs, mule deer, pronghorn antelope, coyotes, red-tail hawks, meadowlarks, and a snake or two.

Ask about the summertime, weeklong day camp programs for kids and the special Fri evening overnights in the tepees for families that include box dinners, wagon rides, campfires, games, and breakfast. Also check on the dates for "Harvest at the Homestead," a

KidSpree

This annual two-day event in mid-July transforms Aurora's twenty-nine-acre Bicentennial Park into a joyful playland for ages 1 through 12. Colorado's largest outdoor festival designed specifically for kids had more than 47,000 parents, children, and volunteer attendees at the free celebration in 2009, its 13th-year anniversary. The activities are seemingly endless. Here kids can try to scale a 25-foot-high climbing wall, bounce on giant inflatables, play house in a playhouse, create crafts, stroll though Kandy Lane, explore the Pink Castle, slide down Gumdrop Mountain, crawl through the 24-foot-long Lifesaver Tunnel, and amble along a path in the Licorice Forest. Squeals of laughter penetrate the air as youngsters play lost-and-found and hide-and-seek in the a-maze-ing, 2,500-square-foot Jungle Maze. When the energy levels (theirs and yours) begin to droop, kids can ask the clowns to paint their faces, pick up a free bottle of water donated by the Rural/Metro Ambulance Service (they also treat boo boos and owies), find a place under a shade tree, and be entertained by magicians, musicians, performing dogs, and professional dancers.

Kidspree takes place on a Sat and Sun in mid-July, 10 a.m. to 5 p.m., in Bicentennial Park, 13655 East Alameda Ave.; (303) 326-8386; www.auroragov .org/kidspree). Phone for dates. Free.

heartwarming celebration with music and costumed interpreters, and "Christmas in the Soddies," with carols sung around a tumbleweed Christmas tree. Fees for special events are used for further improvements of the site.

Where to Eat

Atlanta Bread Company, 14262 East Cedar Ave. (located in the Aurora City Place shopping complex, east of I-225 and Alameda Avenue); (303) 341-6200; www.atlanta breaddenver.com. Open Mon through Sat 6:30 a.m. to 9 p.m., Sun from 8 a.m. to 7 p.m. When you want to treat your family to a nutritious meal made with quality ingredients and, at the same time, keep them happily satisfied, forget the fast-food places and bring them to this family-run restaurant. Soft classical music sets the peaceful tone while you indulge in homemade soups like those that come from Grandma's kitchen, wholesome sandwiches made from bread that was baked only a few hours before, delicious pastries, and fresh fruit-flavored smoothies. The adults will appreciate the House Latte, the Atlanta Bread Company's own concoction of espresso, steamed milk, honey, vanilla, and cinnamon topped with whipped cream, and their Caramel Macchiato, a caramel, steamed milk, and whipped cream delight. And here's a glimpse into this restaurant's community spirit: Every night, all baked goods not sold that day are donated to local charities. $–$$

Las Hadas Mexican Restaurant, 15264 East Hampden Ave.; (303) 693-9519. The best Mexican dining in Aurora is prepared by Miguel Navarro and family. Excellent food, a full bar, courteous service, generous helpings, and reasonable prices make this restaurant a favorite for families. They have a children's menu for those age 10 and under. Over a period of time, my friends and I have tried nearly everything on the menu and have not once been disappointed. For dessert, try their fried ice cream, xango, sopapillas, and flan. You are greeted like friends when you enter, and after a few times dining here, you will find that you and the staff have become friends. A mariachi band often entertains on Fri evening from 6 p.m. to 9 p.m. $–$$

Where to Stay

Double Tree Hotel, 13696 East Iliff Place (I-225 and Iliff Avenue), Aurora; (303) 337-2800 or (800) 222-8733; www.denversouth east.doubletree.com. Amenities here include an indoor pool and Jacuzzi, exercise room, Fitzgerald's Cafe and Pub, and complimentary shuttle service to Denver International Airport and within five miles of the hotel. Centrally located. $$–$$$

Gateway Inns & Suites, 800 South Abilene St.; (720) 748-4800. This Best Western-accredited hotel generously provides a **free** deluxe continental breakfast including a waffle bar, **free** cookies in the lobby every afternoon, and **free** local phone calls. All rooms have refrigerators, microwave ovens, coffeemakers, and high-speed Internet connections. Other amenities include an indoor pool, a jacuzzi, a fitness center, and **free** access to the Bally Total Fitness complex. Centrally located. Children age 12 and under stay **free.** $–$$

La Quinta Inns, 1011 South Abilene St. (off I-225 and Mississippi Avenue), Aurora; (303) 337-0206; www.lq.com. Centrally located in the heart of the city. High-speed Internet access in all rooms. Children age 18 and under stay **free.** $–$$

For More Information

Aurora Chamber of Commerce, 14305 East Alameda Ave., Suite 300, Aurora, CO 80012; (303) 369-8400; www.aurorachamber .org. Open Mon through Fri 8 a.m. to 5 p.m.

Castle Rock

The center of Colorado's fastest-growing county, Castle Rock is 28 miles south of Denver on I-25.

Castlewood Canyon State Park (all ages)

CO 83, 6 miles south of Franktown (east of I-25 at Castle Rock); (303) 688-5242; http://parks .state.co.us/parks/castlewoodcanyon. Open every day of the year, weather permitting, sunrise to sunset. $ per car.

Castlewood Canyon—with turkey vultures drifting overhead, grazing pronghorn antelope, leaping leopard frogs, and tracks of bobcats and porcupines—offers nature and wildlife just thirty minutes from Denver. This popular hiking and picnicking day-use area also attracts technical rock climbers. One-mile-long Canyon View Nature Trail, leading to four overviews, is stroller and wheelchair accessible—a good choice for young children or "flatland" visitors. The park is 1,000 feet higher than Denver, so those—even children— not acclimated to the altitude may huff and puff with exertion. Hardier hikers choose trails into the colorful canyon, to a waterfall or the remains of Castlewood Dam, and along Cherry Creek. Keep your eyes open for prairie falcons, great blue herons and golden eagles flying overhead. Both nest in remote areas of the park.

A visitor center presents a fourteen-minute slide show and encourages children's curiosity with interactive displays. Check schedules for junior-naturalist programs or pre-school storytime. Almost every Sat there's a program or special event. Call for informa-tion and trail conditions during winter months.

Devil's Head Trail & Fire Lookout Tower (ages 6 and up)

From Castle Rock north 8 miles to Sedalia, southwest on CO 67 to junction with Ram-part Range Road (at the Indian Creek Campground), and south approximately 7 miles. Campground, picnic sites, parking, and trailhead are 1 mile east of Rampart Range Road. Free.

Here's a hike with a special reward when you arrive. From parking lot to tower, this National Recreation Trail climbs more than 1,000 feet in less than 1½ miles. Whiners (adult or child) may become almost insufferable, but this is a classic Colorado family hike. As you enter a clearing, you find the last manned fire lookout tower in Pike National Forest awaiting your climb. Consider taking time for a snack and drink before ascending the 143 stairs to the look-out. During summer the ranger will show you around and even sell you a Forest Service T-shirt or cap. This may be the most scenic shopping you'll do in Colorado. The views stretch from Rocky Mountain National Park in the north to the

Devil's Head **Folklore and Legends**

All that glitters just might be gold. In the 1870s an outlaw gang robbed a government train, making off with an estimated $60,000 in gold eagle coins. They buried the loot in the Devil's Head area, marked the spot with a knife stabbed into a tree, and left, a posse fast on their heels. It is said that the loot was never recovered. Could *you* be the one to find it? Keep your eyes open.

Rock hounds still search for topaz on Devil's Head slopes. In 1883 W. B. Smith discovered a rich deposit of the gems, some of the best found in the United States. The mother–lode is yet to be found.

The first woman fire lookout, Helen Dow, served three summers at Devil's Head beginning in 1921. That first summer she reported sixteen fires.

Sangre de Cristos south of Pikes Peak, and west to the Continental Divide, spiked with the spires of the Collegiate Range. It's worth putting up with the whiners, big or little.

Southwest Metropolitan Denver

Denver Botanic Gardens at Chatfield (all ages)
8500 Deer Creek Canyon Rd., Littleton (southwest of C-470 on Wadsworth Boulevard); (303) 973-3705; www.botanicgardens.org. Open daily year-round, 9 a.m. to 5 p.m. $ per car; free the first Fri of each month.

A good place for pleasant walking, this 700-acre preserve maintains open grassland, a woodland river ecosystem, and ten acres of wetlands. There also are two 19th-century farms and a one-room schoolhouse, which functions as the visitor center. Kids will enjoy checking out the old-fashioned playground.

Along 2 miles of walking trails, self-guiding material helps you learn about plants. The survival garden has edible, medicinal, and poisonous plants. Stop in the wildlife blind overlooking the wetlands to observe birds. Deer, elk, and rabbits frequent the area.

During the second weekend in Oct, the Denver Botanic Gardens at Chatfield hosts a terrific Pumpkin Festival and Corn Maze, one of the very best in the area. Allow at least three hours to take in the eight-acre maze, craft booths, food stands, hayrides, and pick-your-own-pumpkin patch. A great way to celebrate fall. Call (303) 973-3705 for information.

Chatfield State Park (all ages)
One mile south of C-470 on Wadsworth Boulevard (follow the signs to the state park entrance on the left); (303) 791-7275; http://parks.state.co.us/parks/chatfield. Open daily 5 a.m. to 10 p.m. $ per car.

Another great place for family hiking! This state park is less crowded than most, yet there's lots to do and 5,600 acres in which to do it. Trails lead you through grasslands, to ponds, along a reservoir, and through the woods. If you're quiet, you may spot lizards, frogs, toads, and turtles. There are good places to practice skipping rocks across the water.

Great blue herons nest within the park. Learn about them at an outdoor exhibit on the park's south side. At 4 feet tall with a 6-foot wingspan, they are a spectacular sight.

From Memorial Day through Labor Day, cool off at the swim beach. Lifeguards are not always on duty. Check on this if you plan for any members of your family to enter the water. The chilly temperature of the reservoir doesn't seem to faze kids. There's a sandy beach, so bring your castle-building equipment. Floats are allowed in the water; lifeguards are on duty. The concession stand has reasonable prices, and there are restrooms with showers and changing facilities. It's perfect! There is a separate entry fee for the swim beach: $1 per person.

If you still have energy after hiking and swimming, boat rentals and fishing await, and horseback riding is available within the park at Chatfield Stables, (303) 933-3636.

Roxborough State Park (all ages)

C-470 to the Santa Fe exit, south to Titan Road, which makes a sharp left turn, becoming Rampart Range Road. There are well-marked signs to the park; (303) 973-3959; www.colorado parks.org. Open daily. Summer hours generally 8 a.m. to 7 p.m.; winter hours vary monthly. Call ahead. $ per car.

History, geology, flora, and fauna—it's all here, but many visitors come just to enjoy Roxborough's gentle looping hikes among stunning red-rock formations similar to those at the Garden of the Gods. Inside the visitor center, a fifteen-minute slide program gives an overview of the park. (Good family hint: Restrooms here are open even if the visitor center is closed.)

A strong program of one-day workshops, lectures, guided hikes, and concerts includes many that are good for kids. Call the park for a schedule of activities for children.

Trailhead of the **Colorado Trail**

North of Roxborough State Park, at the mouth of Waterton Canyon, hikers find mile marker "0" for the Colorado Trail. Completed in 1987 after massive volunteer efforts, this is a continuous trail from Denver to Durango (in southwest Colorado) that is 461 miles long. Each summer hundreds set off to complete the entire trek; many others enjoy a few miles at a time. The first segment follows a Denver Water Board road to Strontia Springs Dam. While not a favorite section with hikers, the reward here is frequently spotting bighorn sheep. During travels in Colorado you will often be near segments of the trail. Take time to experience one of the state's great treasures.

Morrison

Tiny Town (ages 1 to 8)

6249 South Turkey Creek Rd. (5 miles west of the C-470 and US 285 interchange); (303) 697-6829; www.tinytownrailroad.com. Open Memorial Day to Labor Day, 10 a.m. to 5 p.m. Open Sat and Sun only during May and Sept, $, children 2 and younger free.

This miniature, child-size village delights young visitors with its one hundred colorful buildings constructed to a one-sixth scale. You can play the game of "Who Lives Here?" and let your youngsters choose homes for their grandmas and grandpas, aunties and uncles, or for imaginary families. The structures are big enough so that kids can peek in windows, and you can use them as backdrops for photos of your little ones. The Tiny Town Railway takes big and little passengers on a 1-mile journey around the early-20th-century town and up scenic Turkey Canyon. The railway station features a grown-up-size gift shop and snack bar.

Morrison Natural History Museum (ages 6 and up)

501 Highway 8 (½ mile south of Morrison); (303) 697-1873; www.mnhm.org. Open daily 10 a.m. to 4 p.m. Closed Easter, Thanksgiving, Christmas Eve and Day, and New Year's Day. $.

This museum is housed in the Leland Cox cabin, built in 1945 as a replica of a stagecoach stop. It's located just a few miles from Dinosaur Ridge and is a good first stop. A twenty-minute video gives an orientation to the ridge. The collection includes bones of the original stegosaurus found on Dinosaur Ridge in 1877. There are hands-on exhibits where you can handle dinosaur bones, touch live reptiles native to this area, and learn what it's like to dig for fossils.

Dinosaur Ridge (ages 4 and up)

16831 West Alameda Parkway; (303) 697-3466; www.dinoridge.org. Visitor Center open May through Oct, Mon through Sat 9 a.m. to 5 p.m., Sun 11 a.m. to 5 p.m.; Nov through Apr, Mon through Sat 9 a.m. to 4 p.m., Sun 11 a.m. to 4 p.m. Free.

Dinosaurs once lived right here—about fifteen minutes from downtown—when Denver was an ocean. Dinosaur Ridge contains footprints and fossil remains of the giant creatures that roamed here 100–150 million years ago. Ocean waves are preserved in large sections of rock.

Parking is available at the visitor center on the east side of the ridge. Follow the 1-mile self-guided tour provided by Friends of Dinosaur Ridge, a nonprofit group. Sixteen interpretive signs describe important features. Guidebooks, giving more complete information for each stop, may be purchased. You'll be walking on the shoulder of a public road, so hang on to your children. It's easy to wander out onto the pavement.

One Saturday a month, from Apr through Oct, the road is closed to normal traffic for "Open Ridge Days," and a shuttle bus provides rides over the ridge. Tour guides are on board with lively explanations.

While some of the geological information is likely to be uninteresting to younger ones, everyone loves the giant dinosaur footprints. If you have dino fanatics in the family, you can arrange a guided tour by calling at least one week in advance. A minimum fee of $36 is charged for one to twelve students. Groups of thirteen or more pay $3 per person.

If you have surefooted kids with you, climb up the wooden stairs on the east side of the ridge. They lead to the narrow Dakota Ridge Trail, which has magnificent views. Watch out for mountain bikers on the trail. Check out "Trek Through Time," a **free** indoor exhibit highlighting various environments at different prehistoric times. The hands-on fossils always create an interest.

Red Rocks Park and Amphitheater (all ages)

Fifteen miles west of downtown Denver, south of I-70 on CO 93; (720) 865-2494; www.red rocksonline.com. Park hours are daily from 5 a.m. to 11 p.m. **Free** **park admission, fees charged for events.**

You'll see lots of faces and forms in the unusual red-rock formations here. Although remarkable geology surrounds visitors, most come here for the music. The outdoor amphitheater, wedged between spurs of 300-million-year-old sandstone, has been the setting for popular summer concerts since it opened in 1941.

Try to visit on a nonconcert day. The amphitheater is a great place to bring a picnic. Enjoy the panoramic view of downtown Denver. Your kids will love standing on the stage and singing to you in the stands. The natural acoustics are phenomenal. They'll also love to run up and down the rows of seats. Don't follow them for too long, or you'll be sorry tomorrow.

Stop in at the Trading Post, a curio store in a Pueblo-style building. You'll find restrooms here with entry on the outside of the building. (The restrooms at the top of the amphitheater are sometimes locked.)

Evergreen

Located 20 miles west of Denver, Evergreen sits in pine-and-aspen forest at the base of 14,260-foot Mt. Evans. For generations prominent Denver families maintained mountain homes in this area. Today many residents live here year-round and commute to jobs in Denver.

Evergreen Lake (all ages)

29614 Upper Bear Creek Rd.; (720) 880-1300; www.evergreenrecreation.com. Open for ice-skating daily when the lake is safely frozen. Skating, $; rentals, $. Open for boating Memorial Day through Labor Day, weather permitting. $$.

Spin, twirl, and glide along the frozen lake under sparkling blue Colorado skies and snow-blanketed mountain peaks. Our version of Currier and Ives, Evergreen Lake has been a winter tradition for many families for generations. When the chills set in, retreat to the log

Evergreen **Round-trip**

I-70 to the Evergreen Parkway is the fastest route from Denver to Evergreen. Make it a round-trip by following US 74 along Bear Creek back to Morrison and US 285. The route passes through or near to numerous Jefferson County Open Space and Denver Mountain Parks that provide many opportunities for outdoor recreation or picnics.

warming house for hot drinks and snacks. There's even an espresso bar. Lights make it possible to skate until 7 p.m., but temperatures drop sharply after sundown.

During the summer, pedal or paddle using rental canoes and paddleboats, or spend some quiet time fishing. Since the lake serves as a water supply, swimming and wading are not permitted. A boardwalk through wetlands connects to a trail circling the lake and to a wheelchair-accessible fishing pier. Picnic tables, a playground, and adjoining public golf course make this an outdoor stop for everyone.

Hiwan Homestead Historical Museum (ages 4 and up)

4208 South Timbervale Dr. (just off Meadow Drive); (720) 497-7650; www.frontrangeliving .com/architecture/Hiwanhomestead.htm. Open year-round, Tues through Sun; June through Aug, 11 a.m. to 5 p.m.; Sept through May, noon to 5 p.m. Free **tours.**

The seventeen-room log lodge illustrates summer mountain living from 1890 to 1930. Rooms are furnished in an eclectic blend of Old West, Native American artifacts, and period pieces. One of the two octagonal towers has a Gothic-inspired chapel on the second floor. Numerous smaller buildings contain quilt and doll collections, carpentry and printing workshops, and cowboy gear. Some exhibits are hands-on. There's a real saddle to climb onto; perhaps you can try a little roping.

After-school programs feature historical crafts: whittling, papermaking, beadwork, and yarn dolls, among others.

Adjacent is Heritage Grove Park, a lovely shaded site for picnics and a popular spot for special events throughout the year.

For More Information

Evergreen Area Chamber of Commerce,
28065 Highway 74, Evergreen, CO 80439;
(303) 674-3412; www.evergreenchamber.org.

Golden

HOWDY, FOLKS. This large welcome sign that arches over Washington Avenue sets the tone in Golden. Once this region was the dividing line between Arapahoe and Utes—the meeting of plains and mountains. Today this thriving town is most famous as the home of Coors Brewery. But Golden also boasts museums, art galleries, a bustling downtown, and the Colorado School of Mines.

Colorado Railroad Museum (all ages)

17155 West 44th Ave.; (303) 279-4591 or (800) 365-6263; www.crrm.org. Open daily, June through Aug, 9 a.m. to 6 p.m.; Sept through May, 9 a.m. to 5 p.m. Family rates available. $–$$.

If your family is into trains, plan to spend two or three hours here. More than 50,000 rare railroad photos, documents, and artifacts reside inside the replica of a ca. 1880 train depot, while outside on the museum's fifteen acres, more than one hundred locomotives and other railroad memorabilia await. Your family can climb aboard many of the trains. And Santa comes by on the first weekend in Dec to hand out candy from the little red caboose. Several times a year an 1881 narrow-gauge steam locomotive is fired up, and visitors are offered **free** rides with museum admission. Take along a lunch or snacks to be enjoyed at one of the picnic tables, stay as long as you like, and be sure to bring your camera for some memorable happy snaps.

Heritage Square (all ages)

18301 West Colfax Ave. (take exit 259 from I-70 and travel north on US 40 for 1 mile); (303) 279-2789; www.heritagesquare.info. Hours vary greatly depending on season. Open times for entertainment facilities and summer hours vary; phone for exact times. Free admission.

If you haven't been to Heritage Square recently, you are in for a grand surprise. A more than one-half-million-dollar renovation of this Victorian-style shopping and entertainment center has resulted in a great place to take the family. You can shop for gift items, have an old-time portrait taken, and maneuver a paddleboat or bumper car. Younger children will delight in taking a spin on the colorful carousel and climbing aboard the miniature steam

Don't Miss **the View**

Heading west from Denver on I-70, especially if this is your first visit to the Colorado Rocky Mountains, be sure to note the view as you crest the hill at the Genesee exit. The award-winning overpass bridge perfectly frames a majestic scene sweeping to the Continental Divide. For eastbound travelers the bridge frames Denver and the Front Range.

engine-powered train for a ride around the perimeter of the park. Older youngsters are sure to talk you into a game of laser tag, a ride on the Ferris wheel, and an exhilarating sweep down the alpine slide. When you're ready for a rest, popcorn, ice cream, and soft drink outlets come to the rescue, or consider having dinner at the Garden Grill Cafe.

Heritage Square Music Hall (ages 6 and up)

Located at Heritage Square; (303) 279-7800; www.hsmusichall.com. Performances year-round, Wed through Sat evening; Sun matinee. Additional performances during Christmas holidays; phone for schedule. Dinner and show, $$$$; performance only, $$$.

If your family enjoys live theater, they are sure to love the performances at the Heritage Square Music Hall. Multitalented producer, director, and actor T. J. Mullin and his cast of merrymakers present outrageous comedy shows along with musical renditions ranging in nature from honky-tonk to nostalgic, old-time tunes—all family oriented and in good taste. Your kids will delight in hissing the villain and cheering for the hero and heroine. Special productions such as *Cinderella* are nearly always on the bill for children. Consider indulging in the all-you-can-eat buffet and show package. Or dine earlier and come for the performance only.

Genesee Buffalo Herd Overlook (all ages)

West of Golden on I-70, exit 254 (follow signs to overlook). Free.

As you climb into the foothills on I-70, the highway cuts through a Denver Mountain Park. Genesee is home to a herd of approximately forty bison. With 500 acres to freely roam, including their own tunnel under the interstate, I can't promise you'll always be able to spot these mighty American native beasts, but it's worth a try. Fall and winter, when they are hay-fed, provide the best opportunity to view them close to the highway. In the summer's heat check the shaded gullies north of I-70.

The park also keeps an elk herd of about the same size. They can usually be seen from the park road to the south toward the picnic grounds and shelter. By following Genesee Mountain Road and Genesee Drive, you can get back on I-70 at the Chief Hosa exit, 253.

Genesee Park Braille Trail (all ages)

I-70 to exit 253, Chief Hosa; turn right onto Stapleton Drive and continue 1 mile to a gate across the road and a parking area. Free.

The Stapleton Braille Trail leads hikers along a 1-mile nature loop. Informative signs, printed and in Braille, enlighten as you follow the cleared, cabled path. Bask in the sun's warmth from the log bench on a south-facing slope. All visitors can enjoy this quiet stop. Bring a lunch; there is a picnic site with tables.

Buffalo Bill Memorial Museum and Grave (ages 4 and up)

987½ Lookout Mountain Rd.; (303) 526-0747; www.buffalobill.org. Open daily May through Oct, 9 a.m. to 5 p.m.; Nov through Apr, open Tues through Sun 9 a.m. to 4 p.m. Closed Christmas Day. No charge to view the gravesite. Museum: $, children 5 and younger free.

William F. Cody, better known as Buffalo Bill, is immortalized in this museum, located high atop Lookout Mountain, above the city of Golden. The assemblage, begun in 1921 by Buffalo Bill's foster son, Johnny Baker, showcases a comprehensive history of Cody's life, including old photographs, documents, and quality paintings. Also on display are Buffalo Bill's saddles and costumes from his Wild West Show and treasured gifts from his Native American friends. The latter include a ghost shirt, a hair shirt, Chief Iron Tail's headdress, and Chief Sitting Bull's bow and arrow. The museum also highlights the women of Buffalo Bill's Wild West Show. Would-be cowhands are sure to go for the "Kids' Cowboy Corral," an interactive area where they can design a brand, dress up like a cowboy, and sit in a saddle and try to lasso a calf.

Lookout Mountain Nature Center and Preserve
(all ages)

910 Colorow Rd. (from I-70 take exit 256, turn right and follow the brown signs); (720) 497-7600; www.co.jefferson.co.us/openspace. Open year-round, Tues through Fri 10 a.m. to 4 p.m. and Sat and Sun 9 a.m. to 5 p.m. Free.

Looking for something a little more active on Lookout Mountain? Head over to the Nature Center and Preserve, a premier Jefferson County Open Space Park. Hike the nature trails, picnic under towering ponderosa pines, or participate in one of many naturalist-guided activities. Events like the Junior Naturalists, Junior Rangers, and Toddler Times are designed for specific age groups, parent/child, or the entire family. Topics change with the season, so there is always something new and exciting.

Golden Walking, Hiking, **and Biking Trails**

The city of Golden is blessed with numerous easy walking, hiking, and biking trails that are perfect for families with children of different ages. Here are a few. For more request the *Hiking and Biking Trails in Golden* and the *Golden Walk* brochures from the Golden Chamber of Commerce (303-279-3113).

The **Clear Creek Trail** runs west from Washington Avenue through a park and along the river. It has an easy grade with fine gravel and is ½ mile in length, one way.

The **Tucker Gulch Trail** begins at Vanover Park, located at Ford and Water Streets. This paved, 1¹⁄₁₀-mile (one way) trail leads through north Golden and ends at Norman D. Memorial Park.

The **Golden Walk** is actually a 1½-mile, self-guided walking tour of the city, with designated cultural and historical sites along the way. This fascinating excursion includes the Clear Creek Living History Park, the ca. 1861 Territorial Capitol Building (now a restaurant), the 1867 Astor House Hotel Museum, the Foothills Art Center (free), and the Geology Museum (free).

Jefferson County **Open Space Parks**

More than twenty-five years ago, citizens of Jefferson County elected to tax themselves to set aside and preserve lands within the county. Urban nature areas, rolling plains, wildlife habitats, craggy peaks, serene mountain meadows, historical sites, and trail corridors enrich the experiences of residents and visitors. Parks offer varied opportunities and facilities. Whether you hike, bike, cross-country ski, or just take in the view, these Open Spaces are a gift. Hiwan Homestead Historical Museum and Lookout Mountain Nature Center (both listed separately in this chapter) are good places to pick up maps and brochures for the Open Space Parks. For complete information call (303) 271-5925 or consult http://open space.co.jefferson.co.us. Here's just a partial sampling:

- **Alderfer/Three Sisters Park.** Dramatic rock outcroppings, trails, deer, and wildflowers.

- **Apex.** 661 acres with 8 miles of hiking trails near Lookout Mountain.

- **Crown Hill.** Wheelchair-accessible trails lead around a fishing lake; hiking, biking, wildlife preserve, fitness circuit.

- **Elk Meadow Park.** Meadow and forest trails, good cross-country skiing, wildlife from squirrels to elk.

- **Lair o' the Bear Park.** 1½ miles of stream frontage with loop trails, wheelchair-accessible fishing pier, picnic tables, and grills.

- **Matthews/Winters Park.** Popular with mountain bikers; shady picnic grove, historic town site and cemetery; connects to Red Rocks Park.

- **Mount Falcon Park.** Trails with magnificent views of the Front Range and Continental Divide; shelter, picnic tables, historical ruins.

- **Pine Valley Ranch.** This southern-most park offers outstanding scenic views, hiking and biking trails, observatory programs, and river fishing,

- **Reynolds Park.** Interpretive trail, hiking, overnight camping (by permit only) for hikers and equestrians.

- **White Ranch Park.** Trails, very popular with mountain bikers; picnic sites and shelter, designated cross-country ski trails, and overnight camping (free by permit only) for hikers and equestrians.

Inside the nature center you'll find Discovery Corner, with interactive self-guided activity areas for the curious of all ages. Explorer theme packs to use while visiting the preserve may be rented for a small fee. If you find a book, game, or entire theme pack your child really relates to, new ones may be purchased. They're good ideas for gifts, too.

Enviroramas present the complex ecological system of the Ponderosa Pine Community. The facility exemplifies sustainable design, using environmentally responsible materials and promoting human health. Landscaping demonstrates fire-wise/low-water planning. Dedicated staff help visitors connect with nature's community.

Golden Gate Canyon State Park (all ages)

3873 Highway 46 (from Golden travel north on CO 93 for 1 mile, turn west on Golden Gate Canyon Road, and continue 13 miles to park entrance); (303) 582-3707; http://parks.state.co .us. Open daily year-round, weather permitting. Winter visitors are encouraged to call the park office for current conditions. $ per car.

In 1860 the road up Golden Gate Canyon was a toll road carrying fortune hunters to the gold fields near Black Hawk and Central City. Today, shorter routes lead to those old mining towns, while Golden Gate Canyon Road leads to outdoor adventure. Miles and miles of mountain trails keep hikers, mountain bikers, and horseback riders busy (bring your own horse, no stables). From Panorama Point you can view more than 100 miles of the Continental Divide, a great backdrop for family pictures.

Stop in the visitor center for the interactive displays and audios or to put the ecosystem puzzle together. Just outside, a wheelchair-accessible nature trail winds around a pond stocked with rainbow trout. This is an excellent spot for young children to practice their fishing skills. If they get lucky, you'll find picnic tables and grills nearby.

As the quiet solitude of winter settles on the park, opportunities abound for snowshoeing, ice fishing, skating, sledding, tubing, and cross-country skiing—even winter camping for really hardy souls.

Junior Ranger booklets lead families to new discoveries during their park visit. Show the completed booklets to a ranger for **free** certificates and badges. Interpretive programs are available throughout the summer.

Where to Eat

Table Mountain Inn, 1310 Washington Ave.; (303) 732-5447. Open daily for breakfast, lunch, and dinner; weekend brunch. Superb southwestern cuisine draws locals here regularly. Generations of families often gather for the food, friendly service, and relaxed atmosphere. From burgers to fire-roasted chile rellenos, there's something for everyone. Favorites include the southwestern Caesar salad and house-baked, green chile corn muffins. The children's menu offers more typical kid fare. For dessert try the chocolate taco or apple chimichanga—creative, great flavors, and outstanding presentation. $$–$$$

Where to Stay

The Golden Hotel, 800 11th St.; (303) 279-0100; www.thegoldenhotel.com. This hotel has sixty-two rooms and a full-service restaurant. The junior and executive suites work nicely for families. The inn is adjacent to the

Lookout Mountain **Loop**

Another great circle trip. Approach Lookout Mountain on I-70. From exit 256 follow the signs to Lookout Mountain Nature Center and/or Buffalo Bill's Museum and Grave. For the return trip wind down the mountain on Lariat Loop Road. There are great views of Denver and the prairie beyond. If the weather conditions are right, passengers can observe hang gliders and parasailers. Drivers need to proceed slowly and keep a close eye on the curvy, switchback road. At the foot of the mountain, follow 19th Street into Golden for further adventures, or turn right on US 6; it will intersect with I-70.

bike and walking paths along Clear Creek, and across the street from the chamber of commerce, handy for finding even more things to see and do. Nearby are two city parks, and a recreation center with swimming pools and other sports facilities. $$–$$$

The Stage Stop Guest Cottages, 807 9th St.; (303) 279-2667 ; www.stagestopcottages .com. Attractively furnished in southwestern style, The Cottage and The 1873 House feature handcrafted furniture, antiques, kitchen facilities, and sofa beds that work nicely for bedding down children. Both accommodations have porches that lead to a tree-shaded courtyard. Dining, shopping, and numerous attractions are located within walking distance. $$$

Table Mountain Inn, 1310 Washington Ave.; (303) 732-5447 or (888) 292-8331. In the early 1990s this property underwent total renovation. The resulting southwestern adobe-style exterior and decor add warmth and comfort to the seventy-four-room inn. Friendly staff gladly accommodate families with cribs and other special needs. There's no pool, but they provide passes to Golden's great recreation center with indoor pool. $$–$$$

For More Information

Golden Chamber of Commerce/Visitor Center, 1010 Washington Ave., Golden, CO 80402; (303) 279-3113 or; www.goldenco chamber.org.

Boulder

"The little town nestled between the mountains and reality," the *Denver Post* aptly describes Denver's neighbor. "The People's Republic of Boulder" and "Berkeley of the Rockies" are other lighthearted references to Boulder's ambience.

University of Colorado students and staff make up almost one-third of the population. Several scientific institutions—National Center for Atmospheric Research (NCAR), Ball Aerospace, National Institute of Standards—also draw professionals to this well-educated community.

Hugging the majestic Flatirons, so named because of the mountains' resemblance to old-fashioned irons, Boulder's beautiful setting and sunny, mild, four-season climate encourage an outdoor lifestyle. Hiking, biking, skiing, skating, rock climbing—Boulderites are rarely indoors.

Boulder's food, festivals, and fashion all reflect the ethnically diverse cultural life of a university town.

National Center for Atmospheric Research (NCAR)
(ages 6 and up)

1850 Table Mesa Dr. in southwestern Boulder; (303) 497-1174; www.ucar.edu. Open Mon through Fri 8 a.m. to 5 p.m. and Sat, Sun, and all holidays 9 a.m. to 4 p.m. Free.

Perched high above Boulder against the Flatirons, Mesa Laboratory, designed by famed architect I. M. Pei, is visible for miles. Here scientists study weather and climate, and exhibits explain their work. Much of the information is the highly technical type (read boring), but six interactive exhibits from the Exploratorium museum in San Francisco grab your attention. Learn how lightning works or how a tornado spins.

Free guided tours are given at noon daily. Self-guided tours are always available. Within the building two art galleries highlight the work of local artists; the cafeteria and library are open to the public on weekdays.

Many visitors come to NCAR to hike. The Walter Orr Roberts Nature Trail, which crosses the site, provides signs with information about local weather phenomena. It's the only wheelchair-accessible nature trail in Boulder, and it works very well for strollers, too. Take some time to enjoy the spectacular setting. Forgot the picnic basket? There's a handy cafeteria on the premises that is open to the public for breakfast and lunch.

Chautauqua Park (all ages)
900 Baseline Rd.; (303) 442-3282; www.chautauqua.com.

Boulder's first city park was acquired in 1898 as part of a national Chautauqua movement. Centers were established for education, culture, and recreation and named for Lake Chautauqua in New York, where the first site was established. Today, this popular twenty-six-acre park offers hiking trails, cultural events, and a historic dining spot.

> **Hiking.** www.chautauqua.com/hiking. **Free.** Extensive trails draw hikers of all abilities. Two circle hikes popular with families are the Chautauqua Loops, each about 2 miles. But neither is a simple walk in a park, so don't be misled. Be sure your group is properly attired; remember the sunscreen and water. To sort out the best hike for your family, stop in the Rangers' Cottage for maps and advice. Plan on breathtaking scenery. You'll know you're not in Kansas, Dorothy.
>
> Boulder Mountain Parks offer family-friendly guided hikes throughout the year. Check www.bouldercounty.org/openspace/recreating/index.htm for a listing of these **free** events.
>
> **Cultural Events.** (303) 440-7666; www.chautauqua.com. Built in 1898, the Chautauqua Auditorium is now on the National Register of Historic Places. It's a favorite venue for performers and guest lecturers. Concerts are scheduled throughout the

Local **Transit**

Park the car for the day and forget worrying about traffic, directions, and finding a parking space at each destination. Shuttles make getting around Boulder easy and convenient. For an excellent animated transit map, stop in at the **Boulder Convention and Visitors Bureau,** 2440 Pearl St.; (303) 442-2911 or (800) 444-0447.

summer season. The Silent Film Festival offers the chance to show kids what going to the movies used to be like. The films are accompanied by live organ music.

Chautauqua Dining Hall. (303) 440-3776; www.chautauqua.com. Although this dining hall was built in 1898, the food is definitely up-to-date. Check it out after a hike or before an event. Open year-round. Breakfast and lunch, Mon through Sat 8 a.m. to 2 p.m.; Sun buffet brunch 8 a.m. to 2 p.m.; dinner, May through Oct, Wed through Sun 5 to 9 p.m. Reservations accepted. $.

University of Colorado

(303) 492-1411; www.colorado.edu.

It's never too early to take your kids to college. A simple walk across the campus may spark an interest—plant a seed that comes to life years down the road. Casual campus visits with youngsters develop a base of comparison and build personal knowledge that could be invaluable to later decision-making.

The University of Colorado (CU) campus could be a model for all college campuses: attractive architecture (rural Italian-style buildings of Colorado sandstone punctuated with red tile roofs) on a 600-acre tree-lined campus nestled against the mountains.

Founded in 1876, this university was under construction before Colorado became a state. Its history includes legislators riding on horseback between Denver and Boulder to secure funding in time for a critical vote. One faction wanted Boulder to be the site of Colorado's first university, while another group wanted a prison to be built here.

Old Main (still in use) constituted the entire university from 1876 to 1884. Today more than 25,000 students are enrolled. Famous former students include Supreme Court Justice Byron White, bandleader Glenn Miller, and actor Robert Redford.

On a walk across campus you'll discover great people-watching. Many trees in Norlin Quadrangle are more than one hundred years old. Basking turtles can be found at Varsity Pond; basking students are everywhere.

The university offers campus tours led by student ambassadors Mon through Sat. It's best to make a reservation (303-492-6301).

Finding a parking space in the area can be trying, so head to Euclid Avenue Auto Park, just east of the University Memorial Center. Parking 7 a.m. to 5 p.m. is $1.75 per hour.

The CU Museum of Natural History. You can touch fossils here. This two-floor museum of natural history is low key, a delightful change from larger metro facilities. Dinosaur Hall is a favorite with families. You can't miss the spectacular triceratops head. Check out Discovery Corner, an area specifically designed for children. Try on a giant tortoise shell or deer antlers—lots of objects to touch here. Ask about the museum's changing exhibits. Some are pretty intriguing—past shows included Body Art (tattooing) and Dinosaur Tracking.

In the Henderson Building on the University of Colorado campus; (303) 492-6892; http://cu-museum.colorado.edu. Open Mon through Fri 9 a.m. to 5 p.m., Sat 9 a.m. to 4 p.m., and Sun 10 a.m. to 4 p.m. **Free.**

The CU Heritage Center. Old Main, completed in 1876 and renovated in 1982, is home to The Heritage Center. This small museum chronicles university life, highlighting special achievements of alumni and faculty. It's more interesting than it sounds.

Highlights include CU in Space, an exhibit featuring space-travel artifacts from fifteen alumni astronauts. The Athletics Gallery features proud reminders of CU's fine sports performances: trophies, photos, and autographed footballs along with a display of athletic equipment from the past. The mounted head of Ralphie, the Buffs' first mascot, is revered.

In Old Main on the University of Colorado campus; (303) 492-6329; www.cuheritage .org (under alumni). Open Mon through Fri 10 a.m. to 5 p.m. during the school year; 10 a.m. to 4:30 p.m. during summer. **Free.**

Fiske Planetarium and Science Center. Cosmic Collisions, Galaxies at the End of the Universe, and Mars Quest—just some of the star shows and live star talks that are the main offerings here. Once-a-month laser light shows set to rock or reggae music draw a crowd to special late-night performances. Adjacent to the planetarium, Sommers–Bausch Observatory is open for **free** observing sessions after most Fri-evening shows.

Browse the lobby, where you can touch a meteorite, split light into rainbows with prisms, learn about magnetic force, and view the Earth and planets as if you were in space. Toys in Space is a nostalgic look at toys for exploring distant worlds.

On Regent Drive on the University of Colorado campus (look for the geodesic dome); (303) 492-5002; www.fiske.colorado.edu. The building is open Mon through Fri 9 a.m. to 5 p.m. For recorded show information call (303) 492-5001. $.

Colorado Scale Model Solar System. This self-guided walk starts in front of Fiske Planetarium, continuing north across Regent Drive and through the campus. On a scale of one to ten billion, the model planets illustrate the inconceivably vast distances in our solar system. Each step you take along the way represents 10 million kilometers; the *Voyager* spacecraft took ten years to go this same distance!

This model solar system is dedicated to the memory of University of Colorado alumnus Ellison S. Onizuka and his six crewmates of the space shuttle *Challenger*.

Pearl Street Mall (all ages)

Pearl Street from 11th to 15th Streets; (303) 449-3774. Free.

This is city living at its best. Eclectic shops and ethnic restaurants line this pedestrian mall. Street musicians, jugglers, and magicians entertain. Hundreds of seasonal flowers, intriguing sculptures, and the Rocky Mountain backdrop encourage visitors to relax on one of many benches. You won't find better people-watching! Always colorful, always fun.

A favorite stop for kids is Into the Wind, (303) 449-5356. Colorful kites and banners attract customers immediately. This shop is filled with toys, games, alternative sports, and equipment that entire families love.

Peppercorn (303-449-5847) is a must-stop for all cooks. A feast for the eyes begins the moment you look in the window. This store practically overflows with food-related items. The extensive collection of cookbooks includes a children's section.

You may not want to take children in here. Touching is so tempting! The narrow aisles and volume crowds make it tough to roll a stroller around, but a playground is conveniently located right outside the door, and a Ben & Jerry's is nearby. So leave the little ones with the noncooking parent while you take twenty minutes to visit kitchen heaven.

Boulder Creek Path (all ages)

16 miles of paved path from Boulder Canyon to 55th Street. Free.

Walkers, joggers, runners, cyclists, in-line skaters, those in strollers, and those in wheelchairs—they all love this path, which follows the creek. On bikes it's a convenient way to get around Boulder and avoid street traffic. Or it's a pleasant recreational ride that takes families to or near many appealing attractions. During warm weather you'll enjoy watching water-lovers in kayaks, canoes, and inner tubes.

Along the route near the Clarion Harvest House, stop at the Fish Observatory. Just off the path, stairs lead down to an almost hidden nook with four portholes looking into Boulder Creek. On a good day you can watch trout swim by. On a bad day the portholes are covered with scum and you won't see anything. But there are interesting signs that tell about what you would have seen!

Scott Carpenter Park (all ages)

30th Street and Arapahoe Avenue; (303) 441-3427 (pool). Pool open Memorial Day through Labor Day. Hours vary greatly; call ahead. Pool, $; park, free.

Named for the Boulder astronaut, this park is a real haven for families. Conveniently located along Boulder Creek Path, it's a great destination for cyclists. During summer months the outdoor pool is the draw. There's a diving area, water slide, and separate toddler pool. The playground has a rocket ship, in keeping with the astronaut theme.

Boulder Skateboard Park (ages 8 and up)

In Scott Carpenter Park; (303) 441-3429. Open from dawn to dusk. BMX bike hours are from 7 a.m. to 10 a.m. daily. $.

Nirvana for the serious skateboarder and great fun for observers. The YMCA runs this park, a fenced-in area of ramps where teens and preteens strut their stuff on skateboards and in-line skates. Parents will be happy to know that helmets, kneepads, and elbowpads are required. Each can be rented for $1 if you didn't bring your own.

Celestial Seasonings (ages 5 and up)

4600 Sleepytime Dr.; (303) 530-5300; www.celestialseasonings.com. Hours of business vary greatly so it's best to phone before heading out. Tours are run daily on the hour beginning at 10 a.m. Mon through Sat and at 11 a.m. on Sun. Closed during May and on all holidays. Children must be at least 5 years old to participate in factory tours. Free.

The largest herbal-tea company in the United States gives a great tour! In fact, it's rated as one of the top-ten factory tours in the country. You get to see, hear, taste, and smell. You'll remember your visit to the mint room long after you've left. Get your **free** tickets for the tour as soon as you arrive. Be prepared for a wait during the summer and on school holidays. Browse the art gallery, investigate the outside herb garden, or sample tea. The gift shop tempts young and old. The company logo, Sleepytime Bear, embellishes merchandise from boxer shorts to pâté spreaders. There's a nice selection of children's items. An amazing array of Celestial Seasonings teas is sold at a hefty discount. You might want to stock up.

The Celestial Cafe, with indoor and outdoor dining areas, is just the spot to regroup. Nearby, wide grassy areas offer younger visitors room to move about. Please note that children under 5 are not allowed on the tour through the factory.

Leanin' Tree Museum of Western Art (ages 5 and up)

6055 Longbow Dr.; (303) 530-7768; www.leanintree.com. Open Mon through Fri 8 a.m. to 5 p.m. and Sat and Sun 10 a.m. to 5 p.m. Free.

Fans of Leanin' Tree greeting cards come to see where they are made and discover a world-class art museum. Owner Ed Trumble started a business in the 1940s by reproducing original artwork on greeting cards. Through the years he amassed one of the country's largest private collections of contemporary western art. The **free** museum is tucked into their corporate building, which combines offices, printing plant, and distribution center.

Acrylics, oils, watercolors, and sculptures depict weathered cowboys, Native Americans, wildlife, landscapes, and western humor. Easy-to-read biographies of artists are mounted by their work. Your kids won't want to spend all day here, but a quick walkthrough gives them some experience with western art.

Savvy shoppers come to the gift shop with lists of birthdays and anniversaries. All 2,500 Leanin' Tree greeting cards are available for purchase along with mugs, calendars, magnets, and posters.

Where to Eat

Boulder Dushanbe Teahouse, 1770 13th St. (between Arapahoe Avenue and Canyon Boulevard); (303) 442-4993. Open daily 8 a.m. to 9 p.m. This brightly colored teahouse was a gift from Boulder's sister city, Dushanbe, Tajikistan, in the former Soviet Union. It arrived from Asia in 200 crates. The intricate designs, both painted and carved, elicit many oohs and aahs. Stop for a look, inside and out, even if you don't want refreshments. The teahouse is operated by staff affiliated with the Naropa Institute, a local school started by Tibetan Buddhists. They serve international cuisine in addition to tea. $–$$

Lucile's Creole Cafe, 2124 14th St.; (303) 442-4743. Open for breakfast and lunch 7 a.m. to 2 p.m. weekdays and 8 a.m. to 2 p.m. Sat and Sun. Beignets (New Orleans-style doughnuts) and chicory coffee are served here. This is where you'll find a taste of Louisiana—including praline waffles and Creole omelettes—right in the middle of Boulder. Be prepared for a wait on the weekends. A basket of toys on the stairs entertains toddlers. Although Lucile's doesn't have a children's menu, you can get half-orders. $–$$

Noodles & Company, 2770 Pearl St.; (303) 444-5533. Open Sun through Wed 10:30 a.m. to 9 p.m.; Thurs through Sat 10:30 a.m. to 10 p.m. Here you will find the very best noodle dishes from around the world made with fresh produce, grilled meats, and artisan pastas. From spicy to comforting (mac and cheese) and healthy to indulgent, you'll find it here. $–$$

Where to Stay

Boulder University Inn, 1632 Broadway St.; (303) 417-1700; www.boulderuniversity inn.com. Located four blocks from the University of Colorado campus and only two blocks from the Pearl Street Mall, this motel is kid and pet friendly. Families on a limited budget who are looking for a great downtown Boulder location will be pleased to find that this lodging provides an outdoor heated pool, free high-speed Internet access, cable TV, spacious rooms, and complimentary continental breakfasts. For a small fee, microwave ovens and refrigerators can be provided, and a coin-operated laundry is available for guest use. Just across the street is the Wild Oats Market, which, in addition to groceries, offers picnic options and an array of meals to go. $–$$

Hotel Boulderado, 2115 13th St.; (303) 442-4344 or (800) 433-4344; www.boulder ado.com. Located in the heart of Boulder's lively downtown, this restored hotel provides contemporary comfort. Two-room suites give families plenty of space and privacy. Children under 12 stay free. Walk to activities, restaurants, shopping, playgrounds, and shuttle buses. Even if you don't stay here, stop in and admire the lobby's elegant stained-glass ceiling, the richly detailed woodwork, and the cantilevered staircase. $$$$

Quality Inn & Suites, Boulder Creek. 2020 Arapahoe Ave.; (303) 449-7550 or (888) 449-7550 (outside Colorado); www.qualityinn boulder.com. This casual but upscale property offers a full range of services and amenities, including rooms with coffeemakers, microwave ovens, irons and ironing boards, refrigerators, and deluxe suites with mini-kitchen areas. A sauna, Jacuzzi, Life Fitness workout room, and heated indoor swimming pool offer activities for the whole family. The inn is located a short walk from Boulder's famous Pearl Street Mall. Rates include a complimentary hot breakfast buffet and the use of all fitness facilities and the business center. $$–$$$

For More Information

Boulder Convention and Visitors Bureau, 2440 Pearl St.; (303) 442-2911; www .bouldercoloradousa.com.

Nederland

Eldora Mountain Resort

21 miles west of Boulder (take CO 119 to Nederland, turn left at the roundabout, continue south on CO 119 for one mile. Turn right onto US 130 and follow signs to the ski area); (303) 440-8700; www.eldora.com. Open from mid-Nov until the snow melts in late spring. $$$$.

The emphasis at Eldora is on skiing and snowboarding, not luxury lodging or fine dining. This area even has public bus transportation from Boulder. Little Hawk Family Zone offers families and learners of any age their own terrain. The Mountain Explorer package includes a lift ticket, ski rental, lunch, and a four-hour lesson ($$$$).

Professional ski school classes start at age 4, downhill or snowboard. *Half-pipe, gaps, tabletops,* and *transfers*—your preschooler may soon be talking a language you don't understand.

At the Nordic Center options include telemark, snowshoeing, cross-country skiing, and skate-skiing. Lessons, rentals, groomed tracks, and trails make trying something new easy and exciting.

Whichever activity you choose at Eldora, there are mountaintop and base lodges to keep you warm and nourished.

Lafayette

WOW! Children's Museum (ages 1 to 10)

110 North Harrison Ave.; (303) 604-2424; www.wowmuseum.com. Open Tues and Wed 9 a.m. to 5 p.m., Thurs through Sat 10 a.m. to 6 p.m., and Sun noon to 4 p.m. Children $$, adults and children under 15 months free.

WOW stands for World of Wonder. Appropriately named, it is a museum dedicated to children's discovery. A 22-foot pirate ship, a model railroad, dance studio, theater, and playhouse entice youngsters to learn through play and activities. Special features include an after-school game room for children five and up, weekend face painting, a gift shop with educational items, and monthly Friday-night family programs.

Active, exploratory, and quiet experiences are designed for young children to develop gross and fine motor skills. To get the most out of a visit with your toddler, ask for the information sheet called Visiting with Young Children. Toddler-only events for those age five and under are available. Days and times vary so it's best to phone. Toddlers also are welcome during regular business hours.

Longmont

Rocky Mountain Pumpkin Ranch (all ages)

9057 Ute Hwy.; (303) 684-0087; www.rockymtnpumpkinranch.com. Open daily, mid-July through Oct, 10 a.m. to 5 p.m. Phone for exact dates. Rides and some amusements oper-ate on Sat and Sun only. Free admission, but there is a small charge for pumpkins and amusements.

When you're a kid, what could be more fun than picking out your own Halloween pump-kin at a genuine pumpkin patch? At the Rocky Mountain Pumpkin Ranch, some kids, toy wagons in tow, choose the first pumpkin they see, while others wander up and down the rows, determined to find just the right size and shape for their jack-o'-lantern-to-be. This event has evolved into a fall harvest festival with fresh produce, home-baked goods, Halloween items, homemade cider, sizzling bratwurst, fresh-roasted corn, and caramel apples. Kids can have their faces painted, take an antique car ride, visit Uncle Oscar's Hay Maze, walk through the petting corral, get a free apple from Wanda the Good Witch, and ride a pony.

Sunflower Farm (all ages)

11150 Prospect Rd. (from Longmont turn right on Hover Street, left on Pike Road, right on Main Street [US 287]. Immediately enter left turn lane, turn left on Prospect Road [dirt road at Green Spot Nursery], and proceed for ¾ mile); (303) 774-8001; www.sunflowerfarminfo .com. Open Sat, May through Nov 10 a.m. to 3 p.m. Open Sun 10 a.m. to 3 p.m. Sept and Oct only. Suggested donation, $ adults, $$ children, infants under 1 year free.

The couple that owns this fifty-acre working farm and their three children are so happy living the country life, they decided they just had to share it with other families. Accord-ing to owners Bren Frisch and John Roberts, "Most of what we've done here was for our own kids and we thought why not share it with the community." If you and your kids love farms the way I do, you aren't going to want to leave this place. You will find cute little

Sweet as Sugar, and **Twice as Sticky**

If you are driving between Longmont and Lyons and it's time to let the kids out of the car to stretch, stop in at **Madhava Mountain Gold Honey Shop.** Your youngsters can see busy bees at work making honey in a glass-sided hive. While there, pick up some HoneyStix in several flavors for snacking on later. Also for sale are honey, honey spreads, pretty honey containers, bees-wax candles, and gift packs. The shop, at 4689 Ute Hwy., 1 mile east of Lyons, is open year-round, Mon through Fri 8 a.m. to 5 p.m.; Sat 9:30 a.m. to 2:30 p.m.; (303) 823-5166; www.madava-honey.com.

pygmy goats, huge draft horses, Bessie the Cow, a llama family, sheep, rabbits, peacocks, and a cat, most of which are safely penned so your little ones won't be frightened. There are hammocks to stretch out in, tricycles to pedal, ride-on toys to scoot along on, a self-propelled merry-go-round, a massive tree house with a slide for an exit, tire swings hanging from giant cottonwood trees, and a super-sized sandbox beside a playhouse. You can go egg hunting in the hen house, feed the animals, and climb aboard vintage tractors.

Light refreshments are available from the cart of a local vendor, and restroom facilities are provided. Ask about special touring days. The entire area is stroller friendly. Wear comfortable shoes and put play clothes on the kids because that's what Sunflower Farm is all about—playing down on the farm.

For More Information

Longmont Chamber of Commerce, 528 Main St., Longmont, CO 80501; (303) 776-5295; www.longmontchamber.org. Open Mon through Fri 8:30 a.m. to 5 p.m.

Greeley

Historic Centennial Village (ages 4 and up)

1475 A St.; (970) 350-9220; www.greeleymuseums.com. Open mid-Apr through Oct 10th, Tues through Sat 10 a.m. to 4 p.m. Also, open at other times during the year for special celebrations. For event days and fees, phone (970) 350-9216. Regular admission: $.

The Historic Centennial Village provides visitors with an appreciation for what it was like to live on Colorado's northeastern High Plains from 1860 to 1920 (the good times and the not-so-good times). The site's thirty restored structures include German, Swedish, and Hispanic homesteads. Your youngsters can crawl into an authentic Cheyenne tepee, view a one-room schoolhouse, go into the Union Pacific train depot to see an operational telegraph office, and enter a country church. Perhaps not of interest to children but respected and admired by adults are the homes' Victorian-era splendor and their Italianate, Queen Anne, and Colonial Revival architecture.

Plumb Farm Learning Center (age 3 and up)

955 39th Ave.; (970) 350-9220; www.greeleygov.com/museums/plumbfarm.aspx. Open during summer. Call for exact dates. $–$$$$.

This farm is dedicated to teaching children about early farm life through a variety of hour-long and daylong visits, and even weeklong camps, always in a fun, hands-on manner. Classes such as "Kid's Carpentry," "Art Farm," and "Short Chefs," are among the many choices. And then there is "Baby Animal Day" when local farmers loan their animals along with their animals' newborn babies to the Learning Center for the day and teach the kids about their care and feeding. Pets 'n' Popsicles is another special animal event, held on a weekday from 2 p.m. to 3:30 p.m. Kids have a Popsicle treat and play games among the animals. When you remember that some little ones think that milk is somehow made in paper cartons, potatoes live in plastic bags and pumpkins grow in the supermarket's vegetable bins, just think how much fun it would be to introduce them to a real farm. There are many learning possibilities here for children of all ages.

Centennial Park (all ages)
23rd Avenue and Reservoir Road, west of the University of Northern Colorado campus; (970) 330-2837. Pool open daily Memorial Day to Labor Day, 1 to 5 p.m. Admission to the park is free, but there is a small charge for use of the pool.

If it's one of those days when you just have to cool off, stop for a swim at Centennial Park. Plenty of green grass, picnic tables and shelter, tennis courts, ball fields, and a skate park make this a good family spot.

For More Information
Greeley Convention and Visitors Bureau, 902 7th Ave., Greeley, CO 80631; (970) 352-3567 or (800) 449-3866; www .greeleycvb.com.

Loveland

Backed up against the foothills just 25 miles east of Rocky Mountain National Park, Loveland is the "Gateway to the Rockies." Don't be fooled by the quaint small-town look. Loveland is a cultural hot spot—a major center for art, especially bronze sculpture. Two important sculpture shows each August draw top-notch artists and art lovers from around the country. More than fifty well-known artists live here year-round, and many welcome visitors to their studios. Two foundries cast the work of local sculptors and international artists. Ask about scheduled tours—the bronze casting process is fascinating!

Loveland displays its art in easy-to-find public places. Watching for them as you drive through town can be fun for all ages. Circle past the firehouse, library, newspaper office, and baseball field.

Benson Park Sculpture Garden (all ages)
29th Street and Taft Avenue, City of Loveland Public Park. Free.

A showcase for sculptural art, this park, just 3 blocks long with a lagoon at one end, is home to more than forty sculptures. Meander along the paths and marvel at the realism of the coiled boa and the great blue heron. "Unsteady Steadiness," two boys riding double on a bike over uneven pavement, will make you smile. Kids love coming upon the alligator in the streambed and climbing on the turtles (all bronze!).

Foote Lagoon (all ages)

At the Civic Center, 700 East 4th St. Free.

A walk around the lagoon and a romp in the playground make a great break from driving. Outside the library, a young boy pulls a wagon filled with little girls and books in "Overdue" by Jane DeDecker. You can almost hear the music from the quintet under a maple tree in George Lundeen's "Joy of Music." The meaning of "Twist of Fate" will be a good conversation topic as you get back in the car. Don't miss the opportunity to share quality art in Loveland's pleasant surroundings with your family.

Sylvan Dale Guest Ranch (all ages)

2939 North Country Rd. 31 D (off US 34, west of Loveland); (970) 667-3915 or (877) 667-3999; www.sylvandale.com. Open year-round. One-night to weeklong accommodations and ranch activities. Call for rates. $$$–$$$$.

Nearly 50 percent of all guests at Sylvan Dale Guest Ranch are children. And it's easy to see why. This family-owned, family-run operation has been providing dude ranch accommodations, activities, and meals along with authentic western hospitality for more than fifty years. Horseback riding, cattle drives, overnight pack trips, and breakfast rides are only a few of the horse-related activities. Your family can swim together in the outdoor pool, go for a horse-drawn wagon ride, and go fishing in the river and lakes of the Sylvan Dale Valley. You can watch cattle being branded, play a set of tennis, and even help clean the barn, if you are so inclined. No sitting in circles, cutting and pasting for kids at this

Won't You Be **My Valentine?**

The city of Loveland earns its moniker, "The Sweetheart City."

In 1946 the Loveland Postmaster and his wife decided to share the romantic name of their town with the whole world, and the Valentine Remailing Program was born. Volunteers hand-stamp a special four-line rhyme, new each year, on all valentines mailed from Loveland. The Loveland Post Office creates a special cancellation mark for the holiday. An average 300,000 valentines are remailed from this small town every Feb to destinations in fifty states and 104 countries.

How can you add this special touch to your valentine? Before Feb 9, pre-address and stamp your valentine. Enclose it in a larger first-class envelope and mail to:

Postmaster
Valentine Re-mailing
446 East 29th St.
Loveland, CO 80538-9998

ranch. No siree, "pahdner." Depending on their ages, the little buckaroos can help groom the horses and soap the saddles, take off on accompanied nature hikes and scavenger hunts, float on inner tubes on the pasture ponds, pan for gold, or take a farm tour. This is where memories are made.

For More Information

Loveland Chamber of Commerce, 5400 Stone Creek Circle, Suite 200, Loveland 80538; (970) 667-6311; www.loveland.org. Open Mon through Fri 8 a.m. to 5 p.m.

Estes Park

Adjacent to Rocky Mountain National Park and just 65 miles northwest of Denver, this town of 9,000 residents has been a Colorado favorite for more than one hundred years. Its tree-lined streets are accented with Victorian-style lampposts, flower boxes, and sidewalk benches. More than 200 shops and thirty restaurants tempt browsers and diners with an amazing variety of goods and edibles. An attractive Riverwalk offers families a place to stroll off the main street. Nearby Rocky Mountain National Park offers hands-on experiences with nature. Fun with the family comes easily in this mountain valley.

Aerial Tramway (all ages)

420 East Riverside Dr. (1 block south of the post office); (970) 586-3675; www.estestram .com. Open daily mid-May to mid-Sept, 9 a.m. to 6:30 p.m. $–$$.

If you don't have much time but you'd like a mountain experience, this attraction is for you. A gondola whisks you up the mountain in less than five minutes, affording panoramic views of Longs Peak, the Continental Divide, and the town below. There are picnic tables at the top and a snack bar in case you didn't pack your lunch. Easy hiking trails appeal to families.

Remember, though, this is a commercial operation. I suggest that you also drive into Rocky Mountain National Park and stop for a hike in pristine wilderness, away from machinery and fast food.

Colorado Bicycle Adventures (all ages)

184 East Elkhorn Ave.; (970) 586-4241 or (888) 586-2149; www.coloradobicycling.net. Shop and rentals open Mon through Sat 9 a.m. to 8 p.m. and Sun 9 a.m. to 6 p.m. Both morning and afternoon tours are available. Phone for times. $$$$, includes bike rental.

You will find downhill tours for nearly all ages here. Bike seats, tandems, tagalongs, or trailers are available for the younger crowd. Three-hour trips on paved roads wind through grand scenery, while friendly guides keep you focused on fun. You might want to try their number-one family tour, the Cinnamon Roll Ride. This 10-mile downhill adventure takes you through a gorgeous canyon where bighorn sheep frequently graze on the steep slopes. The tour stops at the general store for a cinnamon roll—with butter cream icing.

Estes Park Mountain Shop & Climbing Gym

(ages 4 and up)

2050 Big Thompson Ave.; (970) 586-6548 or (866) 303-6548; www.estesparkmountainshop
.com. Open daily year-round 8 a.m. to 9 p.m. $$–$$$$.

Family adventure is this outfit's middle name. In the store you'll find quality outdoor gear and clothing and knowledgeable salespeople. But even better, they also offer family adventures in climbing, rafting, and fly-fishing.

What your kids are apt to love most here is the indoor climbing wall. Keep this place in mind on a rainy afternoon. "Never-Evers" to "Thrill Seekers" are welcome. The fully trained staff assists in making your climbing adventure safe and rewarding. As sponsors of an afternoon program with the Estes Park schools, they have had lots of experience working with youth. Learn the basics and try three climbs for just $15, adult or child.

Miniclinics to full days, ladies only, large groups, or just your family, indoors or out, there is a climbing program for everyone from ages 4 to 94.

Kid's Adventure Program: *NOTE:* It will be hard to top this one! A hike, tramway ride, orienteering, outdoor ropes course, mountaintop lunch, ecology, and indoor climbing make for an active day. Each participant is provided with a pack containing map, compass, poncho, water bottle, climbing harness, helmet, gear, and other necessities. Bring a lunch, or a box lunch can be supplied for a small additional fee. All instructors (no more than six students to one instructor) are extensively trained, and most have classroom teaching experience.

After riding the Aerial Tramway to Prospect Mountain, the kids will participate in activities that include using map and compass skills to hike to the summit, plant and animal identification, knots, rock climbing, and rappelling. After lunch your adventurous ones return to the indoor gym for high-tech climbing practice. Excitement and confidence radiate as kids demonstrate new proficiencies for parents at the end of the day.

A program as comprehensive as this one can not be offered every day but the proprietors are always willing to design one that is sure to please. For ages 7 to 14. Held during the summer, Mon through Sat 9 a.m. to 3 p.m. Reservations at least one day in advance required. $$$$.

Fly-fishing: Just outside the shop's back door, the Big Thompson River beckons. In a one-hour lesson you'll experience the basics of casting, fly presentation, and reading the water. If you rent your gear from the store, you can keep it for the rest of the day to practice. This program is a very popular way for grandparents to introduce grandchildren to the sport. Full- and half-day sessions are available. For ages 10 and up. $$$$.

Stanley Hotel (ages 5 and up)

333 Wonderview Ave.; (970) 577-4000 or (800) 976-1377; www.stanleyhotel.com. $$–$$$.

Built in 1909 by F. O. Stanley, inventor of the Stanley Steamer, this hotel offers your family a glimpse of what life was like for Estes Park tourists almost one hundred years ago. Its more recent claim to fame was as the inspiration for Stephen King's book *The Shining*. The made-for-television miniseries was filmed here. Stroll through the lobby and public rooms of this 138-room hotel. Visit its small museum on the lower level. Tours of the hotel are available (reservations are required, $) through a nonprofit organization that operates the museum.

Trout Haven Ranch (all ages)

810 Moraine Ave. (1½ miles west of downtown on US 36); (970) 586-5525; www.trouthaven ranch.com. Open daily late Apr through Sept, 8 a.m. until 5 p.m. $.

You can take kids fishing in lakes and streams all around the Estes Valley, but if you want to be sure that they catch something, head to Trout Haven. No license is required, and you pay only for what you catch (95 cents per inch). Bait, poles, and help are provided. They'll even do the yucky part—clean and pack your trout on ice.

Estes Park Center, YMCA of the Rockies (all ages)

2515 Tunnel Rd.; (970) 586-3341; www.ymcarockies.org. Open year-round. Rates vary widely due to numerous accommodation, meal, and activity choices. $–$$$$.

Mention "YMCA," and most people think of swimming classes, a workout room, and perhaps a day-care facility. The Estes Park Center, YMCA of the Rockies, however, is a year-round low-key resort catering to conference groups and individual families. Here you can ride horses; hike, bike, and fish; play miniature golf, tennis, basketball, volleyball, and softball; swim in the indoor pool; and roller-skate at the indoor rink. Cross-country skiing is right outside your door during the winter. There is also a small library, and a museum.

The Mootz Family Craft and Design Center, a $1.3 million, 7,500-square-foot structure was added in 2009 for guests to use for creating traditional crafts, such as ceramics, tie-dying, leatherworking, silk painting, basket weaving, woodworking, beading, and mosaics, as well as contemporary art projects. The Craft and Design Center provides space for classrooms, weekend workshops led by individual artists and an artist-in-residence program, all of which have proved to be very popular,

Guests have access to dining facilities, including all-you-can-eat buffets, and accommodations range from lodge rooms to two- to four-bedroom cabins. Several of the latter will sleep up to ten people. Some families have made the center a gathering place for several generations. What a great place this would be for a family reunion!

Enos A. Mills Cabin (all ages)

6760 Highway 7 (8 miles south of Estes Park); (970) 586-4706; www.oldestes.com/enosmills .htm. Open Memorial Day through Labor Day, Tues through Sat 11 a.m. to 4 p.m. Winter

hours by appointment only. It's a good idea to phone for reservations, even in summer. Free (donations welcome).

Enos Mills is the man to thank for Rocky Mountain National Park. An early conservationist and dedicated educator, he lobbied the government to establish this area as a national park and was successful in 1915.

This one-room cabin served as his home base for twenty years. Inside you'll see photos taken by Mills, his journals, and letters written to him with some impressive signatures—Helen Keller, Theodore Roosevelt, and John Muir, for example.

While all of that can be boring to younger children, the area outside the cabin is just right for them. Three short nature trails beckon with handmade signs identifying trees, rocks, and flowers. Weathered tables hold collections of rocks and natural treasures waiting to be touched. Look for two llamas behind the small gift shop. A bench in the peaceful glen encourages young and old to experience what Mills called "the gentle influence of nature." It's all very homey and noncommercial. There are no restrooms here.

Two of Enos' descendents, Elizabeth and Eryn Mills, own and operate the cabin as a labor of love and devotion to Enos.

Horseback Riding

For many vacationers it just wouldn't be a trip "out west" without swinging into a saddle and taking in the view from atop a horse. Whether it's pony rides for toddlers or overnight pack trips, area stables can accommodate your family's adventure.

Hi Country Stables (all ages)

Hi Country Stables has two locations within Rocky Mountain National Park: Glacier Creek Stables, (970) 586-3244, and Moraine Park Stables, (970) 586-2327; www.som brero.com.

Hi Country Stables operates the only stables within the park, and it has had this concession for forty years. You can call ahead (even months ahead) to reserve a ride. Your two- to eight-hour ride begins in the heart of the park. Real cowpokes ride even if the sun isn't shining—ponchos are provided for the "mist." They'll take riders as young as 1 year old. Children under 6 ride double with an adult. $$$$.

SK Ltd. (all ages)

Many area residents recommend this outfit for a good family experience. It has ponies for your younger cowhands, is authorized to ride within Rocky Mountain National Park and Roosevelt National Forest, and also has two locations. Reservations are recommended; www.nationalparkgatewaystables.com. $$$$.

- **Cowpoke Corner Corral;** on CO 66, 3 miles from downtown; (970) 586-5890. One-hour to four-hour rides with flexible departure times.
- **National Park Gateway Stables;** on US 34 at the Fall River Entrance to Rocky Mountain National Park; (970) 586-5269. Two-hour rides depart on the hour,

beginning at 8 a.m. The departures times for half-day rides vary. Six- and eight-hour rides depart at 8 a.m.

The Livery at Aspen Lodge (ages 8 and up)

6120 Highway 7 (8 miles south of Estes Park); (970) 586-8133 or (800) 332-6867; www .aspenlodge.net. Open year-round; June through Aug, every day; Sept through May rides by reservation only. Walking rides have a minimum age of 8 years old. Hay wagon and sleigh rides all ages. $$$–$$$$.

Want to ride on a clear, crisp winter day? The Livery at Aspen Lodge remains open year-round when weather and trail conditions are safe.

Summer hay wagon rides through a field of longhorn cattle followed by a cowboy dinner delights families of all ages. October brings scary Halloween weekend rides and when the snow flies it's time to take out the sleigh and warm woolen blankets, and Belgian draft horses complete with bells. A warm fire and dinner in the lodge await your return.

Lake Estes Marina (all ages)

1770 Big Thompson Ave. (½ mile east of town on US 34); (970) 586-2011; www.estesvalley recreation.com/marina.html. Boat rentals $–$$$; bike rentals $–$$.

Lake Estes Marina and adjoining Stanley Park are good places to stop when your kids need to work off steam. Take a boat out for an hour. Choose a canoe, sailboat, or three- to five-passenger paddleboat. If you've brought along the whole troop, you might need the nine-passenger pontoon. They've got life jackets for all sizes. The wakeless speed limit ensures a gentle boating experience—and better fishing. Bait, tackle, and fishing licenses are available at the marina store. Your children will also enjoy the beach and wading area. Sand toys are provided.

The pirate ship playground offers more activity. Although it's designed primarily for ages 6 and up, there are some toddler-size swings. Or rent a bike and take to the paths. Child carriers, tagalongs, and tandem cycles allow families to ride together. For the ultimate group ride, rent a surrey cycle.

Other Estes Valley Recreation and Park District facilities near the marina include an indoor pool, tennis courts, a skateboard park, and two golf courses. Phone the park district at (970) 586-8191 for more information.

Books Especially **for Kids**

The Denver Museum of Nature and Science publishes a series of well-done nature books for children. Titles include *Above the Treeline* and *In the Forest* by Ann Cooper and *Field Guide for Kids* by Elizabeth Biesiot. If your children have watched the pikas scampeabring about on rocks, they are sure to want *The Pika's Tail* by Sally Plumb, published by the Grand Teton Association. These make great souvenirs instead of one more T-shirt.

Cowboy Sing-along (all ages)
Downtown in Bond Park; (800) 44-ESTES (800-443-7837). Mid-June through Aug. Check at the Chamber Resort Association (970-586-0144) for days and times. Free.

Wander over to Bond Park after dinner for a good old-fashioned sing-along, western style. Sit around the campfire. Everybody's welcome and encouraged to participate.

Where to Eat

Baldpate Inn, 4900 South Hwy. 7; (970) 586-6151; www.baldpateinn.com. Open late May through mid-Oct for lunch and dinner. This rustic lodge got its name from the novel/movie *Seven Keys to Baldpate,* which also inspired its famous key collection. It's the largest such collection in the world, and your family will have a good time perusing it and reading the labels. You can even add a key of your own. One family with two preteens was overheard locating the key Mom and Dad had donated before the kids were born. What fun! But how about the food? It's outstanding—an all-you-can-eat buffet of salads, breads, and homemade soups that's available all day long. The array is continuously refreshed, so it's always inviting. This is a good place to know about when everyone is suddenly hungry at 3 in the afternoon. A huge deck with porch swings and rockers overlooks some of America's best scenery. Did I mention the homemade pie? $–$$

Ed's Cantina, 390 East Elkhorn Ave.; (970) 586-2919; www.edscantina.com. Open for breakfast on Sat and Sun only. Lunch and dinner daily, beginning at 11 a.m. and ending "when we close." Burgers and sandwiches, along with Mexican specialties, make up most of the menu. Nothing fancy, just good food at reasonable prices. And it's easy to find Ed's, "The Hottest Place in Town," right on the main street. $–$$

Mama Rose's, 338 East Elkhorn Ave., on the Riverwalk in Barlow Plaza, downtown; (970) 586-3330; www.mamarosesrestaurant.com. Open year-round for dinner, Buon Appetito! Mama Rose's looks like Grandma's old Victorian home. Her welcoming front porch overlooks the river. All food items are homemade with an Italian flair. Children's pasta dinners include salad and garlic bread. Bring hungry diners. $–$$

Penelope's, 229 West Elkhorn Ave.; (970) 586-2277. Open for lunch and dinner; closing hour varies with season. "The Hometown Place with the World Wide Reputation." Locals know Penelope's as the place for the best burger in Estes Park: 100 percent fresh ground beef, never frozen, and cooked when you order. Crispy fries come from potatoes cut on the premises. An old-fashioned malt is the perfect beverage. Soup, sandwiches, and vegetarian choices are also offered. There's no wait staff here. You order, eat, and get back to the great outdoors in minimum time (and expense!). $

Poppy's Pizza & Grill, on the Riverwalk in Barlow Plaza, downtown; (970) 586-8282: www.poppyspizzaandgrill.com. Open daily year-round, at 11 a.m. Kids will love Poppy's pizza, and so will you. Poppy's offers lots of choices: five different sauces and toppings from traditional to smoked trout. There's a soup-and-salad bar and lots of sandwiches, including burgers, on the menu for that rare no-pizza person. Save room for homemade desserts. $–$$

Sweet Basilico, 430 Prospect Village Dr.; (970) 586-3899; www.sweetbasilico.com. Open for lunch and dinner. Pizza, pasta, and sandwiches in a funky, friendly setting. Hearty portions of exceptionally tasty food make Sweet Basilico popular with the local crowd. $–$$

Where to Stay

As the gateway to Rocky Mountain National Park, Estes Park is a popular summertime destination. Visitors from around the world come to experience the scenic beauty here. Many families return year after year for their vacations. In some cases, it's become a tradition. While the area is full of hotels, motels, condos, cabins, and inns, the accommodations fill quickly. Lodging owners encourage everyone to plan ahead and reserve early. Make your summer plans by Feb to ensure a wide range of choices.

With more than 175 lodging facilities, finding the right match for your needs can be time consuming. The Estes Park Visitor Center (800-443-7837) provides a **free** lodging referral service and can pair you with the perfect property. If you do find yourself in the area without reservations in summer, stop in at the visitor center. The staff keeps up-to-date on vacancies, and they will do their best to save you a lot of time, effort, and frustration.

Aspen Lodge, 6120 Highway 7 (8 miles south of Estes Park); (970) 586-8133 or (800) 332-6867; www.aspenlodge.net. This dude ranch features a broad selection of summer activities beyond horseback riding. Located next to Rocky Mountain National Park, possibilities abound for hikes, tours, mountain biking, fly-fishing, canoeing, and kayaking. Three-, four-, and seven-day family vacation packages include children's programs for ages 3 to 12 and teen adventures. $$$$

Winter guests have just as many choices: guided snowshoe hikes, cross-country ski lessons, ice skating, hockey, broomball, sledding, tubing, and sleigh rides. Read beside the fire, or gather your family around a board game while it snows outside your cabin. Lodge rooms also available. Nightly lodging rates Labor Day to Memorial Day; separate activity fees. $$$–$$$$

Boulder Brook, 1900 Fall River Rd. (2 miles west of downtown on US 34); (970) 586-0910 or (800) 238-0910; www.boulderbrook.com. Fall River tumbles past Boulder Brook with a soothing sound. This top-of-the-line inn sits between Estes Park and Rocky Mountain National Park. Facilities combine the best of motel lodging with the favorite amenities of a cabin. Each large suite includes daily housekeeping service and a full or partial kitchen. Beautifully maintained grounds include a picnic area, and there's fishing right outside your door.

While many couples choose Boulder Brook for getaway weekends, the staff welcomes families and accommodates those with children in a section away from the romantic spa suites, so all guests are comfortable and happy. $$–$$$$

The Stanley Hotel, 333 Wonderview Ave.; (970) 577-4000 or (800) 976-1377; www .stanleyhotel.com. The Stanley Hotel is a fine example of elegant Georgian architecture, both inside and out. Children will enjoy the playground, tennis courts, and heated outdoor swimming pool (open summers only). The hotel's dining room is rather pricey, but less expensive restaurants and snack shops are close by. $$–$$$$

Wildwood Inn, 2801 Fall River Rd.; (970) 586-7804 or (866) 586-7025; www.esteswildwoodinn.com. Fully equipped kitchens and large condo suites (up to 1,630 square feet), some with hot tubs, are the draw here.

There's lots of area to run; the property borders Rocky Mountain National Park. A playground and picnic area complete with grill make family travel easier. If you have a large family, this is the place for you. $–$$$$

For More Information

Estes Park Chamber Resort Association, 500 Big Thompson Ave., Estes Park, CO 80517; (970) 577-9900; www.estesparkresort.com.

Rocky Mountain National Park

Spectacular scenery, snow-capped peaks, rugged wilderness, and wildlife draw three million visitors a year to Rocky Mountain National Park. No matter how long you stay (the average summer visit in Estes Park is three nights), it won't be long enough to do everything. So sample a variety of activities, and plan to return, perhaps in another season.

The park is open year-round. Trail Ridge and Old Fall River Roads are seasonal. The Park Service strives to clear Trail Ridge by Memorial Day and keep it open until late Oct. Old Fall River's season is even shorter.

Park entrance fees are valid for seven consecutive days, $$$ per car. Annual passes ($$$$), the national Golden Eagle Pass ($$$$), the Gold Access Passport (**free**), and the Golden Age Passport ($$, one-time charge) are also honored. For more information log onto www.rocky.mountain.national-park.com. This Web site is fantastic! My advice is to print out all that interests you on the site and then take the printed material with you on your visit to the park.

Beaver Meadows Visitor Center/Park Headquarters (all ages)
At the east entrance to the park on US 36; (970) 586-1206; www.nps.gov/romo. Open daily year-round; summer, 8 a.m. to 9 p.m.; fall through spring, 8 a.m. to 5 p.m. **Free.**

For most visitors this is the first stop for orientation to the park. Pick up a copy of *High Country Headlines*, a seasonal park newspaper for schedules of events. *Fountain of Life*, a somewhat dated film heavy on the environmental message, runs every half hour from 8:30 a.m. to 4:30 p.m. Park personnel are available to answer questions and help plan your visit. Evening programs are presented nightly during the summer.

Need maps, guidebooks, posters, or postcards? The Rocky Mountain Nature Association operates a bookstore within the visitor center. Check out the series of inexpensive (less than $3) informative booklets on specific park locations published by the association.

Fall River Visitor Center (all ages)

3450 Fall River Rd. (on US 34); (970) 586-1415. Open daily year-round; summer, 9 a.m. to 5 p.m.; hours vary fall through spring. Free.

Moraine Park Museum and Nature Trail (all ages)

South of US 36 on Bear Lake Road; (970) 586-1206. Open daily May through Sept, 9 a.m. to 5 p.m. Free.

This restored lodge with log fireplace mantels and wooden rockers reminds visitors of the park's early days, but the exhibits created by the Denver Museum of Nature and Science are very "today." After learning about glaciations, spend time on the second-story glassed-in porch where the moraine lies before you. Were you caught in an afternoon thunderstorm? The weather and climate displays explain rapidly changing conditions. An art gallery and bookstore are on the lower level.

Looping behind the center is a ⁹⁄₁₀-mile nature trail that even little legs can manage. See how many plants and animals the family can identify, and enjoy the great views.

Alpine Visitor Center (all ages)

Atop Fall River Pass on Trail Ridge Road. Open daily June through Sept, 9 a.m. to 5 p.m. Free.

At 11,796 feet, the aptly named Alpine Visitor Center is the highest facility in the park. A stop here feels like you're on top of the world, and the views are spectacular. There could be snow in July or balmy sunshine in Sept; it's always a surprise. Parking facilities are often crowded, but it's still worth a stop.

Trail Ridge Store (all ages)

Next to the Alpine Visitor Center (970) 586-2133. Open daily June through Aug, 9 a.m. to 6 p.m.; Sept through mid-Oct, 10 a.m. to 5 p.m.

This store, the only souvenir shop within the park, sells much more than T-shirts and post-cards. Select from handmade Native American crafts, jewelry, and original art. Outdoor

Reasons **for Rules**

Throughout the park you'll see warnings not to feed the wildlife. Many people think that applies just within the park boundaries, but there are very good reasons not to feed wildlife in any location. You put animals at risk with improper diet and a loss of ability to survive on their own. You put yourself at risk to injury and disease. That cute chipmunk you're tempting with peanuts may be carrying rabies or fleas infected with bubonic plague. Watch from a distance. Do not come in contact with wild animals even if they appear to be tame. Do your part by letting them remain wild.

A Park Visit **Checklist**

- **Take a hike**—even ½ mile makes a difference in what you see.

- **Participate in a ranger-led event, hike, or program**—learning is part of the experience.

- **Drive high**—drive above timberline into the tundra, where you will find a unique landscape.

- **Stop near water**—whether it's the quiet solitude of a backcountry lake or the roar of a waterfall. Reflect on the importance and impact of this vital natural resource.

- **Observe wildlife**—enjoy the inhabitants of the park in their natural environment.

enthusiasts find quality packs, boots, and clothing and the snack bar satisfies hungry shoppers.

There are plenty of items for young buyers, too. We are told to set a price limit for their souvenirs, not to influence them too much, and let them make their own choices. We try. (But how are we going to feel about that drum 10 miles down the road?)

Junior Ranger Program (ages 6 to 13)

Ask for a Junior Ranger Log Book at any of the visitor centers. Free.

Use the Log Book as your family explores the park. Keep a checklist of wildlife spotted, learn conservation and mountain safety, and attend a ranger-led program. When you've completed the requirements, show your book to a ranger to have the certificate signed, and receive your official Junior Ranger badge.

Trail Ridge Road

One of America's most scenic roads, Trail Ridge carries travelers across the Continental Divide from Estes Park to Grand Lake. The 48-mile trip includes 11 miles that run high above the timberline through alpine tundra, a world of fragile and fascinating beauty. From beaver meadows and mountaintops to river valleys, you'll view a world much as it was when Native Americans followed this route long ago. Numerous pullouts, viewpoints, and trailheads dot the way, so it's easy to get out of your car. Feel the power of the wind, examine tiny tundra flowers, or watch the eagles in soaring flight.

Old Fall River Road

Construction on this road began in 1913, two years before the area was designated a national park. Seven years later the first motor route across the park was completed. Eleven miles in length, the one-way, mostly gravel roadway leaves Endovalley near the

Be **Prepared**

Mountain weather changes rapidly and frequently. For good reason, there's a mountain range here named "Never Summer." Always have jackets with you for every member of the family. Don't leave them in the car when you leave for a hike. Coats with hoods are a good choice since most body heat is lost through the head. Stuff pockets with fleece headbands and stretchy gloves for protection without a lot of additional bulk. By being prepared you'll enjoy your adventure even when conditions fluctuate.

Fall River Entrance Station and joins Trail Ridge Road at the Alpine Visitor Center. From there you can continue to the west side of the park or complete a loop back to Estes Park. Because of the narrow roadbed and sharp hairpin turns, vehicles more than 25 feet long and pulled trailers are prohibited, but four-wheel drive is not required.

Along your journey you'll pass through three distinctive ecosystems: the montane, subalpine, and alpine tundra. Geography, geology, botany, and ecology aren't just textbook subjects here. Witness evidence of glaciers, avalanches, wind, and man. Chasm Falls, a popular stop, tumbles 25 feet into a whirlpool a short walk from the road.

Family Hiking

Park personnel report that most visitors ask, "Where can we take a hike?" With more than 300 miles of trails, there's an option for every age and ability, from boardwalk nature walks to the arduous Longs Peak climb. Whether you have less than an hour or several days, there is a trail just right for your family. Out of the car you can listen for birds and other animals, smell the ponderosa pine, and see nature unfold. Kids' natural curiosity will lead to discovery along forest, meadow, rocky slopes, or tundra trails. Brochures and detailed guidebooks are available for purchase at visitor centers. Ask rangers, local residents, and other visitors about their favorite destinations, or choose one of these. (Distances are one way except where noted.) **Free.**

> **Sprague Lake.** This ½-mile nature trail, which is stroller and wheelchair accessible, circles the lake. Bug enthusiasts will love the variety of insects to study. Riding stables and picnic tables are nearby.

> **Alberta Falls.** Almost everyone loves waterfalls. This one is just ⁶⁄₁₀ mile from Glacier Gorge Junction. Listen for the sound of the falls long before you see it. Aspens along the trail make this a great autumn hike. Hardier hikers can continue to Mills Lake (1⁹⁄₁₀ miles farther) or the Loch (2¹⁄₁₀ additional miles from the falls).

> **Bear Lake Area.** This is one of the most popular areas of the park. Try to visit here very early or late in the day or, even better, in the off-season. At the peak of the summer, when the parking lot fills, **free** shuttle buses access the area.

The ⁶⁄₁₀-mile walk around the lake is fairly level, a good choice for a mixed-ability group. You are almost guaranteed to see chipmunks along the way. Remember to observe, not feed or touch.

A chain of lakes above Bear Lake lures hikers farther up the trail: Nymph Lake, ½ mile; Dream, 1¹⁄₁₀ miles; Emerald, 1⁸⁄₁₀ miles. Climbing upward, the vistas are ever changing and rewarding. Go as far as your group is comfortable, but remember: The only way back to the car is on foot.

Lily Lake. Along the ¾-mile walk around Lily Lake, you're sure to spot summer wildflowers. The trail and fishing are wheelchair accessible. Longs Peak, the highest mountain in the park at 14,255 feet, towers majestically to the south.

Wild Basin Area. In the park's southeastern corner, this trail leads to waterfalls, cascades, and lakes. At ³⁄₁₀ mile you'll find Copeland Falls, hardly worthy of its name. The more interesting Calypso Cascades are 1½ miles farther. A bridge provides views of the rushing creek below. The trail gets steeper if you tackle an additional ⁸⁄₁₀ mile to Ouzel Falls, a watery plunge definitely worthy of its name.

This area is a popular winter location for cross-country skiing and snowshoeing.

Gem Lake. For a hike with a different view, try the Gem Lake trail. Outcroppings of rounded rock in weird formations are a kid's delight. Lumpy Ridge is a favorite with technical rock climbers; just watching can be dramatic. The nearly 2-mile route of moderate difficulty takes you past Twin Owls and Paul Bunyan's Boot (check out the hole in the sole). Make a game of naming formations along the way to divert tired hikers.

Special Programs

Hikes, slide shows, workshops, or campfires will enrich your experience at Rocky Mountain National Park. Some are for families; others, for children only. Watch your kids absorb knowledge from new adventures while they have a great time. Try Rocky after Dark, a nighttime guided hike; learn about beavers in Rocky's Engineers; or attend the "Children's Adventure," a ranger-led program. Ask for a printed schedule of programs at visitor centers. Some require advance reservations. **Free** to $$$$.

Hiking with Rangers. From one-hour nature hikes that unravel mysteries and sharpen your senses to strenuous four-hour treks along the Continental Divide,

Water **Ouzel**

Ouzel Falls is named after a fascinating bird found in the park. About the size of a robin, the gray bird named water ouzel or dipper dives underwater to catch aquatic insects. Watch as it bobs up and down from a midstream rock.

ranger-led hikes are a great way to see the park beyond the roadway. You'll find out about native wildlife, forces that formed the park, and humans' impact. Or take one of the photography walks and learn techniques for better outdoor photos. **Free.**

Campfire Talks. At campgrounds and the Beaver Meadows Visitor Center; daily during the summer. **Free.**

Experience the age-old ritual of gathering around a fire, sharing information, telling tall tales, and singing. Campfire themes differ, so you can go every night without a repeat. Remember to dress warmly. No matter how hot it was during the day, evening temperatures can chill.

If the kids are too tired and cranky to attend an evening campfire program, there's an alternative at Moraine Park. Bring a mug—the hot beverages are provided—for a morning chat (9 a.m.) with a ranger around a campfire.

Camping. Campgrounds in the park are often filled during the summer. Reservations for Moraine Park and Glacier Basin (800-365-2267) may be made six months in advance; cost is $20 per site per night ($14 during the winter months). Aspenglen, Longs Peak (tents only), and Timber Creek sites are available on a first-come, first-served basis and may be filled before noon; cost is $20 per site per night ($14 during the winter months). There are no showers or RV connections in any park campground.

Permits are required for all backcountry camping; reservations are accepted starting Mar 1 each year. The Backcountry Office (970-586-1242) near the **Beaver Meadows Visitor Center** is open during the summer, 8 a.m. to 9 p.m.

Fort Collins

Agriculture meets academia in this town of approximately 140,000 residents. While farms and ranches surround Fort Collins, and nearby mountains gently roll into plains, the city itself is home to Colorado State University. Here, small-town friendliness mingles with the cultural advantages of a college town. Add to this the beauty of the Poudre River Valley and a backdrop of majestic mountains, and you have an outstanding blend of Old West/ New West.

Swetsville Zoo (ages 2 and up)
4801 East Harmony Rd. (off I-25, southeast of Fort Collins); (970) 484-9509; www.roadside america.com. Open daily year-round, dawn to dusk. Donations are appreciated, but admission is **free.**

This "zoo" is like none other, and it's a great place for kids. It all began when owner Bill Swets decided to make a dinosaur out of some old rusty nuts, bolts, shovels, and plough shins he had lying around his farm. It took about five weeks, but when he was finished, there stood in his front yard a 900-pound Tyrannosaurus Rex that came all the way up to the eaves on the Swets's farmhouse. And now there's Harry the Hitchhiker and his companion, Penny the Dimetrodon, Dino the Brontosaurus, and scores of other sculptures, including flowers, windmills, animals, and more dinosaurs, all made from farm machinery, car parts, and scrap metal. Bring lunch and stay as long as you please. Picnic tables are provided.

Kids love exploring this whimsical menagerie to see what sort of creature they can find next. Don't miss the wealthy old Chinese dragon named Kyle the Kyleeasaurus and the ferocious fighter Polly the Polacanthus.

Discovery Science Center (all ages)

200 Mathews St.; (970) 221-6738; www.fcmdsc.org. (At the time of this writing, the Center is building a new facility and is temporarily located in the Fort Collins Museum.) Open Tues through Sat 10 a.m. to 5 p.m.; Sun noon to 5 p.m.; closed Mon. $, children under age 2 are free.

Have fun together while you learn about gravity, pulleys, sound waves, and electricity at the only museum in Colorado devoted entirely to science. Started more than ten years ago by volunteers, Discovery Science Center now has more than 120 exhibits, from aerodynamics to zoology, which are all interactive. Build with pipes and joints, use levers, make arcs and sparks. Learn how a fax works, and use a videophone. A full program of classes and workshops for ages 3 and up is offered.

Old Town (all ages)

Downtown Fort Collins. Free.

Shady trees, brick sidewalks, and one-hundred-year-old buildings present a bit of nostalgia while the shops, galleries, and restaurants are definitely "now." Take a self-guided historic walking tour, or just browse on your own.

Children's Mercantile Company (all ages)

111 North College Ave. (in Old Town); (970) 484-9946 or (888) 326-8465. Open Mon through Sat 9:30 a.m. to 8 p.m. and Sun 11 a.m. to 6 p.m.

Quality and quantity! One look in the window, and you won't be able to bypass this toy store.

City Park (all ages)

1500 West Mulberry St.; (970) 221-6655. Free.

Picnic tables, a large playground, grassy running room, an outdoor swimming pool, and a miniature train make this a pleasant all-day excursion. The small lake has a wheelchair-accessible fishing pier and paddleboats to rent.

Miniature Train (all ages)

1599 City Park Dr.; (970) 416-2264. Open daily June through Aug, Mon through Fri 10 a.m. to 4 p.m., Sat and Sun 10 a.m. to 6 p.m. $, one parent may accompany each child under age 2 for free.

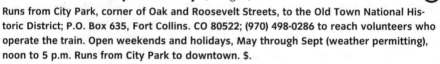

The park's miniature train has been entertaining Fort Collins's families since the 1950s.

Swimming Pool

(970) 416-2489, code: 3463. Open June through Labor Day Mon, Wed, Sat and Sun 10 a.m. to 5:30 p.m.; Tues, Thurs, and Fri 10 a.m. to 8 p.m. $.

Paddleboats

Open June through Labor Day Mon through Fri 3 p.m. to 7 p.m., Sat and Sun 10 a.m. to 5 p.m. Half-hour rental $.

Fort Collins Municipal Railway (all ages)

Runs from City Park, corner of Oak and Roosevelt Streets, to the Old Town National Historic District; P.O. Box 635, Fort Collins. CO 80522; (970) 498-0286 to reach volunteers who operate the train. Open weekends and holidays, May through Sept (weather permitting), noon to 5 p.m. Runs from City Park to downtown. $.

Ride back in time on the only original restored city streetcar in the western United States. Car 21 and 1½ miles of track were renovated by the volunteers who operate and maintain this line.

Environmental Learning Center (all ages)

3745 East Prospect Rd. (1 mile east of Timberline); (970) 491-1661. Visitor Center open daily mid-May through Aug; weekends only Sept through Apr, 10 a.m. to 5 p.m.; closed Dec and Jan. Trails open daily year-round, sunrise to sunset. Free.

Colorado State University operates this environmental education center along the Poudre River. You'll see four major ecological habitats as you explore 2½ miles of trails. The Visitor Center houses interpretive displays and a gift shop.

The Rocky Mountain Raptor Program is located here, so you'll be sure to see eagles and other birds of prey. Be sure to notice the nesting and feeding towers for osprey along the river.

Anheuser–Busch Tour Center (all ages)

I-25 north to Mountain Vista Drive, exit 271, turn right onto Busch Drive; (970) 490-4691; www.budweisertours.com. Open daily June through Aug, 10 a.m. to 4 p.m. Oct through May, Thurs through Mon 10 a.m. to 4 p.m. Free.

Bring your family to visit the famous Budweiser Clydesdales in their Rocky Mountain home. The Fort Collins Brewery serves as a training center where the horses learn to pull a wagon before they join an eight-hitch team.

The magnificent horses, weighing more than 2,000 pounds each, are often outside in the morning and late afternoon. Otherwise, walk over to their home, Clydesdale Hamlet. This grand, gleaming building is no ordinary stable. As you walk along the stalls, consider that each horse consumes fifty to sixty pounds of hay, twenty to twenty-five quarts of feed, and up to thirty gallons of water every day. Take time to watch the twenty-five-minute video and peruse the exhibits interesting to both children and adults. Compare the size of an average horseshoe to one of the Clydesdales' shoes—quite a difference.

Be sure to say hello to Suds, the Dalmatian mascot, who resides in his own fancy digs near Clydesdale Hamlet.

On the first Sat of each month, you can get even closer to the Clydesdales. On Budweiser Clydesdale Camera Day, from 1 to 3 p.m. a trainer escorts one of the horses onto the grounds outside the visitor center. Bring a camera to immortalize your family standing next to a gentle giant. Touching is allowed! In case of bad weather, the photo session takes place inside.

Anheuser–Busch even welcomes visitors who choose not to take the brewery tour.

The Farm (all ages)
600 North Sherwood St. (at Lee Martinez Park); (970) 221-6665. www.fcgov.com/recreation/thefarm.php. Dates and hours vary greatly by season and weather for the museum, gift shop, pony rides, and trail rides. Call ahead or check their Web site. $–$$.

Chickens, pigs, goats, sheep, cows, ponies, and horses—they're all here, along with pony rides for kids 12 and under. (Parents lead ponies around the arena.) Purchase packets of feed to entice the animals closer to the fence. You are allowed to reach through and pet them.

At this quality museum depicting farm life over the last one hundred years, grandparents enjoy showing their families how things used to be. See if you can identify the mystery tool. The gift shop sells arts and crafts with a farm theme.

Horsetooth Reservoir and Lory State Park (all ages)
South on Taft Hill Road to County Road (38E west). Follow the signs to the reservoir, about ten minutes from town. Open daily year-round. $ per car.

Horsetooth Reservoir is a real treasure in landlocked Colorado. Besides being popular with water-skiers, it has a swim beach and covered picnic tables, perfect respites on a hot summer's day. At Horsetooth Yacht Club near the beach, you can purchase lunch or dinner.

Lory State Park borders the reservoir with 2,400 acres of grassy open meadows, ponderosa pine forests, sandstone hogbacks, and unique rock outcroppings. A variety of trails attracts hikers, bikers, joggers, and horseback riders. In winter months, cross-country skiing, sledding, and tubing are the draw. No snowmobiling is allowed.

Main Street **U.S.A.**

You might think you're on Main Street U.S.A. in Disneyland—and with good reason. Disneyland's quintessential hometown street was actually based on this very place, and the Magic Kingdom's Main Street Fire Station is an exact model of Fort Collins's 1882 city hall/firehouse.

Disc **Golf**

It's been called the sport of the future, and Fort Collins is one of the hot spots for it.

Played much like traditional golf, but using discs (Frisbees) instead of balls and clubs, disc golf can be enjoyed by everyone. It doesn't require special skills to begin, and the initial equipment investment is less than $10 and easily transported.

Bill Wright, owner of Wright Life, a downtown Fort Collins sporting-goods store, has been a driving force in the development of this activity soon to be included in the World Games. To learn about disc golf and to purchase or rent discs, stop in to see him at Wright Life, 200 Linden St. (970-484-6932). Then head out for some great family fun. A round of disc golf takes one and a half to two hours.

- **Boltz Junior High.** This course is on the grounds of a junior high school and is one of the easier ones since it was designed for school kids.

- **Edora Park,** 1420 East Stuart St. This park also has a playground, fitness course, BMX track, trails, and the EPIC recreation center (disc golf course map available here) with indoor pool and ice arena.

Many Colorado ski areas have disc golf courses for summer use. The one atop Aspen Mountain has great views. Look for more than two dozen other courses throughout the state during your travels.

Pawnee National Grasslands and Pawnee Buttes

(ages 5 and up)

East of Fort Collins, north of Fort Morgan. County Road 129 north from CO 14 at New Raymer (970) 346-5000. Access to within 1½ miles of West Butte is via dirt and gravel roads. Not recommended in inclement weather. **Free.**

The Pawnee National Grasslands cover 193,060 acres of short-grass prairie ecosystems alive with wildlife habitats and archaeological resources. Here you are apt to see pronghorn antelope, mule deer, coyotes, foxes, badgers, snakes, and prairie dogs. Birdlife includes the golden eagle, hawks, the burrowing owl, and the lark bunting, Colorado's state bird. More than 400 species of plants thrive in the grasslands. Depending on the season, you will see an abundance of wildflowers, including the pink, yellow, and red blossoms of prickly pear cactus, sunflowers, and coneflowers. Walkers and hikers are welcome, but motorized vehicles must stay on routes marked by numbered posts to prevent erosion and unintentional trespass onto private land.

The Pawnee Buttes rise 250 feet above the prairie surface, approximately 11 miles northeast of the small town of Keota. A dirt road provides access to the trailhead and overlook, and a 1½-mile trail takes you to the base of the western butte. The eastern butte is nearby but can't be accessed without crossing private land. Because hawks and other birds of prey use the buttes for nesting, the north overlook and the cliffs near the buttes are closed to the public Mar through June. With binoculars it is possible to observe birds searching for field mice or even to see young birds in the nests, but it is important to stay at least 300 yards away from the nests. Climbing on the buttes is not recommended due to the crumbling sandstone. Watch for antelope and birds, and watch out for rattlesnakes.

Where to Eat

Egg and I, 2809 South College Ave.; (970) 223-5271; www.theeggandirestaurants.com. Open daily for breakfast and lunch. This is the place to go for one of the best breakfasts in town, according to local residents. $

Sundance Steakhouse and Country Club, 2716 East Mulberry St.; (970) 484-1600. Open nightly, except Mon, for dinner and entertainment. Forget your idea of a cosmopolitan country club; real local cowboys eat here. There's a collection of old "retired" boots on one wall. If you choose, you can even learn to line dance here. The country-western entertainment won't be for everyone, but the steaks are the best. Perhaps you'd like to try some bison. $$$

Where to Stay

Best Western Kiva Inn, 1638 East Mulberry St.; (970) 484-2444; www.bestwesterncolorado.com. **Free** continental breakfast; exercise room, outdoor swimming pool, guest laundry, in-room microwave ovens and refrigerators. $–$$$

Motel 6, 3900 East Mulberry St.; (970) 482-6466. Outdoor swimming pool; **free** HBO and ESPN; kids under 12 stay **free.** $–$$

Treats in **Town**

Homemade ice cream and chocolate call your name at this shop in the Fort Collins Old Town area. Try it for a memorable treat.

- **Kilwin's Chocolates and Ice Cream,** 114 South College Ave.; (970) 221-9444. Choosing is difficult—there are thirty-two flavors. Toasted Coconut or Fort Collins Mud? Try a **free** sample of fudge. You won't be able to leave without a purchase. They make it on the premises. The hand-dipped caramel apples also are irresistible. And then there's Kilwin's chocolates—creams, truffles, caramels, oh, my!

Sterling

The town of Sterling, 125 miles northeast of Denver on I-76, is a laid-back community of friendly people and intriguing attractions.

City of Living Trees

Sterling is sometimes referred to as the "City of Living Trees" due to the fascinating works of former resident Brad Rhea, a gifted artist who became a one-man beautification project for the town. Early in his career, this highly acclaimed sculptor took dead trees, stripped off their bark, and carved wondrous sculptures from them. Although Rhea has long since become a renowned sculptor of marble and now lives in the nearby town of Merino, his work still draws thousands of visitors to Sterling to seek out his tree art. Take a walk around town to see who in your family can spot the next carving. Keep score to determine who has found the most at the end of your trek. In the process you will discover a herd of five giraffes carved from a single tree in Columbine Park. See if you can find the clown, a mermaid, and an actor with the masks of comedy and tragedy. Thankfully, several of the sculptures are housed inside public buildings to avoid the destructive effects of the elements. A map of the sculpture locations is available at the visitor center across from the Overland Trail Museum on US 6.

Overland Trail Museum   (ages 2 and up)

Take exit 125 off of I-76 onto US 6, east of Sterling; (970) 522-3895; www.sterlingcolo.com. Open Apr through Oct, Mon through Sat 9 a.m. to 5 p.m., Sun 1 to 5 p.m. Nov through Mar, Tues through Sat 10 a.m. to 4 p.m., closed Sun, Mon and holidays.

Built in the form of an old fort, this museum displays artifacts from the days when pioneers traveled the Overland Trail from Kansas City to Denver. From 1862 to 1868, this branch of the trail, which led along the South Platte River, was the most heavily traveled road in the entire country. The museum grounds reveal a Concord stagecoach, a covered wagon, old farm machinery, and a shaded, well-equipped picnic area. You can enter the old country store, a blacksmith shop, a 1900s barber shop, a country church, and the one-room Stoney Buttes Schoolhouse. During the summer your children can attend short classes held in the old school.

The indoor exhibits showcase items that once belonged to the westward-bound pioneers and to the Native Americans who inhabited the area for so many generations. You will find antique dolls, sunbonnets, bottles, and period wedding dresses. Native American artifacts include buckskin clothing, arrowheads, and stone metates, used to grind corn. Bring along a lunch, and after touring the museum, sit under a shade tree and suggest that each member of your family tell what he or she liked best about the museum and why. Then make a game of imagining what the people were like who once owned these items and lived, studied, and worshipped in these buildings.

North Sterling Reservoir State Park (all ages)
13 miles north of Sterling; (970) 522-3657; http://parks.state.co.us.

This is a boaters' paradise on the high plains, with coves and lake fingers to explore with expansive views of buttes and bluffs. Three campgrounds, a sandy swim beach, visitor center with interpretive summer programs, picnic sites, and fishing and wildlife viewing lure visitors to this northeastern Colorado park.

Where to Eat

Country Kitchen, in the Ramada Inn, I-76 and US 6; (970) 522-2625. Children's menu. $

Where to Stay

Ramada Inn, I-76 and US 6; (970) 522-2625 or (800) 272-6232. Tropical courtyard with indoor swimming pool, sauna, whirlpool, and games. Special packages for family escapes. $$–$$$

Super 8 Motel, 12883 Highway 61, (970) 522-0300. Indoor swimming pool. Free continental breakfast. $–$$

For More Information

City of Sterling, 421 North 4th St., Sterling, CO 80751; (970) 522-9700; www.sterlingcolo .com.

Logan County Chamber of Commerce, 109 North Front St., Sterling, CO 80751; (970) 522-5070.

Keenesburg

The Wild Animal Sanctuary (all ages)
1946 County Rd. 53, Keenesburg. (303) 536-0118; www.wildanimalsanctuary.org. Open daily year-round, except for Christmas, New Year's Day, Fourth of July, Thanksgiving, and during very bad weather. From Denver, take I-25 north to I-76. Proceed northeast on I-76 in the direction of Fort Morgan. From I-76, take exit 31 at the town of Hudson. At top of off-ramp, turn right onto County Road (CR) 52. Proceed 4 miles east on CR 52 to CR 53. Turn right (south) onto CR 53. Go 3 miles to Sanctuary entrance, on left side of road. Follow signs to parking lot. $$.

This is not a zoo. No popcorn, balloons, or cotton candy. And no cages. This is a sanctuary with a clear-cut, two-fold mission: To provide every one of the 210 lions, tigers, bears, jaguars, mountain lions, leopards, lynx, bob cats, servals, wolves, and other wildlife the very best care possible in order to try to make up for the grievous lives most of them lived before being rescued. The goal also is to try to educate the public regarding the problems involved with trying to make pets out of captive wildlife.

Situated on 320 acres of rolling grassland, 30 miles northeast of Denver, the sanctuary is cleverly arranged to allow the animals to have large, natural habitats like they would have in the wild, where they can run freely and play with members of their own species. The bears and tigers have natural ponds and lakes in which to swim and play. The habitats range in size from five to twenty-five acres, depending on the types, needs, and habits of the particular animals that occupy them.

Visitors view the animals from 35 feet above the ground on a uniquely designed, elevated system of walkways and large observation platforms that span a major portion of the sanctuary. A heated, centralized roundhouse protects the wildlife during extreme weather conditions

On-site educational tours are offered and are well worth taking. The sanctuary is a 501 (c) 3, nonprofit, state and federally licensed zoological facility that works closely with city, state, and federal agencies to help provide a good home for confiscated animals that were illegally possessed, abandoned, abused, housed in extremely cruel situations, facing euthanasia due to over–breeding for commercial use, or because they became too large for the owners to handle. The stories are enough to break your heart, but you need only to see how healthy and playful the animals are now to be convinced that they have finally found a good home.

The sanctuary provides safe, permanent, comfortable, natural environments for the animals. They do not breed them, sell them, or use them in any commercial way. The admission fees help support the sanctuary but, of course, do not even come close to the cost of food and care. The refuge relies heavily on donations and volunteer help.

Brighton

Barr Lake State Park (all ages)
13401 Picadilly Rd. (I-25 north from Denver to I-76, northeast on I-76 to Bromley Lane, east to Picadilly Road, and south to park entrance); (303) 659-6005; http://parks.state.co.us/ parks/barrlake. Open daily 5 a.m. to 10 p.m. Visitor Center hours vary greatly according to seasons and weather. Call for exact days and times. $ per car.

The forty-minute drive from town through flat, dusty farm country is not a high point with kids, but this state park offers pleasant, low-key family fun. The lake, surrounded by 2,600 acres of park, is the nesting site of bald eagles and more than 350 other species of birds. A boardwalk leads out to the gazebo, where you can do some bird-watching in relative comfort. Deer, red fox, rabbits, toads, turtles, and snakes also call this home. **Free** public programs include guided nature walks.

Fishing and boating are allowed on the northeast end of the lake. Boats with electric trolling motors or gasoline motors of 10 horsepower or less are allowed. Kids like the visitor center with its many hands-on exhibits. There usually are some live animals on display (snakes, turtles, and toads are popular). Take the 13-passenger Eagle Express motorized cart on a naturalist-guided tour of wildlife viewing, departing the Nature Center every Sat at 10 a.m. and Sun at 11 a.m., from mid-May through Sept.

Limon

It may come as a surprise to be told that the small prairie town of Limon, with an approximate population of 2,050 residents, would be referred to as "The Hub City of the Eastern Plains." When you consider, however, that I-70, US 24, US 40, US 287, US 71, US 86 all cross paths here, it seems only natural that Limon would qualify for the title. Located a little over one hour's drive southeast of Denver or northeast of Colorado Springs, makes this a popular stop for travelers to stretch their legs or relax for the night before heading on west to the larger cities and the mountains of Colorado's Front Range.

Limon Heritage Museum & Railroad Park (age 3 and up)

899 1st St.; P. O. Box 341, Limon CO 80828. From Denver, take I-70 southeast for 86 miles to exit 359 or 361 and proceed one mile to downtown Limon. From the stoplight, travel 2.5 blocks south to the Town Hall. The museum complex is immediately behind the Town Hall. (719) 775-8605; www.townoflimon.com. Open Memorial Day through Labor Day, Mon through Sat, 1 p.m. to 8 p.m. free.

Community pride is obvious at the Limon Heritage Museum and Railroad Park. If possible, plan to spend several hours here. There is so much to see.

Restored and maintained by Heritage Society volunteers, the ca. 1910 Limon Depot has been placed on the National Register of Historic Places. Formerly a "Union" depot that served both the Union Pacific and the Rock Island railroads, it showcases a restored railroad office, a working "N" scale model of Limon's ca. 1940s railroad yard, a permanent display called, "Trains of the Plains," and several changing exhibits.

Day Trip to **Limon**

Arrive shortly before noon. Either bring along a lunch or choose from several fast food establishments for "take out" and proceed to a picnic table in the garden, park, and play area of the Limon Heritage Museum and Railroad Park. Spend a slow, relaxed afternoon exploring the park and letting your family's imaginations wander as you stroll through the museum complex, check out Limon's shops and antiques stores, and select a restaurant for dinner. During your meal would be a good time to get a lively conversation going by having each member of your family say what they liked best about the museum and why, a great tradition to establish for expanding excursions into learning experiences.

Dinner over and kids having run out of energy, you can opt to spend the night in one of Limon's many motels or drive home with the little ones, no doubt, snoozing in the back seat.

Outdoors, in the Railroad Park, adjacent to the Depot, you will find antique machinery and vintage windmills. You can walk through a Western Saddle boxcar, a rail dining car, and a Union Pacific caboose.

Next, in the Exhibit Building, imagine what life on the plains was like in the prairie kitchen, barber shop, old-fashioned gas station, and mercantile store, and think about how it might have been to study in the one-room schoolhouse, and live in the Cheyenne tipi or the sheep herder's wagon.

Where to Stay

Holiday Inn Express and Suites, 803 Highway 24; (719) 775-9033; reservations: (800) HOLIDAY. Indoor pool and spa, guest laundry, elevator, fitness center, complimentary breakfast bar, gift shop. $$–$$$

Comfort Inn, 2255 Ninth St.; (719) 775-2752; I-70 at exit 359. Complimentary deluxe continental breakfast, indoor pool and spa, exercise room, premium cable channels. $$–$$$

Genoa

Genoa Wonder View Tower and Museum
95 miles east of Denver on I-70; (719) 763-2309; www.ourjourney.info/myjourneydest inations/wondertower.asp. Open June through Oct, 9 a.m. to 5 p.m.; shorter hours Nov through May. $.

You will spot a gigantic red-and-white tower on the north side of the highway at Genoa. Welcome to the Genoa Wonder View Tower and Museum. It is said that Ripley, of "Believe It or Not" fame, proved that six states could be seen from the top of this tower.

Inside the twenty-room museum you will find an unbelievable assortment of priceless items alongside those of total gimcrackery. Old bottles, jars, and inkwells; 300 different kinds of barbed-wire fence strands; more than 1,000 paintings rendered more than fifty years ago by Raven Wing, a Sioux princess; a buffalo hairball (!); a stuffed, two-headed calf; a pair of woolly mammoth tusks; washboards; antique guns; fish fossils; and more than 20,000 Native American artifacts haphazardly line the floors, hang on walls, and reside in dusty showcases.

The museum is the pride and joy of Jerry Chubbuck, who has been its owner and curator since 1974. According to Chubbuck, "If it ain't here, it don't exist." After wandering through this museum, you just might agree.

Chubbuck has antiques and inexpensive curios for sale. The buildings are unheated, so although they bring a welcome relief from the heat of summer, they are bone-chillingly cold in winter. Bundle up if you plan to come by during fall, winter, or early spring. It's best to call ahead during the off-season to make sure someone is around to let you in.

Burlington

Located off I-70 in extreme eastern Colorado, almost to the Kansas border, the small town of Burlington provides an opportunity to experience turn-of-the-20th-century life in the heart of the Eastern Plains.

Old Town (all ages)

420 South 14th St.; (719) 346-7382 or (800) 288-1334; www.ourjourney.info/myjourneydest inations/oldtownmuseum.asp. Open daily year-round; Mon through Sat 9 a.m. to 5 p.m. and Sun noon to 5 p.m. $.

Old Town is a six-and-one-half-acre complex of twenty-one fully restored historic buildings filled with artifacts from the area. The entire facility is wheelchair and stroller accessible. Here you will see a schoolhouse built in 1911 for the children of homesteaders, a "soddie" made of thick slabs of buffalo grass because there were few trees or rocks for house building, and a drugstore that sold everything from hot water bottles to milk of magnesia toothpaste. Your children will want to see the playhouse filled with a unique collection of dolls, one of which was made from bread dough.

Stop in at the Longhorn Saloon to purchase peanuts, popcorn, and beverages. During the summertime see can-can girls dance on tabletops and roughhousing cowboys settle arguments with their shootin' irons. (Phone ahead for performance times.) Peek into the jail, sample old-fashioned candy in the general store, and order a root beer float while listening to the jukebox at the soda fountain. In the Emporium you will find handmade crafts such as barbed-wire wreaths, pottery, wheat weaving, wood carvings, and carousel figures.

Kit Carson County Carousel (all ages)

Open daily Memorial Day to Labor Day, 11 a.m. to 6 p.m.: www.kitcarsoncountycarousel .com. The 25-cent admission fee includes a twenty-minute tour and a memorable four-minute ride.

When you have finished touring Old Town, wait out front of the Emporium (on weekends only but it is a short walk to the carousel if you happen to be there on a weekday) for a horse-drawn wagon ride aboard the Old Town Express to the Kit Carson County Carousel. This treasure was built in 1905, number six of only seventy-four manufactured by the Philadelphia Toboggan Company. Now designated as both a National Historic Site and a National Landmark (one of only thirteen in Colorado), it is the only antique carousel in the United States still maintaining its original paint on both the animals and the scenery panels.

Forty-six intricately hand-carved horses, lions, giraffes, deer, zebras, and a camel "Mar" (the animals are stationary and do not move up and down) to festive melodies played by a restored ca. 1912 Wurlitzer Monster Military Band Organ, a one-hundred-key instrument measuring almost 7 feet high and 10 feet wide and with musical output equal to a twelve- to fifteen-piece band. Your kids will long remember riding on this carousel. Bring plenty of film.

Where to Stay

Comfort Inn, 2825 Lincoln St.; (719) 346-7676; www.comfortinn.com. $–$$

Super 8 Motel, 2100 Fay St.; (719) 346-5627; www.bestlodging.com. $–$$

For More Information

State Welcome Center at Burlington, just off I-70; (719) 346-5554; www.colorado.com.

Annual Events

MAY

Kinetic Conveyance Race, located at the Boulder Reservoir in spring; (303) 442-2911; www.bouldercoloradousa.com. "Wacky" best describes this Boulder springtime celebration. Witness human-powered machines struggle through deep water and across muddy beaches. Themes and costumes are definitely creative. $$

Bolder Boulder, Boulder, late May; www.bolderboulder.com. This high-altitude championship competition is considered to be one of the nation's top footraces. You can watch as runners from around the world compete in the 10-kilometer road race through the city streets. Runners $$$$, observers **free.**

JUNE

Greeley Independence Stampede, Greeley, mid-June to July 4; (970) 356-7787 or (800) 982-2855; www.greeleystampede.org. This celebration has grown from a small rodeo to become one of the top twenty PRCA rodeos in the world. Performances from country music stars, flapjack feeds, chili cook-offs, barbecues, carnival rides, trail rides, and a Fourth of July parade and fireworks make this a family-friendly event. $$–$$$$

Renaissance Festival, Larkspur (I-25 south from Denver to the Larkspur exit), eight weekends in June and July; (303) 688-6010; www.coloradorenaissance.com. King and queen, lords and ladies, strolling minstrels, jousting knights—you're back in the 16th century. More than 200 costumed artisans sell hand-crafted goods. Continuous entertainment and tempting food booths. $$$

Wool Market, Estes Park, mid-June; (970) 586-6104; wwww.estasnet.com/events. Celebrate wool! Live animals (sheep, llamas, alpacas) and lots of demonstrations make this festival interesting for kids. Techniques in loom weaving, rope weaving, and spinning are taught in the Children's Tent. **Free.**

JULY

Rooftop Rodeo, Estes Park, early-July; (970) 586-6104; www.estesnet.com/events. This rodeo is a favorite not only with audiences but with the cowboy athletes as well. Six nights of PRCA rodeo, wild horse racing, and "mutton bustin'." It's all kicked off with a festive parade. $$

KidSpree, Bicentennial Park, Aurora, mid-July. Colorado's largest outdoor festival designed specifically for children. Bicentennial Park, 13655 East Alameda Ave., Aurora; corner of Alameda and Potomac avenues. **Free** parking and shuttle at Aurora Town Center (formerly Aurora Mall). Twenty-nine-acre playland with over sixty activities just for kids. Call for exact dates and times, (303) 326-8FUN; www.auroragov.org/kidspree. **Free.**

Arapahoe County Fair, Arapahoe County Fair Grounds, Aurora, mid- to late July; (303) 795-4955; www.arapahoecountyfair.com. Begun in 1906, this annual, weeklong affair provides activities for the entire family: a carnival, catch and release fish tank, petting zoo, entertainment, draft horse shows, farm animals, 4-H competitions, livestock auction, contests, food vendors, pancake breakfasts, and fireworks exhibitions. $, children age 3 and under **free.**

Buffalo Bill Days, Golden, late July; (303) 279-3113; www.goldencochamber.org. You will see lots of Buffalo Bill look-alikes at this festival put on in his honor. Activities include a Wild West Show, a burro race, craft and food booths, and a parade. **Free.**

SEPTEMBER

Longs Peak Scottish–Irish Festival, Estes Park, early Sept; (970) 586-6308; www .scotfest.com. You've heard of the "wearin' of the green." Well, during these festivities, Estes Park celebrates the "wearin' of the plaid" as the traditions of both Scotland and Ireland bring forth bagpipe band concerts, Celtic competitions, and a parade. **Free** admission to some events; others, $–$$$.

Potato Day at Centennial Village, Greeley, mid-Sept; (970) 350-9220; www.greeley gov.com/museums/centennialvillage. Held at the living-history museum of Centennial Village, Potato Day is a jolly event. You can take part in a variety of old-fashioned family activities, watch a blacksmith at work, explore Buffalo Joe Flier's one-room cabin, and dine on baked potatoes with all the trimmings. $

Festival International, Fletcher Plaza, Aurora; third Sat in Sept; (303) 361-6169; www.aurorabusiness.info/festivalInterna tional. This one-day, annual event provides an opportunity to experience Aurora and metro-Denver's cultural diversity by celebrating the music, dance, food, and crafts of the many ethnic groups residing in this region of the state. You can expect to see nearly two dozen performances representing as many as twenty countries. The children's activity area, Passport to Culture, allows kids to experience global dancing, sports, games, various projects, and the opportunity to try on ethnic attire. **Free.**

OCTOBER

The Pumpkin Festival and Corn Maze, Denver Botanic Gardens' suburban Chatfield nature preserve, second weekend in Oct; (303) 973-3705; www.botanicgardens.org/ content/pumpkin-fest. This celebration of fall offers a you-pick pumpkin patch, hayrides,

and food and craft booths. The eight-acre maze cut among cornstalks provides a giant puzzle for kids to amble through. You won't be able to keep your toddlers from exploring the smaller version, designed just for them. $

Rocky Mountain Pumpkin Ranch Harvest Festival, Longmont, late Sept through Oct; (303) 684-0087; www.rockymtnpumpkin ranch.com. Bring the kids and let them pick out their own Halloween pumpkin amid the gaiety of a fall farm fest. Games, activities, food, a hay and corn maze, pony rides, and farm animals add to the merriment. **Free** admission, $ for activities.

Old Town "Ghost Town," Burlington, late Oct; (800) 288-1334; www.burlingtoncolo .com/oldtown. Old Town becomes a ghost town for an evening of trick-or-treating in a safe and controlled environment. Kids go from building to building to pick up their Halloween snacks and play games for small prizes upstairs in the barn. The lower level of the barn becomes a "haunted house" for those brave enough to enter. There is no charge for this "spooktacular" event, except for a 25-cent admission fee to the haunted house.

Trick or Treat Nature Trail, Morrison Nature Center at Star K Ranch, 16002 East Smith Rd., Aurora. Scavenger hunt during afternoon. Wear Halloween costumes if you like, pick up treats and enjoy fun activities. Call for date and times, (303) 739-2428; www .auroragov.org/nature. **Free.**

Holidays at the Homestead, Gully Homestead, 200 South Chambers Rd., Aurora. An opportunity to admire Aurora's oldest permanent dwelling during its annual sale of antiques, primitives, and handmade crafts. From late Oct through first few days in Dec. Call for dates and times. (303) 326-8630. **Free.**

DECEMBER

Kids Kristmas, downtown Fort Collins; (800) 274-3678; www.visitfortcollins.com. Call for date and time.

Southeastern Colorado

Histury and tradition run deep in southeastern Colorado, and more than a trace of the Spanish explorers, fur traders, mountain men, Native Americans, and pioneers that long ago crisscrossed this land remains today. Cultures as diverse as the landscapes enhance this region of the state.

Colorado Springs

Colorado Springs bustles as the state's second-largest city. A terrific vacation destination, it has one of the highest concentrations of natural and commercial attractions in the state.

TopPicks in Southeastern Colorado

- **Bent's Old Fort,** La Junta
- **Cave of the Winds,** Manitou Springs
- **Cripple Creek & Victor Narrow Gauge Railroad,** Cripple Creek
- **Florissant Fossil Beds National Monument,** Florissant
- **Flying W Ranch,** Colorado Springs
- **The Manitou Cliff Dwellings Museum,** Manitou Springs
- **Olympic Training Center,** Colorado Springs
- **Pikes Peak Cog Railroad,** Manitou Springs
- **Rocky Mountain Dinosaur Resource Center**
- **Santa's Workshop and North Pole**
- **WoodlandPark**

SOUTHEASTERN COLORADO

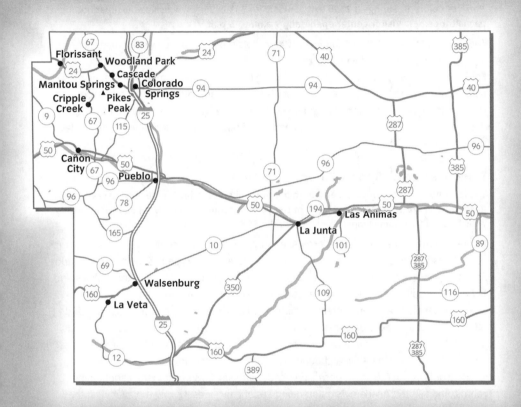

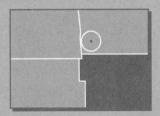

This is Pikes Peak country, and enough activities lie in its shadow to keep a family busy for weeks. Christened "The Long One" by Ute Indians who once hunted in the area, the 14,110-foot mountain became known to white settlers through the efforts of explorer Zebulon Pike in 1806.

United States Air Force Academy (all ages)

North of Colorado Springs (I-25 to exit 156B); (719) 333-2025; www.usafa.edu/superintendent/ pa/visitor-center. Visitor center open daily 9 a.m. to 5 p.m. Free.

The United States Air Force Academy is Colorado's most frequently visited man-made attraction. The Barry Goldwater Visitor Center features exhibits detailing life as a U.S. Air Force cadet, a 250-seat theater, a cafeteria, a gift shop, academy merchandise, and a nature trail leading to the Cadet Chapel. All proceeds from sales at the visitor center go to support collegiate and intramural cadet sports. You are welcome to visit the Protestant, Catholic, and Jewish sanctuaries in the chapel and take a self-guided driving tour to view the extensive wildlife sanctuary.

Falcon Summer Sports Camp (ages 8 to 18)

These camps are very popular, and enrollment is taken on a first come, first served basis. Reservations are accepted after Jan 1 of the year the camp is held. (719) 333-2116; http:// goairforcefalcons.com/camps/afa-camps.html. $$$$.

Offered by the United States Air Force Academy, these three- and five-day summer camps are held each year during the month of June on the Academy campus, north of Colorado Springs. They are designed to challenge and improve existing skill levels and abilities and to help build self-esteem, encourage teamwork, and promote good character qualities. The camps feature Academy intercollegiate head coaches as instructors. Topics include baseball, football, basketball, ice hockey, golf, soccer, lacrosse, tennis, wrestling, track and field, cross-country running, volleyball, self-defense, swimming, diving, gymnastics, strength/power/speed training, cheerleading/dance, and fencing.

Boarders live in the cadet dorms on gender specific floors, eat in the cadet dining rooms, and use the Academy's outstanding athletic facilities. During the evenings, they have a choice of supervised activities, including swimming, ice-skating, basketball, foosball, air hockey, table tennis, watching a movie, playing in the arcade gallery, and more.

"America **the Beautiful**"

In 1893 a young schoolteacher named Katharine Lee Bates joined several other schoolmarms aboard a mule-drawn prairie wagon in an effort to reach the top of Pikes Peak. A sign across the rear of the wagon—PIKES PEAK OR BUST—revealed their determination. Once at the summit, Bates, overcome by the spectacular panoramic view, penned the poem that eventually became the lyrics to the song "America the Beautiful."

Commuter campers attend on a daytime basis but still lunch in the dining halls, use the academy's athletic facilities and participate in the same classes as the live-in attendees.

Your youngsters can count on having a fun, safe, and secure experience overseen by more than 100 staff members, including counselors, supervisors, medical and security personnel, and top-notch instructors.

Garden of the Gods (all ages)

1805 North 30th St.; (719) 634-6666; www.gardenofgods.com. Open daily May through Oct, 5 a.m. to 11 p.m.; Nov through Apr, 5 a.m. to 9 p.m. **Free.**

Located within the Colorado Springs city limits, this 1,300-acre park is a registered National Natural Landmark containing magnificent rock formations more than a million years old. Sculpted by time and erosion, they bear names befitting their various shapes, such as Kissing Camels, Cathedral Spires, and Sleeping Giant. Mainly level cement paths lead among the towering, rusty-red sandstone monoliths. The 1-mile Central Garden Trail, in the heart of the park at the base of the highest formations, is wheelchair and stroller accessible. Depending on the season, you are apt to see cottontail rabbits, chipmunks, rock squirrels, hawks, white-throated swifts, swallows, and black-billed magpies. Watch carefully and you might even see a mule deer or bighorn sheep.

Garden of the Gods Visitor & Nature Center (all ages)

Garden of the Gods east entrance; (719) 634-6666; www.gardenofgods.com. Open daily June through Aug, 8 a.m. to 8 p.m.; Sept through May, 9 a.m. to 5 p.m. **Free,** High Definition Blue Ray presentation, $.

Before entering the Garden of the Gods, stop first at the visitor center to view a fast-paced twelve-minute high-definition show in order to answer the question your kids are sure to ask: "How did those rocks get there?" The center's state-of-the-art interactive exhibits and touch-screen CD-ROMs will intrigue your children as they reveal the geology, ecology, cultural history, and Native American heritage involved in the making of this one-of-a-kind park. The center features a Junior Ranger program for 7 to 12 year olds, nature talks, a large deck for photographing the area, a gift shop, a cafe, restrooms, and **free** maps.

Garden of the Gods Trading Post

Past Balancing Rock, southwest end of the park; (719) 685-9045 or (800) 874-4515; www.co-trading-post.com. Open daily June through Aug, 8 a.m. to 8 p.m.; Sept through May, 9 a.m. to 5 p.m. Cafe open summer only. **Free.**

Built in the early 1920s by local artist and Indian trader Charles E. Strausenback, the Garden of the Gods Trading Post is designed in the adobe style of the Pueblo Indians. It is now Colorado's largest trading post. From the usual T-shirts and trinkets to prized kachina dolls; valuable Santa Clara, Acoma, and Jemez Pueblo pottery; and original paintings by legendary Navajo artist R. C. Gorman, thousands of gift items parade across the shelves, line the walls, and fill the many chambers.

A Taste from **the Past**

While visiting Rock Ledge Ranch, stop in the General Store. Cool off with a frosty bottle of sarsaparilla soda, a refreshing taste Grandpa might have enjoyed. Or choose from a variety of flavored candy sticks. Historical reproductions, books, and unique gifts reflect an earlier era.

Rock Ledge Ranch Historic Site (all ages)

1401 Recreation Way at 30th Street and Gateway Road; near the Garden of the Gods Visitor & Nature Center; (719) 578-6777; www.rockledgeranch.com. Open June through mid-Aug, Wed through Sat 10 a.m. to 5 p.m., Sun noon to 5 p.m. $, ages 6 and under **free.**

Visit this living-history museum in the heart of Garden of the Gods. You'll find an 1868 homestead, an 1890s working farm and blacksmith shop, and the 1907 Orchard House. Interpreters in period clothing bring the history of the area to life. Popular special events include military reenactments and annual holiday traditional celebrations.

Academy Riding Stables (ages 8 and up)

4 El Paso Blvd. (near south entrance to Garden of the Gods); (719) 633-5667 or (888) 700-0410; www.academyridingstables.com. Open year-round, weather permitting, but days and hours vary. Call if you're unsure about weather-caused trail conditions. $$$–$$$$.

The Academy Riding Stables provides guided horseback tours through the Garden of the Gods Park. Whether your family members are experienced equestrians or novices, stable personnel will select a horse that is just right for each individual. Wranglers will identify the various rock formations as you ride along and, with your camera, even snap a family photo or two for you. One-, two-, and three-hour rides are offered. Participants must weigh less than 250 pounds and be at least eight years old.

Flying W Ranch (ages 2 and up)

3330 Chuckwagon Rd.; (719) 598-4000 or (800) 232-3599; www.flyingw.com. Open daily Memorial Day through Sept; chuck wagon suppers served outdoors. (Heated shelter available in case of inclement weather.) Oct until Christmas and Mar to Memorial Day, dinners and shows in the Steak House on Fri and Sat evening. Reservations are required. $–$$$.

Your kids will be happy to know that they don't have to "sit still and be quiet" at this eatery, where chuck wagon suppers are served outdoors at wooden tables and benches. If they drop a biscuit on the ground, they can just go get another one, because this is an all-you-can-eat feast of barbecued beef, baked potatoes, Flying W baked beans, chunky applesauce, hot biscuits, old-fashioned spice cake, coffee, iced tea and lemonade.

During the summer months begin the evening by wandering through the Old Western town to watch the blacksmith at work, visit the underground kiva, and observe Indian women as they weave rugs in ancient Native American patterns.

If you have a toddler in tow, seek out Irene's Homestead for a stick horse for your little cowpoke. Kids delight in exploring the tepee and riding the miniature train through the interior of an old mine and around the village area.

Following dinner, the Flying W Wranglers present an hour-long stage show of wholesome, family-style entertainment, including skits and old-time country tunes accompanied by guitars, fiddles, drums, and piano. During the summer it's best to arrive by 5 p.m. to allow plenty of time to play before dinner. They are often booked two weeks or more in advance, so make your reservations early.

Pro Rodeo Hall of Fame and American Cowboy Museum

(ages 4 and up)

101 Pro Rodeo Dr. (I-25 at exit 148); (719) 528-4764; www.prorodeohalloffame.com. Open daily 9 a.m. to 5 p.m.; closed Mon and Tues, Sept 7 through Apr 1. $, children age 5 and younger free.

This museum pays tribute to the only competitive sport that evolved from a working lifestyle. Two multimedia presentations address the history of the rodeo, from its haphazard origins in Deer Trail, Colorado, in 1869, to its present status as a major spectator sport. More than ninety exhibits—showcasing saddles, chaps, ropes, boots, clothing, trophies, and artifacts—trace the progress of rodeo over the years. Be sure to check out the entertaining anecdotes about the lives and experiences of the men and women who have made rodeo a world-class event. Outside, children enjoy meeting the retired rodeo stock, which includes a live rodeo bull, a bucking bronco, and a longhorn steer. And you may have a difficult time dragging them out of the gift shop, with its more than 1,000 different rodeo and western gift items.

Sky Sox Baseball (all ages)

4385 Tutt Blvd.; (719) 597-1449; www.skysox.com. Mid-Apr through early Sept. $–$$.

The Sky Sox, a Colorado Rockies Triple A team, play in Colorado Springs. Watch future major league players or, sometimes, today's stars on rehab assignment. Players are accessible for autographs before and after each game. Call for information about stadium tours.

Olympic Training Center (all ages)

1750 East Boulder St. (corner of Union Boulevard and Boulder Street) www.teamusa.org/content/index/1374. Open daily year-round; call (719) 866-4618 or (888) 659-8687 for tour schedule. Free.

Striving to perfect their sport, thousands of athletes train at the Olympic Training Center yearly. In the visitor center view a twelve-minute orientation film and browse the U.S. Olympic Hall of Fame. A guided forty-five minute walking tour stops at numerous training facilities: gymnasiums for twenty-three sports, weight training, sports medicine and science, aquatic center, coaching and sports science, and shooting ranges. Sites seen on

Western **Day-Tripper**

Plan a western theme day. Start at Academy Stables with a morning ride in the Garden of the Gods. Bring your camera; the morning light on the rock formations is perfect for outstanding photos. In the afternoon visit the Pro Rodeo Hall of Fame and American Cowboy Museum. On their patio try your hand at ropin'. Return to Garden of the Gods for a chuck wagon dinner and western show at Flying W Ranch.

the tour vary due to training schedules. You might see Olympic volleyball medalists or the German wrestling team—every visit is different.

Opportunities for photos abound along the Irwin Belk Olympic Path, where forty-five Olympic and Pan American Games sports are depicted in colorful two-dimensional sculptures. From the rooftop terrace, the Olympic flame display stands before panoramic views of Pikes Peak. Purchases from the U.S. Olympic Spirit Stores directly support American athletes. Here, you are likely to find the perfect souvenir among the wide selection of unique merchandise.

In addition to being the headquarters of the United States Olympic Committee, Colorado Springs is home to numerous national sports federations. Check the local newspaper to see if there are competitions taking place while you're in town. It's an opportunity to see world-class athletes in peak condition.

Memorial Park (all ages)

1605 East Pikes Peak Ave.; (719) 385-2489; www.springsgov.com. Open year-round; some facilities seasonal. Free.

Need some play time? Just east of downtown, Memorial Park offers what you're looking for and more. Choose from three playgrounds, including Pollywog (designed for disabled individuals), miles of trails and bikeways, a swim beach, boat rentals (paddle, row, sail, or canoe), indoor ice-skating rink, swimming pool, and state-of-the-art skateboard park.

Ghost Town (ages 3 and up)

400 South 21st St.; (719) 634-0696; www.ghosttownmuseum.com. Open Memorial Day through Labor Day, Mon through Sat 9 a.m. to 6 p.m. and Sun 10 a.m. to 6 p.m. The rest of the year, open Mon through Sat 10 a.m. to 5 p.m. and Sun 10 a.m. to 5 p.m. $, children age 6 and younger free.

To capture a bit of the Old West, stop by this museum. A wooden sidewalk leads guests to a blacksmith shop, general store, saloon, jail, livery, Victorian home, and several Main Street shops where animated characters tell about life in this turn-of-the-20th-century town. Your kids can play old-time arcade machines with silent movies, pan for gold, try their luck in the shooting gallery, and pay a visit to the gypsy fortune-teller. Several antique vehicles, including a 1903 Cadillac and the 1867 Wells Fargo Express Concord stagecoach that once carried the railroad payroll between Denver and Cheyenne, Wyoming, are on the street.

Simpich Dolls (ages 3 and up)

2413 West Colorado Ave.; (719) 465-2492; www.simpich.com. Open year-round, Mon through Sat 10 a.m. to 5 p.m. Free.

This Old Colorado City attraction includes a museum, theater, and gallery. The museum features fifty dioramas showcasing the dolls created by Jan and Bob Simpich. The collection highlights many rare and one-of-a-kind pieces. The 70-seat theater presents a variety of string-puppet shows, including *The Secret Garden, Hans Christian Andersen Storybook,* and *Great Expectations,* as well as several seasonal productions. The gallery hosts works by regional artists and those of Jan and Bob Simpich. Of course there is a salesroom—bring your Christmas list.

North Cheyenne Cañon Park (all ages)

2120 South Cheyenne Cañon Rd.; (719) 385-6086; www.springsgov.com/parks. Open year-round, weather permitting. Free.

Explore cascading waterfalls, rock formations, and a botanical reserve within a city park. Begin at the Starsmore Discovery Center near the base of the canyon. A hands-on mineral exhibit, dioramas, climbing wall, small shop with regional books and maps, and interpretive programs introduce you to the area. From the back porch, hike some of the 56 miles of trails or drive up the canyon to Helen Hunt Falls. Here you'll find a small visitor center and, for hearty hikers, a steep trail to Silver Cascade Falls.

Seven Falls (ages 4 and up)

2850 South Cheyenne Cañon Rd.; (719) 632-0765; www.sevenfalls.com. Open daily year-round; summer, 8:30 a.m. to 10:30 p.m.; winter, 9 a.m. to 4:15 p.m. Children age 5 and under are free. $–$$.

Park your car in the parking lot and walk a short distance along a stream to a clear mountain pool inhabited by rainbow, brook, and golden trout. Here seven separate falls splash, crash, and tumble 181 feet down a sheer granite canyon wall. A 224-step staircase runs adjacent to the waterfall. At the top a milelong, forested nature trail is frequented by Abert squirrels, chipmunks, white-tailed deer, and hummingbirds. For families with children unable to climb the many steps, the Mountain Express Elevator transports visitors to the Eagle's Nest platform for a bird's-eye view of all seven falls.

Beautiful during daylight hours, the falls become a spectacular fantasyland at night when enhanced by colored lights. This is when Native American performers present interpretive dances. Visiting children are permitted to participate.

For more than fifty years, Seven Falls has admitted guests free of charge for special night lighting displays during a ten-day period at Christmastime. The proceeds from donations are used to provide toys for less-fortunate children.

Pikes Peak **Ice Cream Pick**

This outstanding Colorado Springs hometown business will satisfy your ice-cream cravings.

- **Colorado City Creamery,** 2602 West Colorado Ave. (in Old Colorado City); (719) 634-1411. Fresh dairy cream with 14 percent butterfat guarantees a rich, smooth ice cream. Pick a flavor and create your own treat at the sundae bar. For a sound from yesteryear, drop a quarter in the forty-four-note electric piano called a pianino. The shop is small and the line can be down the block, but the ice cream is great.

Cheyenne Mountain Zoo   (all ages)

4250 Cheyenne Mountain Zoo Rd.; (719) 633-9925; www.cmzoo.org. Open daily year-round, Memorial Day weekend through Labor Day, 9 a.m. to 6 p.m. The rest of the year, 9 a.m. to 5 p.m. $–$$.

The slogan at this zoo is "The Zoo with a View." And indeed it is. With a base elevation of 6,800 feet, it is said to be the only "mountain zoo" in the United States. The exhibit areas are actually carved out of the lower slopes of a 9,400-foot-high mountain. Set beneath jagged rock cliffs and amid groves of oak, pine, spruce, and aspen, the 700-acre complex houses more than 800 wild and wonderful animals.

Due to the zoo's unique layout, guests gradually ascend the side of the mountain as they go from exhibit to exhibit. This is not a problem for little ones who take tiny steps or those who tire easily, however, because a much-appreciated tram travels up the mountainside while stopping every few minutes for passengers to climb aboard or depart. Strollers and wheelchairs are available for rent and the tram is equipped to handle both modes of transportation. The tram runs from late spring through Labor Day, weather permitting, and costs only $1 per day for unlimited rides

The zoo's hillside location makes it possible for your children to come face-to-face with towering giraffes and hand-feed them the special "animal crackers" available for purchase. Kids able to tackle the slightly rugged terrain can walk to the zoo's highest point; otherwise they can ride the tram to the top. Here they will find picnic grounds, a snack bar, a nature trail, a carousel (seasonal), and an area where they can feed and touch the animals.

Recently added attractions include a state-of-the-art complex that connects zoo visitors with the state's wildlife. The chairlift-style, open-air Sky Ride transports you high above the Rocky Mountain Wild, the Asian Highlands, and My Big Backyard exhibits. Watch for frolicking mountain goats, especially in springtime when the latest crop of baby goats are seen following closely behind their moms

Admission includes entry to the Will Rogers Shrine of the Sun, a granite tower with spectacular views of the Front Range of the Rocky Mountains.

World Figure Skating Museum and Hall of Fame (ages 3 and up)

20 1st St. (off Lake Avenue near the Broadmoor Hotel); (719) 635-5200; www.worldskating museum.org. Open year-round, Mon through Fri 10 a.m. to 4 p.m.; Sat, May through Oct, 10 a.m. to 4 p.m. $, children under 6 free.

Sit spin, Lutz jump, triple-toe-loop—figure skating entertains millions of spectators every year. Here you'll find a tribute to the sport's greatest stars, glittering costumes, Olympic medals, videos of historic performances, and intriguing exhibits. Skates made from animal bone and leather straps from the 8th century, toddler ice walkers, and Japanese skates with cloth toe thongs demonstrate the evolution of equipment. Works by Currier and Ives, Norman Rockwell, and Andy Warhol appear in the largest collection of skating art in the world. A stop here could put dreams in the minds of young skaters.

World Arena (ages 3 and up)

3185 Venetucci Blvd.; (719) 477-2150; www.worldarena.com. Open daily year-round for public skating sessions; times vary. Rentals available. $.

This ice arena, home to training camps for the U.S. Olympic Training Center and professional and collegiate hockey teams, opens daily for public skating. You can also watch future champions in practice sessions. A great way to cool off on a hot summer afternoon.

May Natural History Museum of the Tropics (ages 4 and up)

710 Rock Creek Canyon (9 miles southwest of Colorado Springs on CO 115); (719) 576-0450 or (800) 666-3841; www.maymuseum-camp-rvpark.com. Open daily May through Sept, 9 a.m. to 6 p.m. $, children 5 and younger free.

Most kids are fascinated by bugs, even if it's just for the fun of wrinkling up noses and letting out a squeal or two. That could be the reason this museum is such a hit with children. The only museum in North America entirely devoted to the display and study of giant tropical insects, it attracts students from preschool to college age to see more than 8,000 of the world's largest, rarest, most venomous, and most beautiful insects and related jungle creatures. The irreplaceable collection, comprising over 100,000 specimens in all, represents a lifetime of work by current curator John May and his father, the late James May. It is said that if someone were to begin collecting now, with $1 million and fifty years of time at his or her disposal, it is unlikely that that individual would be able to even come close to duplicating May's collection.

Old Colorado **City**

For five days in 1859, Colorado City served as the first Territorial Capital of Colorado. Today you'll find a National Historic District with the log cabin "capitol," parks, unique shopping, dining, lodging, and a great ice-cream vendor.

Olympic Theme **Day-Tripper**

Make a vacation day an Olympic event. Stop by the World Arena to see Olympic-hopeful figure skaters during a morning training session. Visit the nearby World Figure Skating Museum and Hall of Fame. Tour the U.S. Olympic Training Center and see athletes in action. While you're there, check the schedule for evening games, events, or competitions. Get in the act with some afternoon ice time at the World Arena.

At the museum's entrance stands a designed-to-scale, exact replica of a *Dynastes Hercules,* the world's largest beetle. This gigantic 25-foot-long, 15-foot-high sculpture is only a hint of what is to come, and it is sure to entice your youngsters to want to see more.

Museum of Space Exploration (ages 4 and up)
Admission to the May Natural History Museum of the Tropics includes entry to the adjacent Museum of Space Exploration. Hours are the same for both museums.

This collection depicts man's first attempts at flight up to the present space program. Included are hundreds of official National Aeronautics and Space Administration (NASA) photographs and models of early aircraft, World War II planes, and spacecraft. Visitors can view official NASA films of the first moon landing, the shuttle program, and the exploration of the solar system.

Challenge Unlimited (ages 8 and up)
204 South 24th St.; (719) 633-6399 or (800) 798-5954; www.bikithikit.com. Open mid-May to mid-Oct. $$$$.

This easy 20-mile ride down Pikes Peak via the Pikes Peak Highway provides individuals an exciting journey through five distinct vegetation and animal-life zones. Although this adventure takes place on Pikes Peak, it begins at the Challenge Unlimited office, where, depending on the ride you plan to participate in, you will be treated to a breakfast or a snack. During this time you will have the opportunity to meet the guides and your fellow bikers. Your family will then be driven to the 14,110-foot summit and issued twenty-seven-speed mountain bikes, helmets, all-weather clothing, and souvenir water bottles. Experienced guides with training in first aid and emergency medical techniques will accompany you down the mountain. One van will travel in front of the group and another will follow behind. Periodic stops will allow you to take photos, learn about the area, and rest. Along the route you will stop for either a picnic lunch or a snack, again depending on your choice of ride.

Where to Eat
Conway's Red Top, four locations: 1520 South Nevada Ave., (719) 633-2444; 390 North Circle Dr., (719) 630-1566; 3589 North Carefree Circle, (719) 596-6444; 1228 East Fillmore, (719)

329-1445. Open daily for lunch and dinner. Hungry for a burger? The Conway family—with ten kids and lots of energy—has been serving up giant hamburgers since 1962. Grandma Esther's recipes for soups, stews, and chili are still faithfully followed. The milk shakes are the real thing—thick and frosty. When you see the size of the burger, you'll know why buns are baked especially for Conway's. $

Giuseppe's Old Depot Restaurant, 10 South Sierra Madre; (719) 635-3111; www .giuseppes-depot.com. Daily lunch and dinner, served continuously from 11 a.m. Located in a century-old former railroad depot, Giuseppe's serves an extensive Italian and American menu—stone-oven pizzas, calzones, pasta, sandwiches, and steaks. Try the Italian meatball sandwich. The Baggage Cart salad bar overflows with sixty-five items. Note that Giuseppe's serves all afternoon, so you don't have to settle for fast food when you're hungry at 3 p.m. $–$$

Where to Stay

The Broadmoor, 1 Lake Ave. (719) 577-5775 or (866) 837-9520; www.broadmoor.com. Although staying at The Broadmoor can rather quickly put a hole in your vacation budget, I'd be remiss if I didn't include it for your consideration. Five-diamond, five-star accommodations await at this historic, ca. 1918, world-class resort hotel, including indoor and outdoor swimming pools, a European spa, tennis courts, a golf course, restaurants, and cafes. The children's concierge will provide information on babysitting services, seasonal camp programs, and various family activities. Ask about the Summer Bee Bunch Camp. $$$$

Residence Inn by Marriott, 3880 North Academy Blvd.; (719) 574-0370; www.marriott .com/hotels/travel/cosp-residence-inn-colo rado-springs-central. This fine hotel offers fully equipped kitchens and living areas, a complimentary breakfast buffet, an outdoor pool, a hot tub, and a sport court. All rooms are suites, thus providing ample room for your family to spread out. $$–$$$

For More Information

Colorado Springs Convention and Visitors Bureau, 515 South Cascade Ave., Colorado Springs, CO 80903; (719) 635-7506 or (800) 368-4748; www.experiencecolorado springs.com.

Pikes Peak Country Attractions Association, 354 Manitou Ave., Manitou Springs, CO 80829; (719) 685-5894 or (800) 525-2250; www.pikes-peak.com. Check the Web site for online coupons.

Manitou Springs

Geographically adjacent to the northwest section of Colorado Springs but totally different in lifestyle and tempo, Manitou Springs thrives as a laid-back artisan community. The Ute and Arapahoe Indians considered this area to be a sanctuary where they could gather in peace to worship the god Manitou.

Good Old Summertime Ice Cream and Pie Baking Social (all ages)
Soda Springs Park; (719) 685-5089 or (800) 642-2567. Annually in mid-July, 5:30 to 8 p.m.

Along with ample supplies of ice cream from a local dairy, this annual affair brings a popular homemade ice cream contest. Prizes are awarded in a variety of categories, including "best vanilla ice cream," "most creative ice cream," and "best ice cream made with Manitou Springs mineral water." Musical entertainment is provided.

Miramont Castle (ages 4 and up)

9 Capitol Hill Ave.; (719) 685-1011; www.miramontcastle.org. Open daily Memorial Day through Labor Day, 9 a.m. to 5 p.m.; after Labor Day to Memorial Day, Tues through Sat 10 a.m. to 4 p.m., Sun noon to 4 p.m. $.

Built in 1895 by Jean Baptiste Francolon, a Catholic priest from France, the grandiose castle is a composite of nine architectural styles—Queen Anne, Romanesque, English Tudor, Fleming, Domestic Elizabethan, Venetian Ogee, Byzantine, Moorish, and Chateau—all beautifully blended together. Exquisite antiques will require that little ones not touch, but your children are likely to be intrigued by a sojourn through the magnificent castle to see a ceiling sheathed in gold, a 200-ton sandstone fireplace, and an elaborate 400-square-foot bedroom that once belonged to the priest's mother, Marie Francolon.

After a tour through the mansion's many rooms, reward your well-behaved youngsters with a stop at the castle's Museum of Miniatures and Model Railroad Museum, followed by a snack in the Queen's Parlor Tearoom.

From late Nov until Christmas Day, Miramont Castle is decorated in grand Victorian style. A tour through this opulent masterpiece during the holidays is a lovely way to celebrate the season.

The Manitou Cliff Dwellings Museum (ages 5 and up)

West of Manitou Springs, on US 24; (719) 685-5242 or (800) 354-9971; www.cliffdwellings museum.com. Open daily June through Aug, 9 a.m. to 6 p.m.; Sept through May, 9 a.m. to 5 p.m., weather permitting. Hours depend largely on weather conditions so it would be best to phone ahead for exact times. $–$$, children 6 and younger free.

Nineteenth-century architecture, stately Victorian bed-and-breakfasts, art galleries, and craft shops line Manitou Springs's narrow, curving streets, while just outside of town are former accommodations and artwork of a different sort. The Manitou Cliff Dwellings Museum allows visitors to experience a culture created by the Ancient Pueblo People (formerly called the Anasazi) during the peak of their civilization, from A.D. 1100 to 1300.

Although the structures were relocated here from McElmo Canyon in southwestern Colorado, the reasons for moving them are well founded. At the time the museum was established, in 1904, looters and "pot hunters" were vandalizing these structures, and it was in the interest of preserving them for future generations that they were transplanted to this location. The Federal Antiquities Act, which makes it a federal offense to destroy or remove artifacts, was not enacted until 1906.

Your children can pretend to be explorers and archaeologists on your self-guided tour through the forty rooms, which include a lookout tower, sleeping quarters, and a kiva—a sunken, circular, dome-covered structure once used for ceremonial purposes. One three-story dwelling housed nine families in its tiny rooms that average 6-by-8-feet wide and 5½-feet high. The upstairs chambers are reached by ladders.

The Springs of **Manitou**

Nine of Manitou Springs's twenty-six constantly flowing mineral springs have been completely restored and are safe for drinking. The water from each tastes a little different, depending on the exact mineral content. Chemists claim that carbonic acid is responsible for the water's bubbles. Indian legend states that the spirit of the great god Manitou breathed into the waters their sparkly effervescence. The Indians brought their sick and aged to drink from the health-giving waters, leaving behind offerings of blankets, bows, moccasins, and knives, which they threw into the water or hung on trees.

The current residents of Manitou Springs continue to advocate the healthful benefits of drinking the spring water. Many townspeople can be seen filling jugs and bottles at the pipes leading from the springs. They drink the water as it is or mix it with fruit juice. Your children will no doubt insist on trying the mineral-laden water. Be prepared, though, for a negative reaction to the taste.

The main building at the museum, modeled after the pueblos of the Southwest, houses examples of the Ancient Pueblo People's pottery, baskets, jewelry, tools, burial urns, and weapons. The gift shops feature Indian-made jewelry, pottery, and crafts. Native American dancing is performed during June, July, and Aug.

Cave of the Winds (ages 7 and up)

North of US 24, 100 Cave of the Winds Rd.; (719) 685-5444; www.caveofthewinds.com. Phone ahead for hours, which vary due to weather conditions and are subject to change. During summer high season, advance reservations are recommended. $$–$$$, children 5 and younger free.

Your children won't soon forget an adventurous journey into these mysterious caves. With Mom, Dad, or grandparents close at hand, youngsters will experience the thrill of being in a cave deep within the Rocky Mountains. They will discover colorfully displayed stalactites and stalagmites in an underground created by nature over millions of years.

On the Discovery Tour, the most popular, guides lead visitors along a well-lighted path past breathtakingly beautiful formations and secretive nooks and crannies that turn-of-the-20th-century explorers suspected were the homes of gnomes and trolls. This tour lasts approximately forty-five minutes.

The one-and-a-half-hour Lantern Tour takes you along pitch-black passageways, illuminated only by your candlelit lanterns. As you venture through the darkness, the lantern light causes fascinating configurations to come alive among the crevices and shadows and dance against the rock walls. This tour is best suited for children age 6 or older. Children age 5 and younger are not admitted.

Where to Eat

Queen's Parlor Tearoom, 9 Capitol Hill Ave. (in the Miramont Castle); (719) 685-1011. Open daily Memorial Day through Labor Day 9 a.m. to 5 p.m. After Labor Day to Memorial Day, Tues through Sat 10 a.m. to 4 p.m., Sun 12 noon to 4 p.m. High Tea is served Tues, Fri, Sat, and Sun at 2 p.m., with reservations required at least seventy-two hours in advance. You can choose from salads, sandwiches, soups, creamy milk shakes or malts, cherry or lime phosphates, ice-cream sodas or sundaes, or go for the works and reserve ahead for High Tea, complete with fancy sandwiches, fruit, chocolates, tempting desserts, and delightful scones with Devonshire cream, lemon curd, and preserves. For the young prince and princess in your family, the Queen's Parlor Tearoom has a special version of High Tea with all the trimmings just for them or those 12 years and younger can order the child's plate, which includes a half sandwich, fruit cup, vegetable cup, either a cookie or a sundae for dessert and soda or lemonade. $–$$$

Mason Jar Restaurant, 2925 West Colorado Ave.; (719) 632-4820; www.masonja colorado.com. Comfort food in a Colorado lodge atmosphere. Casual. $–$$

Front Range Barbeque, 2330 West Colorado Ave.; (719) 632-2596; www.frontrange barbeque.com. Home-style meals, smoke house BBQ, patio dining. $

Where to Stay

The Antlers Hilton Colorado Springs, 4 South Cascade Ave.; (719) 473-5600; www .antlerscoloradosprings.hilton.com. This is a full-service, historic, downtown hotel. $$

Blue Skies Inn Bed & Breakfast, 402 Manitou Ave.; (719) 685-3899 or (800) 398-7949; www.blueskiesbb.com. Secluded along Fountain Creek, within walking distance to shops and restaurants, this bed-and-breakfast welcomes families to enjoy its garden courtyard surrounded by ten beautifully decorated three-room suites. The inn resembles a quaint village situated on two and one-half landscaped acres of lawn, gardens, flowerbeds, trees, and a gazebo outdoor hot tub. $$$

Timber Lodge, 3627 West Colorado Ave.; (719) 636-3941 or (800) 448-6762; www .pikes-peak.com. Twenty-four cabins, some with kitchens, on four acres of land with a stream running through property. Great for families. $–$$$

For More Information

Pikes Peak Country Attractions Association, 354 Manitou Ave., Manitou Springs, CO 80829; (719) 685-5894 or (800) 525-2250; www.pikes-peak.com. Check the Web site for online coupons.

Manitou Springs Chamber of Commerce and Visitors Bureau, 354 Manitou Ave. (they share space with the above Pikes Peak Country Attractions Association); (719) 685-5089 or (800) 642-2567; www.manitou springs.org. They have a terrific Web site.

Up (and Down) the Pike

Historically, Pikes Peak has stood as a challenge to many over the years. Zebulon Pike, for whom the mountain was named, not only failed to reach the top but found the prospect so awesome that he declared, "I believe no human being could have ascended to its pinnacle." In 1820 Edwin James did just that, but it was Zalmon G. Simmons (of Simmons Mattress Company fame and fortune) who, after riding to the top on the back of a mule in the early 1880s and proclaiming the beauty to be astounding but the journey dreadful, set about to make the mountain accessible by rail.

Pikes Peak Cog Railway (all ages)

515 Ruxton Ave.; (719) 685-5401; www.cograilway.com. Open year-round, depending on weather; phone for exact hours. Reservations are strongly recommended. $$$–$$$$.

The first locomotives to reach the summit of Pikes Peak were steam operated. These were replaced by diesel engines in the 1940s. Since 1965, Swiss-made railcars, constructed exclusively for the Pikes Peak Cog Railway, have transported millions of riders along the 9-mile track.

The train chugs out of the Manitou Springs station and through aspen glens and steep canyons filled with wildflowers and cascading streams. Arrival at the summit reveals expansive vistas of the Continental Divide and the Great Plains. Traveling at just 8 miles per hour, the locomotive provides photographers ample time to capture the magnificent panoramas.

After nearly an hour-long ride, your children can stretch their legs at the Summit House, get a snack at the concession stand, and browse the curio shop before embarking on the return trip down the mountain.

Cascade

Pikes Peak Highway (all ages)

South of US 24 at Cascade; (719) 385-7325 or (800) 318-9505; www.pikespeakcolorado.com. Open year-round, weather permitting; Memorial Day through Labor Day 7:30 a.m. to 6 p.m.; month of Sept, 7:30 a.m. to 5 p.m.; Oct through the day prior to Memorial Day, 9 a.m. to 3 p.m. Cost $10 for age 16 and older, $5 per child ages 6 to 15 (maximum $35 per car, pass valid two consecutive days).

"Pikes Peak or Bust." It's an American tradition to want to stand atop Colorado's best-known mountain. Pikes Peak Highway makes that a greater possibility than in Zebulon

Hiking **Hints**

Before you set out on a hike, let someone know where you are going and when you expect to return.

The U.S. Forest Service advocates that all hikers carry the ten essentials: map, compass, flashlight, sunglasses, extra food and water, extra clothing, matches, candle, knife, and first-aid kit. And at Colorado's high altitude, sunscreen is a must.

Pike's day. While the drive is still not for the faint of heart—many miles are gravel with no center stripe or crash barriers—the family sedan will get you to the top. The round-trip can be done in less than two hours, but a better choice is to take a full or at least a half day to enjoy activities on the mountain. Crystal Reservoir gift shop, just after mile marker 6, offers boat rentals, fishing, hiking, some interpretive exhibits, snacks, grills and a picnic area, and souvenirs. You'll find Halfway Picnic Ground at the midpoint of your ascent.

Geography and vegetation change frequently as you ascend almost 8,000 feet. Just below timberline, stop at Glen Cove Inn, where you can grab a burger or some barbecue. The rock formations here are favorites of climbers. Note the effect of wind and weather on the gnarled, twisted bristlecone pines. Among the earth's oldest living things, they can be more than 1,000 years old.

Watch for yellow-bellied marmots in the tundra areas below 12,000 feet. This cousin to the woodchuck hibernates for seven to nine months each year. Building up body fat

Popcorn **Stop**

"Family fun is what it's all about," says Mike Myers, owner and proprietor of the **Pikes Peak Gourmet Popcorn** factory and store, at Pikes Peak Highway and US 24 in Cascade (7935West Highway 24; www.pikespeakpopcorn.com), approximately 5 miles west of Manitou Springs. From home milk delivery by horse-drawn wagon in 1925 to filling orders via the Internet, the Myers family has been in the business of pleasing customers for more than seventy years.

This is the sort of place kids beg to stop at, and parents and grandparents don't find it hard to take, either. The first thing that hits you as you enter the door is the wonderful aroma of just about every flavor of popcorn imaginable. For starters there are almond-pecan crunch, cherry cordial, butter rum, mountain raspberry, strawberries and cream—you get the idea—packed in attractive decorator tins of several sizes and every description. Or how about an unusual basket, crafted of corncobs and packed with half-gallon bags of any flavor popcorn you choose? If you are visiting this area as someone's house guest, a tin or basket filled with popcorn would be a delightful gift for your host or hostess. You will be happy to know that you also can purchase smaller quantities in plastic bags, enabling you to satisfy everyone, just in case your youngsters can't agree on a flavor.

Pikes Peak Gourmet Popcorn is open daily Jan through mid-May, Mon through Sat 10 a.m. to 5 p.m., Sun noon to 5 p.m.; mid-May through Dec, Mon through Fri, 10 a.m. to 5 p.m., Sat 10 a.m. to 6 p.m., and Sun noon to 5 p.m. Open dates are approximate, depending on weather. Best to phone. Free samples are always available. Call (719) 684-9174 or (800) 684-1155 for more information.

during the summer requires lots of munching on grasses and wildflowers. If you hear his loud, shrill call, you'll understand the nickname "whistle pig." Devil's Playground earned its name because of the way lightning skips from rock to rock here. If the weather is threatening, stay in your car. Approaching curves, with no view of the road ahead, you feel as if you're driving into the heavens.

It's camera time at the summit—family snowball fights in July, clouds swirling in the valley below, shiny red cars of the Cog Railway. If you're panting and gasping for oxygen at the peak, think about the yearly marathon racers who run up—and back down. Winners have raced in less than three hours and twenty minutes. Check out the souvenir selection in Summit House. How about a "Real Men Don't Need Guard Rails" T-shirt for the trip back down the mountain?

Check out the Pikes Peak Highway Web site before your trip. It has some excellent information that is important to know, such as: The round-trip uses approximately one-half tank of gas; you will probably want to use lower gears during the drive; the round-trip takes two hours minimum (longer if you wisely make many stops along the way to enjoy the scenery); if anyone in your vehicle has a history of severe cardiac or respiratory problems, it is not recommended that you go all the way to the summit.

Santa's Workshop and North Pole (ages 2 to 10)

5050 Pikes Peak Hwy., Cascade; (719) 684-9432; www.santas-colo.com. Open daily mid-May through Aug 24, 10 a.m. to 5 p.m.; Aug 25 to Dec 24, 10 a.m. to 5 p.m. daily except Wed and Thurs; closed Christmas Day. The open days and hours depend largely on the weather. Many of the activities are outdoors and there are no rain checks given, so watch the weather forecasts and then be sure to call before leaving home. This may sound like a bit of a bother but it is truly worth it, especially if your kids are between the ages of 4 and 7. Admission price includes shows and unlimited rides. $$$. Individuals age 60 and above and kids under age 2 admitted free.

In 1940 an eight-year-old girl was asked by one of Walt Disney's artists what Santa Claus's home and village looked like. Blessed with a vivid imagination, the child shared her vision of Santa Claus land. Thus Santa's Workshop and North Pole was created.

Santa's village is a fantasyland that is sure to please your little ones. Here they will find Santa's reindeer, llamas, deer, rabbits, chickens, and ducks. They can watch Elmer the Elf's magic show, swing through the sky on Santa's space shuttle, and climb aboard the carousel, the Ferris wheel, the miniature train, and nearly twenty more rides. You can all shop in gingerbread-style houses with pointy roofs and mail your postcards here so that the postmark will read "North Pole."

Ah, but the best part of a visit to Santa's Workshop and North Pole is when your youngsters enter Mr. and Mrs. Claus's little cottage to sit on Santa's lap and, no matter if it happens to be July or Dec, whisper into his ear the hopes and dreams for Christmases to come. You can snap a photo of the occasion for next year's Christmas card or have Santa take a picture automatically while he listens to your youngster's requests.

Going here with your children is definitely a memory-maker. They will talk about the fun they had for years. Do phone to make sure the facility will be open when you arrive.

Worth **Remembering**

We remember Zebulon Pike (although he never made it to the top), but hardly anyone has heard of Julia Archibald Holmes. She is credited as the first woman to reach the top of Pikes Peak in 1858. At age twenty, with an adventurous spirit, she left her home in Lawrence, Kansas, and walked with a wagon train to the Colorado Territory. That walk must have been great conditioning for the climb to the summit. In a letter to her mother she reported, "Nearly everyone tried to discourage me from attempting it, but I believed I should succeed. . . ." And succeed she did.

Disappointments do *not* make good memories. Have rain gear in the car for summer showers and coats, sweaters, scarves, hats, and mittens for fall and winter days. Unlimited activities are included in the cost so you will want to be prepared for a long, comfortable stay.

Woodland Park

Rocky Mountain Dinosaur Resource Center (age 4 and up)

201 South Fairview St.; 719-686-1820; www.rmdrc.com. Open daily year-round, Mon through Sat 9 a.m. to 6 p.m. and Sun 10 a.m. to 5 p.m. Closed Easter, Thanksgiving, Christmas Day, New Year's Day. $$$$, children age 4 and younger are admitted free.

Just about every kid goes through a dinosaur phase, some more intense and longer lasting than others. If someone in your family has decided that a plush dinosaur makes a better bedtime companion than a Teddy bear, he or she is bound to be thrilled with a visit to the Rocky Mountain Dinosaur Resource Center (RMDRC), home to a fascinating display of dinosaurs, pre-historic marine reptiles, pterosaurs, and fish of North America's late-Cretaceous Period, plus a Paleo laboratory, a children's learning center, and a gift shop.

The RMDRC, located in downtown Woodland Park, encompasses 20,000 square feet, of which 12,000 square feet are dedicated to exhibits showcasing 30 life-size specimens, mainly skeletons, and a large collection of fossilized animals. The working fossil laboratory is especially popular with visitors.

Woody's Paleo Playground is thoughtfully designed for children. Here, they can explore their own "dig site," make a dinosaur rubbing and even create a dinosaur. Educational videos run non-stop. A visit to the gift shop, guaranteed to be a hit with kids, reveals books, videos, bronze, pewter and framed fossil art, cast replicas of claws, teeth, skulls and complete skeletons, games, puzzles, dig kits, toys, dinosaur themed shoes, socks, sweatshirts, T-shirts, hats, and party supplies.

The rotating exhibits at the RMDRC are on loan from Triebold Paleontology Incorporated (TPI). An independent company, founded by
Mike Triebold, TPI provides services for museums and individual
endeavors ranging from paleontological exploration, excavation,
restoration, mold making, and casting. TPI's collected, prepared, and
restored replica castes and specimens are displayed in museums
worldwide. Mike Triebold has been collecting fossils for more than
20 years. His widely respected paleontology expertise has been featured on The Learning Channel's *Paleoworld*, The Discovery Channel's *Bone Head Detectives*, several Fox Channel specials, and
magazines such as *U.S. News and World Report, Newsweek,*
and *National Geographic.* TPI operates dig sites in North and
South Dakota, Montana, and Kansas. The Rocky Mountain
Dinosaur Resource Center is said to be one of the five best dinosaur museums in the United States.

Cripple Creek

From Woodland Park head west on US 24. At Divide, turn south onto CO 67 to go to
Cripple Creek.

In 1890 "Crazy Bob" Womack discovered the largest gold deposit in the history of the
world in Poverty Gulch, near Cripple Creek. Until then Womack's dubious claim to fame
had been his ability to lean down from his horse at a full gallop and snatch a whiskey
bottle with his teeth. Alas, "Crazy Bob" got tipsy one time too many and, during one such
occasion, sold his claim—eventually worth $600 million—for a measly $300. He died
penniless.

By the late 1800s Cripple Creek boasted a population of nearly 50,000 people.
Archives record churches of all denominations, 150 saloons and gambling halls, and
"almost constant sunshine and no tramps, everybody prosperous."

Many celebrities have roots in Cripple Creek. Groucho Marx delivered groceries here.
The Wright brothers won an auto race from Cripple Creek to Colorado Springs. Boxer Jack
Dempsey labored in the mines by day and boxed by night, and cowboy actor Tom Mix
worked as a bouncer in a Bennett Avenue saloon.

Though no longer as wild and woolly as it was during the Gold Rush days, Cripple
Creek is still plenty lively due to legal gambling and several Wild West-type attractions.
Families will find inexpensive dining establishments, reasonably priced lodging, and
numerous family-oriented activities.

Mollie Kathleen Gold Mine (ages 4 and up)

**CO 67, on the north end of Cripple Creek; (719) 689-2466 or (888) 291-5689; www.goldmine
tours.com. Open daily Apr 21 through May 15, 10 a.m. to 4 p.m. May 16 through Sept 20,
9 a.m. to 5 p.m. Sept 21 through Oct 25, 10 a.m. to 4 p.m. Sometimes open during winter
months (depending on weather; call ahead). $–$$$.**

Footloose and **Fancy-free**

As you meander Cripple Creek's narrow streets, listen for a hearty hee-haw or two and watch for a herd of donkeys, the town's mascots, which are looked upon as pets by the locals. They are protected by city ordinance but are owned by the Two Mile High Club, a community booster club not unlike a chamber of commerce. Allowed to roam at will during the summer months and taken to pasture during the winter, the furry critters can be found just about anywhere in town and as far as 6 miles away in the former mining town of Victor. They are said to be descendants of the burros that at one time helped work the mines. Of course, children should use care when approaching the donkeys, but with parental supervision they can feed them "Donkey Treats," available for purchase in local shops.

To learn what life was like for the hard-rock miners of old, plan to take a tour of the Mollie Kathleen Gold Mine. Legend states that while on a family outing in 1892, Mollie Kathleen Gointner discovered the gold outcropping that eventually led to a successful mining operation that lasted from 1892 to 1961. Don't let the touristy exterior discourage you. The tour is an exceptionally good one, led by gentlemen guides who have been associated with gold mining most of their lives.

The tour lasts about one hour. During that time you will board a miner's cage called a "skip" and descend a shaft 1,000 feet into the earth. You will see mining equipment and working areas and learn what stopes, winzes, crosscuts, and drifts are and what they had to do with gold mining. You will see gold veins and a display of various gold ores found in Colorado, and you and your kids will each receive a souvenir ore specimen that contains actual gold.

This tour is easily navigated by children and grandparents. There are no steps, climbing, or rough ground involved.

Cripple Creek & Victor Narrow Gauge Railroad (all ages)
Bennett Avenue and Fifth Street (at north end of Bennett Avenue); (719) 689-2640; www .cripplecreekrailroad.com. Open daily late May through early Oct, 9:30 a.m. to 5 p.m. with trains departing every forty minutes beginning at 10 a.m. Schedule is dependent on weather conditions. Call for exact times. $–$$.

As the engineer blows the whistle, clouds of steam escape from the engine's stack, and the train chugs out of the Cripple Creek station for a 4-mile round-trip journey back in time. The country's only steam locomotive that crosses a historic gold camp district, the fully restored fifteen-ton iron horse of the 0–4–0 type—representative of the early-day steam engines—transports passengers over a trestle and past head frames, ore dumps, "Crazy Bob" Womack's abandoned cabin, Poverty Gulch, and mine site after mine site to the ghost town of Anaconda. A narrator provides an informative and educational talk, highlighting points of interest along the way. The train stops several times so that photographers can obtain some memorable shots of this toylike train brightly painted in primary colors, and when the engineer blows the train whistle at Echo Valley, passengers strain their ears to determine how many times the sound reverberates across the land. This trip is especially beautiful during fall, when aspen leaves of brilliant yellow and burnt ocher remind viewers that there still is "gold in them thar hills."

Mueller State Park (all ages)

Two miles west of CO 67, 15 miles north of Cripple Creek; (719) 687-2366 or (800) 678-2267; http://parks.state.co.us/parks/mueller. Open daily year-round. $ per car.

Five thousand acres of forests and meadows with miles of trails, modern camping facilities, fishing, and abundant wildlife create an ideal state park. Bighorn sheep are abundant. Note the scars on the lower trunks of aspen trees—signs of elk gnawing during the winter when snow covers the natural grasses. Black bears, bobcats, and an occasional mountain lion are spotted in remote areas of the park. Because of the large number of aspen, fall is a golden time to visit.

Some of the more than 50 miles of trails are hiking only, but most are multiuse—hiking/biking or hiking/horse. Difficulty ranges from a relaxed walk along the self-guided Wapiti Nature Trail to all-day treks. During the summer rangers lead hikes, activities, and amphitheater presentations. Kids can participate in a Junior Ranger program, and there's a small playground in the ninety-site campground.

All 50 miles of trails are open to cross-country skiing and snowshoeing thus making this a popular winter day-trip. Sledding and tubing are permitted when there is enough snow to prevent resource damage. When conditions allow, frozen ponds are cleared for skating.

Where to Stay

Gold King Mountain Inn, 601 Galena Ave., P.O. Box 1329, Cripple Creek, CO 80813; (800) 445-3607. Located in a quiet area, ¼ mile out of town, this hotel offers **free** shuttle service to attractions and complimentary continental breakfasts consisting of fresh fruit, cereals, milk, juice, and baked goods. Roll-away beds are available. $$

Victor Hotel, 321 Victor Ave., P.O. Box 185, Victor, CO 80860; (719) 689-3553 or (800) 713-4595; www.victorhotelcolorado .com. Located 6 miles from Cripple Creek, this renovated historic structure has served as a bank, offices for the Western Union Telegraph Company, and the infirmary for Dr. H. G. Thomas, father of author and broadcaster

Lowell Thomas. Children will enjoy riding in the antique "birdcage" elevator, original to the building. Rates include a **free** continental breakfast. $–$$$

For More Information

Prepare Peak Heritage Center, 9283 South Highway 67; P. O. Box 430, Cripple Creek, CO 80813; (719) 243-6769 or (877) 858-4653; www.visitcripplecreek.com. Open daily, year-round, 9 a.m. to 5 p.m. **Free.** Plan to let this interpretive center be your first stop when visiting Cripple Creek. The 11,600-square-foot facility provides fascinating information about the dinosaurs that once roamed this land, the world-famous former gold camp that flourished here during the late1800s, and current activities and attractions. Using interactive technology, the Center's multiple hands-on exhibits educate and entertain. A spacious wall of windows reveals a stunning view of the Sangre de Cristo Mountain Range.

Florissant

Florissant Fossil Beds National Monument (all ages)

US 24, 8 miles west of Divide; (719) 748-3253; www.nps.gov/flfo. Open daily year-round, June through Aug, 8 a.m. to 6 p.m.; Sept through May, 9 a.m. to 5 p.m. $.

Home to an abundance of wildlife, including deer, antelope, cougars, black bears, elk, bighorn sheep, porcupines, golden eagles, and mountain bluebirds, the Florissant Fossil Beds National Monument preserves some of the finest fossil deposits of the Oligocene epoch found anywhere in the world. Today, the paper-thin, light-gray, fossil-bearing shales occur in only a few areas at the monument, so the best places to see the fossils are in the exhibits at the visitor center and on two interpretive trails.

Since the Florissant Fossil Beds were discovered in 1873, numerous paleontologists have come to this mountainous environment to collect specimens that now reside in more than twenty museums, including Harvard University's Museum of Comparative Zoology, the Smithsonian Museum of Natural History, the Denver Museum of Natural History, and the British Museum in London.

Many special programs well suited for families take place at the monument during summer and fall. You can take a "Hike with a Ranger" to some of the less-visited areas of the park. Bring a lunch, water, and sunscreen. You can learn about "Native People and Pioneers" during a two-hour session, including a slide presentation at the Fowler Education Center and a tour of the Hornbeck Homestead. And if you don't mind getting your feet wet, you can accompany your youngsters on the "Junior Ranger Stream Studies," where children in kindergarten through sixth grade earn a Junior Ranger Certificate. For this one, bring a lunch, water, sunscreen, and shoes suitable for wading into the stream. During autumn on designated days, you can participate on a "Wapiti (elk) Watch." This is bugling season for the elk, and during the early evening your group will take an easy hike to see and listen to a herd of these fine animals. Bring warm clothing and a flashlight. (The National Park Service reminds children that the elk bugle only when it is very, very quiet.) There is no charge for these programs, but reservations are strongly recommended. Call for times and dates.

Petrified Forest Loop

The Florissant Fossil Beds National Monument is a marvelous place for picnicking and hiking. There are 14 miles of good hiking trails. Perhaps of special interest to your children would be the self-guided Petrified Forest Loop, a 1-mile trail through ponderosa pine forest to the "Big Stump," a giant sequoia measuring 12 feet tall and 74 feet in circumference. This tree is thought to have stood 200 to 250 feet tall 700 years ago when it was buried in volcanic mud flows. Your children are sure to ask why there are broken saw blades in the top of the stump, and you can explain to them how a failed attempt to cut the stump in quarters and send it to Chicago for the Columbian Exposition was conducted in 1893. Also of interest to children are the numerous animals that frequent the area: ground squirrels, coyotes, elk, and antelope. Watch for the very special Abert squirrel, a pointy-eared little critter that depends on the ponderosa pine for its survival. This trail and the ½-mile Walk through Time route are stroller and wheelchair accessible.

Hornbeck Homestead

While at the Florissant Fossil Beds National Monument, you'll want to take your children through the old Hornbeck Homestead, located at the north end of the park and open during summer months only. Here they can wander through widow Adeline Hornbeck's home and across the land where she raised four children, grew potatoes and garden vegetables, and cut twenty tons of hay. You can tour the main house, the bunkhouse, the carriage shed, the barn, and the root cellar. Plan to bring a lunch and go back in time a hundred years.

Sanity Savers

Every child, no matter how well behaved, gets a little cranky when exposed to just too much fun in one day. Here are a couple of products I have thoroughly checked out and highly recommend for helping to entertain your child while giving him or her some much-needed rest. Before setting off on a weeklong adventure or daylong trip, pick up a colorful, super cozy **My Nap Pak.** Designed for those age 7 and under, My Nap Pak is a washable, easily portable, all-in-one pillow, comforter, and oversized fleece blanket perfect for spreading out under a shade tree at a festival, on the ground beside a picnic table, or in the back seat of the car. Check it out at www.mynappak.com.

Now, when your little one is all settled in his My Nap Pak, hand him one of the best options for keeping kids busy while traveling, the **Story Reader.** This item (a book that reads out loud to your child) combines narration, sound effects, and music. It is a magical reading experience that children can control and learn from all by themselves. With numerous titles featuring favorite characters, this electronic book/toy/teaching/learning device is an ideal take-along for family trips. The *Story Reader* is available at major bookstores. www.storyreader.com.

Pueblo

The city of Pueblo, located south of Colorado Springs at the juncture of I-25 and US 50, is a major center of activity in southeastern Colorado. The remaining destinations in this chapter will be accessible from Pueblo, first to the east, then to the west, and finally to the south.

El Pueblo Museum (ages 2 and up)

301 North Union St.; (719) 583-0453; www.coloradohistory.org/hist_sites/pueblo/pueblo .htm. Open Tues through Sat 10 a.m. to 4 p.m. Children age 5 and under free; children age 12 and under free on Sat. $.

At this museum, kids can climb aboard a saddle, crawl into a full-size tepee to snuggle into furry animal hides, and see artifacts from frontier life prior to 1870.

Nature and Raptor Center of Pueblo (ages 2 and up)

In Rock Canyon on the Arkansas River, 1 mile west of Pueblo; 5200 Nature Center Rd.; (719) 549-2414; www.natureandraptor.org. Free.

You will find a profusion of outdoor family activities here. For starters you can rent bikes at the visitor center to ride the paved, 21-mile River Trails System. The bike path adjoins state lands and the Pueblo Reservoir with 16 additional miles of trail to the west. To the east, another trail extends to the city center and as far as the University of Southern Colorado. Most of the trails nicely accommodate strollers and wheelchairs.

At the Cottonwood Nature Shop you will find nature-oriented items, including bird feeders, books, music, and T-shirts. Other amenities at the Greenway and Nature Center include a playground, a fine picnic area, and a fishing deck.

Buell Children's Museum (all ages)

210 North Santa Fe Ave.; (719) 295-7200 ; www.sdc-arts.org. Open year-round (except for major holidays), Tues through Sat 11 a.m. to 4 p.m. $.

Located in downtown Pueblo, the two-level, 12,000-square-foot Buell Children's Museum offers exciting and innovative hands-on exhibits, programs, and technology focusing on science, history, and the arts. Programs in the colorful Magic Carpet Theatre change regularly, bringing musicians, storytellers, and plays, as well as prerecorded presentations. Kids can even put on their own play, learning about lighting, sound, scenery, and costuming through the use of the theater's cutting-edge technology equipment.

Plan not to rush this stop. Take time to let your youngsters create their own splash of color inside King Kong's Kaleidoscope; make their own masterpiece with boxes, paper, ribbon, wax, and lots of wiggly, gooey material in the Artrageous studio; and watch in wonderment in the Reilly Family Gallery, where a 10-foot kinetic sculpture channels colorful balls around vortexes until, for a brief moment, they drop to the base only to be swooped up for another descent.

Children under the age of 4 have their own Buell Baby Barn, where wee ones nurture their motor skills while playing in a winsome barnyard setting. When energy levels drop and the hungries take over, amble on over to the Kid Rock Cafe for snacks and beverages.

Pueblo Zoo (all ages)

In Pueblo City Park, Pueblo Boulevard and Goodnight Avenue; (719) 561-1452; www.pueblo zoo.org. Open year-round; winter, Mon through Sat 9 a.m. to 4 p.m. and Sun noon to 4 p.m.; summer, daily 9 a.m. to 5 p.m. $, children under 2 free.

The Pueblo Zoo is the only Zoo Historic District in the country. It is small in area, so you can easily see all the animals, 130 different species, in a half day. And it's easily accessible for strollers and wheelchairs. The black-footed penguin exhibit is a "must see." Also called "jackass" penguins, the birds can be heard braying. The state's only underwater penguin-viewing area lets you watch their aquatic antics.

The Discovery Room welcomes families to touch, explore, and learn more about the animal kingdom with living coral tanks, microscopes, insects, and a "What Is It?" table.

Pueblo City Park (all ages)

Pueblo Boulevard and Goodnight Avenue; (719) 553-2790; www.pueblo.us. Park open year-round; pool and rides open June through mid-Aug. Train, kiddie rides, and carousel, 25 cents each; City Park free.

In addition to the zoo, City Park has two fishing lakes, an outdoor swimming pool, play-ground, and lots of room for sports and letting off steam. Young family members will want to ride all eight of the kiddie rides and the miniature train.

Carousel lovers from around the country come to ride a restored 1911 gem. There are fewer than 200 hand-carved wooden carousels still in existence. This community treasure is on the National Register of Historic Places.

For More Information

Pueblo Visitor Information Center, 302 North Santa Fe Ave., Pueblo, CO 81003; (719) 542-1704 or (800) 233-3446; www.pueblo chamber.org.

La Junta

Take US 50 east from Pueblo to La Junta. The name means "the junction," and a lot of other roads converge here as well.

Bent's Old Fort (ages 4 and up)

35110 Highway 194 East (8 miles northeast of La Junta); (719) 383-5010; www.nps.gov/beol. Open daily June through Aug, 8 a.m. to 5:30 p.m.; Sept through May, 9 a.m. to 4 p.m. $, children age 6 and younger free.

Read Me a Story

The perfect book to tuck into your luggage to read to your primary-school-age child the night before you arrive at Bent's Old Fort is *Little Fox's Secret, The Mystery of Bent's Fort* by Mary Peace Finley. This story, about an 11-year-old Native American boy, is bound to stimulate interest and make going to Bent's Old Fort become a personal experience.

Mary Peace Finley (www.marypeacefinley.com) is an award-winning author of children's historical fiction. She was born and raised on the plains of southeastern Colorado, near Bent's Old Fort. Filter Press, LLC; (719) 481-2420 or (888) 570-2663.

On the high plains of southeastern Colorado stands Bent's Old Fort, a masterful reconstruction based on drawings and descriptions from the diaries of early travelers. Originally built in 1828 by brothers Charles and William Bent and Ceran St. Vrain, the massive adobe structure was the only place on the Santa Fe Trail between Boonville, Missouri, and Santa Fe, New Mexico, where travelers could stop to rest their livestock, repair their wagons, and replenish their supplies. Bent's Old Fort became a major trading post where goods manufactured in the East were traded for those of Mexican and Native American origin. Mountain men and fur traders also bartered for needed items here. Cloth, hardware, glass, tobacco, coffee, and firearms were exchanged for Navajo blankets, beaver pelts, buffalo hides, horses, and mules. Kit Carson was hired by William Bent in 1841, at $1 per day, to help hunt for the 1,000 pounds of meat needed daily at the fort.

Today's visitors to Bent's Old Fort can take a ranger-led tour of the premises or wander at will, imagining what life was like here in the 1800s. Enter the kitchen to see where

Annual Events **at Bent's Old Fort**

In early July, Kid's Quarters allows children to spend a half day at the fort learning games, skills, chores, and activities of the 1840s. This day camp helps youngsters ages 7 through 11 better understand the lives of children in earlier times.

In early Oct, this National Historic Site comes alive when volunteers and staff reenact the fort's trading days during the annual Fur Trade Encampment.

For two days in early Dec, your family is welcome to join in as the park's staff and volunteers celebrate Christmas in 19th-century frontier style.

For information on additional events, call (719) 383-5010.

Charlotte Green, the fort cook, managed to bake bread and prepare meals under primitive conditions. Go into the blacksmith shop to see the smithy at work. Consider the plight of Susan Magoffin as you stand in the chamber where the 19-year-old spent ten days resting after suffering a miscarriage in 1846. Her meticulously kept diary made it possible for historians to accurately re-create life at the fort.

Koshare Indian Museum

115 West 18th St. (on the Otero Junior College Campus); (719) 384-4411; www.koshare.org. Open hours vary throughout the year. Call ahead. Extended hours on show nights. $.

A tribute to Native American heritage, western art, dedicated leadership, and American youth stands proudly on the southeastern plains. Since 1933 the Koshares have used proceeds from their dance performances to acquire American Indian art and artifacts. Gifts from artists who respect the Koshare mission enrich the collection. An evaluation team from the American Association of Museums declared this to be "one of the finest collections of American Indian artifacts in the world." Pieces from this collection have been borrowed for display by the Smithsonian Institute.

When you stop to see the pottery, baskets, jewelry, and early Taos paintings, you're likely also to see young men practicing dance steps or patiently completing bead or quill work for their costumes.

At the Kiva Trading Post shoppers find a selection of authentic Native American art and a comprehensive book section.

Who Are the **Koshare Indian Dancers?**

James Francis "Buck" Burshears's dream to incorporate respect and understanding of Native American cultures within the Boy Scout program has become a legend. Since 1933, numerous boys in the La Junta area have spent their teenage years not only camping and hiking but also studying the lore, legends, and lives of Plains and Southwestern Indians. Dancers must be active in a Scout Troop or Exploring Post and meet all Boy Scout of America (BSA) advancement requirements. More than 575 have achieved the rank of Eagle Scout—the highest honor a Scout can earn.

As he learns the songs and dances, each Scout researches, designs, and makes his own dance costume using authentic materials. The troop gives more than fifty performances a year in their kiva and around the United States. Presidents and world leaders have enjoyed the Koshares's precise footwork, intricate regalia, and inspiring devotion to a dream.

Koshare Indian Dances

At the kiva next to the museum. On weekends in June and July (check for additional performances), 8 p.m.; winter ceremonials between Christmas Eve and New Year's Eve; times vary. $.

The pulsating beat of the traditional Taos drum and the haunting call of an Indian flute set the stage for the colorful Koshare dancers. Swirling fringe, feathers, and quills of the fancy dancer; black-and-white stripes of the Koshare clown; and dramatic agility of the fire hoop dancer—all will be a long-remembered performance.

Where to Stay

Holiday Inn Express, 27994 US 50; (719) 384-2900 or (800) 315-2621. This hotel has an indoor pool and spa and serves a complimentary, all-you-can-eat breakfast of bacon, eggs, cheese omelets, cereals, fresh fruit, milk, juice, and baked goods. Guest rooms have refrigerators. $–$$

For More Information

La Junta Chamber of Commerce, 110 Santa Fe Ave., La Junta, CO 81050; (719) 384-7411; www.lajuntachamber.com.

Las Animas

At the intersection of US 50 and US 101, east of La Junta, lies the community of Las Animas with its historical and recreational attractions.

Boggsville (ages 5 and up)

Along the banks of the Purgatoire River, 2 miles south of Las Animas on US 101; (719) 384-8054; www.phsbc.info/boggs. Buildings open Memorial Day through Oct 1, 10 a.m. to 4 p.m.; site and walking trails open year-round. Free. Donations appreciated.

The historic settlement of Boggsville, once an agriculture and commerce center, was founded in 1862 by Thomas O. Boggs and his wife, Rumalda Luna Bent; L. A. Alien; and Charles Rite. Kit Carson and his family lived here for one year before the untimely deaths of both Carson and his wife. Boggs and Bent raised the Carsons' seven children.

A work in progress, the site now includes the restored ca. 1866 Boggs house and one of the three wings of the John Prowers home. Excavations are being conducted to determine the former locations of other structures that once stood here. With sufficient donations and volunteer help, plans are to eventually reconstruct the Kit Carson home, the schoolhouse, and the general store.

John Martin Reservoir and Hasty Lake (all ages)

16 miles east of Las Animas off US 50. (719) 829-1801; http://parks.state.co.us/parks/johnmartinreservoir. Open year-round. Free entry.

You can swim, picnic, camp, jet-boat, water-ski, sail, and windsurf at John Martin Reservoir and Hasty Lake. Especially convenient for families, Hasty Lake provides marked-off swimming areas, restrooms, a playground, a fishing pier, and an enclosed picnic shelter with fireplace on the west side of the lake. Fishing at Hasty Lake is considered good to excellent. The lake is stocked annually with rainbow trout, walleye, and channel catfish.

For More Information

Las Animas–Bent County Chamber of Commerce, 332 Ambassador Thompson Blvd., Las Animas, CO 81054; (719) 456-0453; www.bentcounty.org.

Cañon City

US 50 leads west from Pueblo to Cañon City, a distance of 38 miles. This small town and vicinity harbor several attractions worth checking out.

Dinosaur Depot and Garden Park Fossil Area (all ages)

330 Royal Gorge Blvd.; (719) 269-7150 or (800) 987-6379; www.dinosaurdepot.com. Open daily Memorial Day through Labor Day, 9 a.m. to 5 p.m. (these hours may vary). After Labor Day through Dec 23, open days and hours vary greatly depending on weather. $, children 3 and younger free.

Jurassic dinosaurs inhabited the Cañon City region 150 million years ago. Dinosaur Depot and the Garden Park Fossil Area facilities make learning about them fun. The museum is designed to stimulate an interest in science, instill an appreciation for the vast time spans in the Earth's past, recapture the excitement when dinosaur remains were discovered here in the 1870s, and foster awareness for the importance of protecting fossil resources. Among its exhibits is a stegosaurus skeleton in the process of being removed from rock that has held it captive for more than 150 million years. Knowledgeable guides, regularly scheduled programs geared toward children and adults, a gift shop, and tours of the Garden Park Fossil Area make this a worthwhile stop.

Royal Gorge Canyon and Bridge (all ages)

From Cañon City, follow US 50 West for about 7 miles to sign for Royal Gorge Canyon and Bridge; turn left at sign and proceed for 5 miles; (719) 275-7507 or (888) 333-5597; www .royalgorgebridge.com. The main gate and bridge are open daily from 7 a.m. to dusk. Open days and hours vary greatly, however, depending on weather conditions that can have an effect on the bridge. Entry fees include unlimited rides, shows, and attractions. Some attractions are seasonal, but the bridge, shops, eateries, and several attractions are open daily, weather permitting. $$–$$$, children under 3 free.

The Royal Gorge Bridge, the world's highest suspension bridge, spans the Royal Gorge Canyon. Stretching for nearly a quarter of a mile, 1,053 feet above the rushing Arkansas River, this man-made marvel is truly a remarkable sight. Visitors can ride a trolley or walk across. Those who want an eagle-eye view of the bridge and the massive granite-walled cliffs can take the thirty-five-passenger aerial tram across the chasm. Or you can ride the world's steepest incline railway for a thrilling descent to the river's edge at the very bottom of the canyon.

A 360-acre park surrounds the Royal Gorge Bridge. Here your children can ride a vintage miniature train, go round and round on the carousel, see the friendly mule deer that frequent the area, visit the trading post, and spend time at Kids Krazy Korner to play on the slides and climbing apparatus. They might even meet Gorgeous the chipmunk, Robin the deer, Little John the bear, and Stryker Rick the old gold prospector, all costumed characters that wander the park amusing visitors with their antics. A full-service restaurant and several snack bars stand by to handle big and little appetites.

The Cañon City and Royal Gorge Railroad (all ages)

Trains depart from Santa Fe Depot, 401 Water St.; (719) 276-4000 or (888) 724-5748; www .royalgorgeroute.com. Open days and hours change throughout the year according to the particular package you would like and the weather. It is best to call and make reservations for the ride you wish to take and then hope that one of those 300 days per year of sunshine that Colorado is so famous for arrives on the day you have chosen. Many types of rides—Gourmet Dinner, Gourmet Lunch, Murder Mystery, Santa Express, Observation Dome Class, First Class, Coach Class—are offered. This information is available via phone and Web site. Be sure to arrive at least 45 minutes before your departure time. $$$–$$$$.

A two-hour, 24-mile, round-trip journey along the Royal Gorge Route, aboard the only passenger train with access through this remarkable natural wonder, will take you deep into the canyon beside the mighty Arkansas River. From the open-air observation deck, your children can watch for bighorn sheep and red-tailed hawks. Look up along the way and you will see, 1,000 feet above the tracks, the Royal Gorge Suspension Bridge spanning the chasm and clinging precariously to the edge of the gorge.

As you glide along, the conductor will call your attention to the Hanging Bridge, at a point where the gorge narrows to 30 feet. Here the railroad had to be suspended over the river due to the sheer rock walls that go straight down into the surging water on both sides. Built in 1879, this unique structure has served on a main rail line for more than a century.

The train consists of former Canadian National Railway passenger cars built in the mid-1950s. Two former Chicago & Northwestern Railroad locomotives power the train. Food and beverages are available in the concession car. All coaches are heated in the winter and air-conditioned in the summer.

Buckskin Joe (all ages)

8 miles west of Cañon City on US 50, in the Royal Gorge Park Area; (719) 275-5149 or (719) 275-5485; www.buckskinjoe.com. Open daily, early May through mid-June, 10 a.m. to 5 p.m.; mid-June through Aug, 9 a.m. to 6 p.m. Open Thurs through Mon in the month of Sept, 10 a.m. to 5 p.m. $–$$$.

Buckskin Joe is one of Colorado's most unusual "towns." An authentically reconstructed gold-mining camp, it is modeled after an actual mining town that once thrived

"Are We **There Yet?**"

Traveling as a family can result in memories that last a lifetime or, unfortunately, can create some nightmares you'd rather not recall. If your brood includes daughters between the ages of 9 and 13, I suggest introducing them to the Beacon Street Girls, a series of travel-related, inspiring, multicultural books featuring five lively seventh-grade friends who work through problems, make smart choices, and, in the process, develop self-esteem. Readers easily identify with the characters, suddenly realizing, "These girls think, act, and feel just like I do!" I would begin with *Worst Enemies/Best Friends* (book 1) as an introduction to the series, and I highly recommend *Charlotte in Paris*, an adventure about becoming involved in finding a stolen Picasso while searching for Charlotte's lost cat. Placed in contemporary settings, the stories are pleasurable reading laced with positive messages, sure to keep your girls happily occupied.

90 miles northwest of this location. The original town and this rebuilt version were named after a legendary character who, in 1859, along with several other miners, made a rich placer strike on a small creek near the present-day community of Fairplay. His real name was Joseph Higgenbottom, but he was called "Buckskin Joe" due to his mode of dress.

With vintage buildings resembling those of the original settlement, gathered from several ghost towns throughout the state, today's namesake is similar to a living-history museum, with a general store, blacksmith shop, livery stable, saloon, print shop, "Mystery House," barn and corral with farm animals, and perhaps a few too many gift shops.

Kids can ride a pony through town, pan for gold, explore a make-believe gold mine, take a horse-drawn wagon ride, and view a magic show. In Oct, your family can experience the Town of Terror (not recommended for kids under age 12, however. If you stop for lunch at the Gold Nugget restaurant, you might want to consider ordering a buffalo burger.

Royal Gorge Scenic Railway and
Antique Steam Train and Car Museum (all ages)

Adjacent to Buckskin Joe; (719) 275-5485; www.buckskinjoe.com. Open days and times vary greatly according to weather. Call or check Web site. $–$$.

The Royal Gorge Scenic Railway takes passengers on a 3-mile, thirty-minute excursion around the town of Buckskin Joe and to the very rim of the spectacular Royal Gorge Canyon. When you return to the depot, don't overlook the Antique Steam Train and Car Museum. Here you will see, among other exhibits, a dandy 1915 Model T Highboy Speedster and a cute-as-can-be 1929 Model A.

Where to Stay

Best Western Royal Gorge Motel, 1925 Fremont Dr.; (719) 275-3377 or (800) 780-7234; www.bestwestern.com. Family suites with microwave ovens and refrigerators. Seasonal swimming pool, enclosed hot tub, guest laundry, playground, picnic area with barbecue. $–$$, children under 12 stay **free.**

Comfort Inn, 311 Royal Gorge Blvd.; (719) 276-6900. **Free** continental breakfast. Indoor heated swimming pool and spa. Guest laundry. Pets allowed with deposit. Nearby playground and picnic area. $–$$

For More Information

Cañon City Chamber of Commerce, 403 Royal Gorge Blvd., Cañon City, CO 81212; (719) 275-2331 or (800) 876-7922; www.canoncitychamber.com. The chamber of commerce is located in a lovely old home once occupied by former Colorado governor James Peabody.

Walsenburg

The small town of Walsenburg lies south of Pueblo, on I-25. This community, with a population of 3,900 residents, is surrounded by majestic scenery—the legendary Spanish Peaks to the south, the magnificent Sangre de Cristo Range to the west, and rolling prairie lands to the east. Walsenburg is the gateway to the Highway of Legends, a Colorado Scenic and Historic Byway. The circular route loops around the base of the Spanish Peaks and travels through the small mountain towns of La Veta, Cuchara, Stonewall, and Segundo to Trinidad and back to Walsenburg.

Lathrop State Park (all ages)

70 County Rd. 502; 3 miles west of Walsenburg on US 160; (719) 738-2376; http://parks.state.co.us/parks/lathrop. $ per car.

This 1,600-acre recreational area encompasses Martin Lake and Horseshoe Lake. These two regularly stocked lakes provide good fishing for rainbow trout, bass, walleye, and tiger muskies, Colorado's version of the Loch Ness Monster. These huge predatory fish are said to pop out of the water to glare at fisherfolk, chase boats to shore, and gobble up ducks and other waterfowl. Additional Lathrop State Park activities include windsurfing, water-skiing, boating, hiking, cross-country skiing, camping, swimming, biking, picnicking, and golfing.

La Veta

Seventeen miles west of Walsenburg on CO 12, La Veta is home to many artisans. Painters, poets, photographers, and writers are continually inspired by the spectacular mountain vistas.

Francisco Fort Museum (ages 4 and up)

**306 South Main St.; (719) 742-5501; www.spanishpeakscountry.com/fortfrancisco.aspx.
Open late May through early Oct, Wed through Sun 10 a.m. to 5 p.m. $, children 9 and
younger free.**

Stop at La Veta's ca. 1862 Francisco Fort Museum to view Indian artifacts, ranching items,
and period clothing. Kids will want to check out the old one-room schoolhouse, post
office, blacksmith shop, and gift shop.

Old La Veta Pass Road (all ages)

**For directions inquire at the La Veta Chamber of Commerce; (719) 742-3676; www.laveta-
cucharachamber.com or at one of the local shops.**

Excellent hiking exists in the La Veta area. The summertime trekking trails become outstanding cross-country ski routes during winter. The Old La Veta Pass Road was originally
a narrow-gauge railroad route, and several old structures, including the historic train
depot, remain along the way.

For More Information

**La Veta/Cuchara Chamber of Com-
merce,** located in the Town Hall/Train Depot;
(719) 742-3676; www.lavetacucharachamber
.com.

Annual Events

JUNE

**Pikes Peak International Auto Hill
Climb,** at Pikes Peak Highway, south of US 24
at Cascade; (719) 385-7325; www.pikespeak
colorado.com. This auto extravaganza, that
takes place on the last Sat each June, thrills

onlookers as race cars exceed 130 miles per
hour over the 12½-mile course to the top
of Pikes Peak via a dirt road with 156 turns
and an altitude gain of nearly 5,000 feet. Be
advised that the loud noise from the cars'
engines could frighten little tykes. $$$$, children under 12 free.

Donkey Derby Days, Cripple Creek, late
June; (719) 689-3461 or (877) 858-4653. At
this event, said to be the longest-running
annual festival in Colorado, your kids can
slurp watermelon in the watermelon-eating
contest, and you can all watch the Firemen's
Follies, where fire hoses are used to push
back the opposing team in a spirited game of
tug-of-war. The biggest draw is the donkey
races, when local businesspeople attempt
to guide (push? pull?) their furry friends for 1
block, all uphill, to see who is master, human
or beast. Free.

JULY

Hornbeck Homestead Days, Florissant,
late July; (719) 748-3253. The wonderful
aroma of baking bread emanates from the
kitchen woodstove, and old-time games are
played in the yard during this celebration. $

AUGUST

Colorado State Fair, Pueblo, late Aug; (719) 561-8484 or (800) 876-4567. This seventeen-day affair features top-name country-western entertainers, amusement-park rides, a petting zoo, stock exhibits, craft and food booths, and a rodeo. $–$$$

SEPTEMBER

Chile and Frijole Festival, Pueblo, late Sept; (800) 233-3446. This "hot and sassy" celebration features fiery mariachi music that will have your little ones dancing like Mexican jumping beans. Here you can smell the roasting chilies, taste genuine frontier food, learn how to make adobe blocks, and check out the arts and crafts booths. **Free.**

Aspen History Tours, Cripple Creek, late Sept/early Oct; (719) 689-2634. Take a tour on a guided four-wheel-drive vehicle to mining areas that are usually off-limits to travelers because they are on private property. While passengers admire the golden aspens in their fall splendor, a guide provides information on the region's famous gold rush days. **Free,** but donations go to purchase food for the Cripple Creek Donkeys.

OCTOBER

Fur Trace Encampment, La Junta, early Oct; (719) 383-5010. This event celebrates fur-trading days at Bent's Old Fort by showcasing the bustling activity that was common there in the mid-19th century. $

Northwestern Colorado

Worldld-renowned ski resorts; fascinating dinosaur digs; warm, soothing, natural hot springs; and some of the country's dandiest dude ranches make northwestern Colorado a delightful destination for families.

Idaho Springs

If you travel 32 miles west of Denver on I-70, you will come to the historic town of Idaho Springs. Gold was discovered here in 1859. The community has retained its mining-era

TopPicks in Northwestern Colorado

- **Cross Orchards Historic Site,** Grand Junction
- **Dinosaur Journey,** Fruita
- **Georgetown Loop Railroad,** Georgetown
- **Glenwood Caverns Adventure Park,** Glenwood Springs
- **Glenwood Springs Hot Springs Pool,** Glenwood Springs
- **National Sports Center for the Disabled,** Winter Park
- **Phoenix Mine,** Idaho Springs
- **Ski Programs for Kids,** Steamboat Springs
- **Snow Mountain Ranch/YMCA of the Rockies,** Fraser
- **Two Below Zero,** Frisco

NORTHWESTERN COLORADO

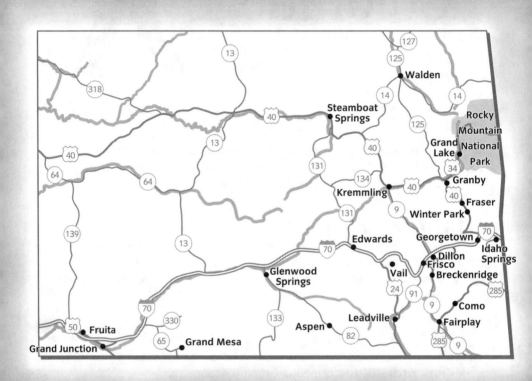

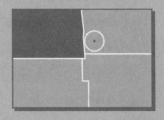

heritage by preserving its gingerbread-trimmed Victorian homes and old-time storefronts, and providing tours of mining facilities.

Argo Gold Mine (ages 4 and up)

North of I-70 (you can see it from the highway); (303) 567-2421; www.historicargotours .com. Open daily mid-Apr through mid-Oct depending on weather, 9 a.m. to 6 p.m. Winter tours by appointment. Children age 7 and under are free. **$$.**

The Argo Gold Mine stands in the heart of Idaho Springs's historic mining district. Visitors interested in the process of removing gold from the remainder of the ore walk 500 feet into one of the mine tunnels and then proceed from level to level of the museum buildings to view the rock-crushing apparatus and grinding equipment. The one-hour tour of this National Historic Site is partially underground, so it's important to wear warm clothing.

Phoenix Mine (ages 4 and up)

4 miles west of Idaho Springs (take Stanley Road west for 1 mile, then turn left onto Trail Creek Road); (303) 567-0422; www.phoenixgoldmine.com. Open daily year-round, May through Oct, 10 a.m. to 5 p.m.; Nov through Apr 10 a.m. to 4 p.m. Children age 4 and under are free. **$–$$.**

Here is an opportunity to visit a working underground gold mine. With a seasoned Colorado hard-rock miner as your tour guide, you will get a realistic idea of what it's like to mine gold. Watch as miners push tons of gold and silver ore in small railcars just as their predecessors did more than one hundred years ago. Your kids can try out the antique tools, listen to fascinating stories about the "Tommyknockers" (mine ghosts), and pan for gold in a mountain stream after the tour. Any gold you find is yours to keep. Bring your camera!

Indian Springs Resort (all ages)

302 Soda Creek Rd.; (303) 989-6666; www.indianspringsresort.com. Open daily 7:30 a.m. to 10:30 p.m. Hours vary for pool, geothermal cave baths, and restaurant. $–$$.

Long before gold was discovered in the Rocky Mountains, both Ute and Arapahoe Indians considered the hot springs that bubble endlessly from the earth at this rather rustic resort to be sacred. Later, miners soaked their tired muscles in the hot pools. The famous, as well as infamous, came as well. The Roosevelt and Vanderbilt families took to the waters here. Notorious outlaws Frank and Jesse James and Billy the Kid dropped in for a spell. Clint Eastwood, James Caan, and other movie greats have also been guests of the resort.

The Indian Springs Resort features an indoor swimming pool, outdoor hot tubs, private bathing rooms, cave hot pools, lodging, a restaurant, and a campground.

Especially popular with families is the large, mineral water-fed swimming pool, covered with a translucent dome and surrounded by banana and palm trees and lush tropical foliage. The pool's water is kept at a comfortable ninety degrees, so kids can splash about as long as they please. The underground cave pools are much hotter, and children ages 12 and under are not allowed in this area.

Knowing that kids and dirt just naturally go together, it comes as no surprise to find whole families sloshing about in the resort's "Club Mud," a large sunken tub filled with mushy mineral-rich clay that reportedly absorbs toxins from the body. You can spread the gooey muck on one another and then shower it off, or sit back and let the mud dry in order to obtain the maximum effect. Your kids won't soon forget the time they had parental permission to wallow in the mud. Definitely a photo moment.

Where to Eat

Beau Jo's, 1517 Miner St.; (303) 567-4376; www.beaujos.com. Open daily for lunch and dinner. Find out what makes Colorado-style pizza special. Beau Jo's has been feeding happy customers for more than twenty-five years. The hand-rolled white or wheat crust is very thick, but it's never left—they serve honey so that you can enjoy it for dessert. Look for Beau Jo's in nine other locations along the Front Range. $

Winter Park

This town's name is a little misleading because Winter Park is both a winter and summer community with loads of family activities available throughout the entire year. Located 67 miles northwest of Denver, it is best reached by traveling west on I-70 for approximately 42 miles to US 40 at exit 232. Follow US 40 north over Berthoud Pass and into Winter Park.

Winter Park Ski Resort (all ages)

85 Parsenn Rd.; (303) 316-1564 or (970) 726-5514; www.winterparkresort.com or www.ski winterpark.com. $–$$$$, depending on activity.

Winter Park Ski Resort in Winter (all ages)

Winter season begins in mid-Nov and runs until about mid-Apr (depending on snowfall). $–$$$$, depending on activity.

Winter Park Resort receives an average of 365 inches of snow per year. Thanks to the twenty-five lifts—including two high-speed six-pack, seven high-speed express quads, five triples, six double chairlifts, three surface lifts, and three magic carpets —36,920 riders can be "lifted" up the mountain per hour. This can be one busy place but lift lines are usually short.

Winter Park Ski Resort is well known for its family-oriented resources. It has outstanding children's ski programs and child care facilities. It also offers adult private and class lessons, including unique learning experiences and specialty clinics throughout the season that cater to mogul skiers, freeriders, women, and telemarkers. Advance reservations are available and recommended. Information pertaining to cost can be had and reservations made by calling the Guest Contact Center at (800) 729-7907 or by visiting www.winterparkresort.com.

Need a Lift?

In Winter Park, the Lift, a local shuttle service, provides **free** transportation between lodging properties and activities to the Winter Park Ski Resort base area. During peak season, buses run every thirty minutes, from 7:30 a.m. to 10:30 p.m. For information call (970) 726-4118.

Wee Willie's Childcare. A nonski program for children two months through six years with indoor activities and outdoor play. Lunch is available on site. A complimentary beeper/pager is provided. Reservations are required. A one-hour private ski or snowboard lesson add-on is available for children two years and older who are enrolled in full-day child care. Parents can take advantage of the Jump Start Program (for children 3 and older), which includes a two-hour lesson and rentals in the morning and all-day child care and lunch. Reservations required by calling (800) 420 8093.

Kids Daily Programs. The program for 3-year-olds is a nonchairlift-riding ski orientation with all-day supervision, playtime, and lunch. Children are introduced to skiing through indoor and outdoor activities designed and paced for each group. Participants must be potty-trained and willing to play outside.

Classes for all other kids are determined by ability level—beginner through advanced—and age 4- to 6-year-olds, and 7- to 14-year-olds. Traditional snowboarding lessons (also for children as young as age 6) can be purchased for a full-day program, which includes lesson, lift, rentals, and lunch. Registration for lessons is either in advance by calling (800) 729 7907 or in person from 8 to 9 a.m. on lesson day at Kids Adventure Junction. Terrain Parks and Pipes. Winter Park Resort features five levels of terrain parks for children ages 6 and up.

Rail Yard: advanced terrain; Dark Territory: a limited access area; Ash Cat: an intermediate system ideal for perfecting skills; Gangway: jib features for skiers and riders; Starter Park: great for the beginner-jibber, it features small rails for first attempts at rail sliding.

Winter Park Ski Resort in Summer (all ages)

Open for the summer season daily from early June through Labor Day. All mountain activities operate from 10 a.m. to 5:30 p.m. except for the Zephyr Express chairlift, which is open from mid-June through Labor Day, 10 a.m. to 5 p.m. All of the following activities may be purchased individually but there is a Park Pass available that offers the best value. The pass includes unlimited all-day use of all activities. Some height and weight restrictions apply. $$–$$$$, depending on activity. Children age 5 and under are free.

Alpine Slide (ages 4 and up). Colorado's longest two-track Alpine Slide is located under the Arrow chairlift. The tracks are 3,030 feet long with twenty-six linked turns. Children 45 inches tall or shorter must ride with an adult.

Zephyr Express Chairlift. Ride up to the 10,700-foot summit for mountain biking, hiking, and disc golf. Consider picking up picnic supplies at the village and then spreading a blanket at the top of the mountain for a meal with spectacular views of the Continental Divide. If you somehow arrived at the summit without vittles and the fresh air has everyone complaining about the hungries, treat yourselves to a delicious lunch at The Lodge at Sunspot, open from mid-June to Labor Day ($$–$$$).

Mountainside Mini Golf (ages 4 and up). Each hole of the course depicts a Fraser Valley scene or a historic site.

Amaze'n Human Maze (ages 6 and up). Located at the base of the Zephyr Express Chairlift, the maze is an enormous wooden network of passages that wind and twist into wrong turns and dead-ends. Afraid you might lose someone? Not to worry. An observation tower lets you give helpful route directions if any of your little "mice" get confused or lose their way in this life-sized puzzle.

Leaps & Bounds Bungee (ages 5 and up). If you have ever wondered how those talented gymnasts do it, here's your chance to give it a try. You will be harnessed with two bungee cords so that you are free to leap, flip, and jump on a high-altitude trampoline that will send you vaulting high into the air.

Gyro Extreme (ages 6 and up). Here's a new one for you. Try testing your ability as an astronaut in this three-dimensional, human-sized, sphere-shaped gyro ride. After a few tries, you'll be able to move yourself upside down and all around until you've created a sensation similar to weightlessness. Best to eat lunch afterward. Must be 50 inches tall to ride.

Outdoor Climbing Wall (ages 4 and up). If climbing Mt. Everest is on your wish list, it's time to begin training. With your harness safely secured, try climbing one of the three routes that vary in difficulty up this 24-foot-high climbing wall. It's perfectly okay to start with the easiest course.

Plenty of Paths **for Pedaling**

Mountain bikers, novice or advanced, will be happy to know that the Winter Park and Fraser Valley area encompasses more than 250 miles of single track and more than 600 miles of interconnected trails and four-wheel-drive roads ideal for this popular sport. You can pick up a mountain-bike map for **free** at any bike shop or at the Winter Park Visitor Center.

National Sports Center for the Disabled (NSCD)
(all ages)

(303) 316-1540 or (970) 726-1540.

NSCD is recognized as the world's finest ski and outdoor activities program for the disabled. Each year, thousands of children and adults with disabilities come to NSCD to learn new skills, feel the freedom of being able to participate in outdoor activities, and to gain confidence. With specially trained staff and its own adaptive equipment lab, the NSCD enthusiastically accommodates individuals with almost any mental or physical challenge. In summer it provides rafting, fishing, golfing, sailing, therapeutic horseback riding, camping, mountain biking, and rock climbing. In winter NSCD offers alpine skiing, cross-country skiing, Nordic hut trips, snowshoeing, snowboarding, and ski racing. Programs are designed for individuals, families, and groups and are available for nearly all levels of ability.

Where to Eat
Carvers Bakery Cafe, 93 Cooper Creekway; (970) 726-8202. Open daily. For a hearty breakfast or lunch, this is the place. Be forewarned, Carvers is as popular with locals as it is with visitors, so there could be a bit of a wait. $

Hernando's Pizza and Pasta Pub, 78199 US 40; (970) 726-5409. Open daily for dinner. Well known for its original pizza pies, this restaurant is a good choice for families. $

Where to Stay
Winter Park Central Reservations, (800) 729-5813 (U.S. and Canada) or (970) 726-5587 (local and international). This is your best bet for accommodations. Be prepared to tell them the number of people in your family, ages of children, what your needs are, and what your price range is. They no doubt will be able to find you a suitable place to stay. Ask about the four-night, learn-to-ski package for families.

For More Information
Winter Park/Fraser Valley Chamber of Commerce, P.O. Box 3236, Winter Park, CO 80482; (970) 726-4118 or (800) 903-7275; www.winterpark-info.com.

Fraser

The resort community of Fraser lies just north of Winter Park along US 40. Families interested in cross-country skiing will find lots of options in this area.

Devil's Thumb Ranch (all ages)

3530 County Rd. 83 (970) 726-7000 or (800) 933-4339; www.devilsthumbranch.com. Open year-round. $$$–$$$$.

Devil's Thumb Ranch, previously known as one of the region's leading cross-country ski centers has become the place for a luxurious wilderness experience. Located 65 miles west of Denver and only 10 minutes west of Winter Park Ski Area, this year-round ranch

High Country Stampede **Rodeo Series**

The John Work Arena, located 1 mile west of Fraser, hosts this Old West extravaganza, featuring the "Best Little Rodeo in Colorado," every Sat evening from early July through Aug. The Junior Rodeo gets under way at 5 p.m. and showcases wranglers ages 9 to 17 who participate in some of the same events as their older counterparts: calf roping, barrel racing, and pole bending. The adult bareback, saddle bronco, and bull-riding events follow at 7:30 p.m. Only the most rugged of cowpokes can hang on to a one-ton Brahma bull with one hand while being tossed from side to side and hither and yon for the eight seconds required to receive a score and qualify for prize money. For information call (970) 726-5491.

resort features luxury log cabins furnished with antiques, pillow-top beds, down comforters, log furniture, and mini- to fully equipped kitchens. Cabin options range from one-bedroom lofts with EPA-approved woodburning fireplaces to two- and four-bedroom log homes. The main lodge boasts fifty-two guest rooms and suites. Other full-service options include the Ranch Creek Spa and the Ranch House Restaurant & Saloon serving homemade soups, salads, specialty sandwiches, cobblers, and pies. A Swiss-style continental breakfast and afternoon wine and cheese are included in the room rate. The ranch's Adventure Center provides professional guides for everything from Nordic skiing, with chariots for the little ones, ice skating, snowshoeing, hiking, mountain biking, fly-fishing, and nature tours. Equipment for all activities is available for kids, adults, beginners, and experts. Downhill enthusiasts have access to Colorado Ski Country Gold Passes, for **free** downhill skiing at Winter Park or Sol Vista at Granny Ranch, both of which are within fifteen minutes of Devil's Thumb. Additional amenities include a heated indoor/outdoor pool, a hot tub, steam room, and sauna. The Cabin Creek Stable offers horseback riding and instructors for riders of all ages. Trail rides and lessons are available from May to Oct. There are summertime hay rides and wintertime sleigh rides when kids can help toss hay to the field horses. The Broad Axe Barn, a reclaimed ca. 1850s barn, serves as a multiuse facility for family reunions and other special occasions, and the outdoor chapel is perfect for weddings. They also have another chapel for small, intimate weddings called the Timber House.

Snow Mountain Ranch/YMCA of the Rockies

(all ages)

Ten miles northwest of Fraser via US 40; (970) 887-2152 or (800) 777-9622; www.ymcarock ies.org. Open year-round. $–$$$.

Snow Mountain Ranch is an affordable family destination in all seasons with overnight lodging in cabins that sleep five to twelve people, in lodge rooms berthing four to six, and at campsites (summer only). Perfect for conferences and large groups, the mountain setting with its varied activities is an ideal choice for a family reunion or a single family get-away.

Hiking, mountain biking, miniature golf, tennis, fishing, canoeing, horseshoes, hayrides, and horseback riding fill the slate for sunny days, while plenty of other options, including an indoor swimming pool, a sauna, a skating rink, a library, Bible studies, and a homestead museum occupy kids and their parents during rare bad weather.

Come winter, you'll find 50 miles of groomed Nordic trails for all abilities, an ice skating rink, wildlife viewing, and sledding and tubing hills. The downhill skiers can venture to nearby Winter Park and Silver Creek Ski Resorts while those who choose, can engage in basketball, swimming, and roller skating, ascend the climbing wall, or make new friends in the comprehensive craft shop where you are apt to find several generations of crafters, from age 3 to 93. Several miles of lighted, groomed track provide an invigorating evening sport.

Fraser Experimental Forest Ranger Station (all ages)

On the west side of US 40, south of Granby, about 4½ miles from Fraser; (970) 887-4100; www.fs.fed.us/r2/arnf/about/organization/srd/index.shtml. The ranger station is not open to the public.

This ranger station provides marked trails suitable for beginning, intermediate, and expert cross-country skiers. There are no food facilities here, and the nearby vault restroom is sometimes locked. In the summer, the trails provide mountain biking courses, and campgrounds are available.

Fraser Valley Tubing Hill (ages 3 and up)

Behind the Alco Shopping Center in Fraser on County Road 72; (970) 726-5954. Open late Nov through mid-Apr, depending on snowfall, Mon through Thurs noon to 9 p.m.; Fri noon to 10 p.m.; Sat 10 a.m. to 10 p.m.; Sun 10 a.m. to 9 p.m. $$–$$$, seniors 60 or older may use a tube at half price.

Snow tubing allows you to take an exhilarating ride down a snow-covered slope on an inner tube, spinning and yelping for joy all the way to the bottom. Then you lie down on your inner tube and hold on for dear life to a minilift that drags you back up to the top of the hill. When fingers and toes begin to feel like icicles, gather your kids and traipse into the warming hut for a hot beverage. Children must be at least 3 years old to participate, and those ages 3 through 6 must ride with an adult. Be prepared for the cold by bringing earmuffs or stocking hats, heavy gloves or mittens, insulated jackets, and snowpants. A change of outfits for the kids is also a good idea, because they are apt to get rather wet from snow spray and from tumbling off their tubes into the snow.

For More Information

Winter Park/Fraser Valley Chamber of Commerce, P.O. Box 3236, Winter Park, CO 80482; (970) 726-4118 or (800) 903-7275; www.winterpark-info.com.

Grand Lake

Sequestered between the western boundary of Rocky Mountain National Park and Grand Lake, the state's largest natural lake, is Grand Lake village, the mountain community that bears the lake's name. The town is small, with hospitable lodging, good eateries, and the ever-present souvenir and gift shops.

The lake provides numerous water sports. You can rent a canoe or bumper boat at one of the two marinas. Or perhaps your family would prefer a rowboat or motorized craft in order to try your luck fishing for rainbow trout, kokanee salmon, or Mackinaw. Trolling and inlet fishing usually bring the best results. Fishing licenses are required for those age 17 or older and can be bought at the marina.

Because Grand Lake village borders Rocky Mountain National Park, the hiking trails are seemingly endless. And if you visit Grand Lake during winter, you will find that those same trails that were so wonderful for summertime treks have become outstanding cross-country skiing and snowmobiling routes. Do remember, though, that appropriate cold-weather clothing is a must, and if you plan to go snowmobiling, it is important to reserve your machine in advance. Other wintertime activities in the Grand Lake area include ice fishing, dogsledding, and snowshoeing.

Kawuneeche Visitor Center (all ages)

1½ miles north of Grand Lake village on US 34; (970) 627-3471. Open daily Memorial Day through Labor Day, 8 a.m. to 6 p.m. (sometimes later); Labor Day through Memorial Day, 8 a.m. to 4:30 p.m. Free guided hikes.

This visitor center hosts several family-oriented programs each day throughout the summer. One of the most popular with kids is the "Come Bug a Ranger" session, where participants learn about the insects that inhabit Rocky Mountain National Park.

"Skins and Things" teaches children and adults about the animals that live in the park—deer, elk, bighorn sheep, bears, mountain lions, otters, squirrels, and rabbits, as well as raptors such as peregrine falcons, hawks, golden eagles, and bald eagles.

Home, Home on the Ranch

One would be hard pressed to find a better family vacation than that spent on a dude ranch. Horseback riding, gold panning, llama trekking, square dancing, rafting, fishing, hiking, swimming, and relaxing are some of the activities families can enjoy together on dude ranches.

Because most dude ranches provide counselors and programs for children and teens, and in some cases even babysitting for infants, parents can spend time alone if they wish without feeling guilty about not including their children. For the single parent, dude ranching may be especially attractive. While children indulge in their own activities, Mom or Dad is free to pursue adult interests. Or parent and child can spend all their time together. The choice is theirs. This outdoor experience allows for complete freedom, because all needs are provided for and you can participate in group activities as much or as little as you please.

Another important plus is knowing the total cost before leaving home. Very little money is spent after arrival. In addition, there is no repeated unpacking and repacking; no getting up in the morning and climbing back behind the wheel for another day of dodging semis and breathing exhaust fumes; no more taking chances on unfamiliar eating places and searching for lodging every evening; and no roar of traffic going by your window all night long. Rates vary according to ranch selected and facilities provided. A ballpark figure would be from $950 to $2,500 per week per adult. Reduced rates are available for children. It's best to call individual ranches for exact costs.

Dress on a guest ranch is casual. Pack a good pair of jeans along with a couple of western shirts for "dress-up" affairs, but be sure to bring along everybody's favorite, most comfortable grubbies, too. Take jackets and sweatshirts, even in summer, and a pair of boots for horseback riding. Forest insects seem to get as hungry as riders, hikers, and anglers, so repellent is a must.

For More Information

The Colorado Dude and Guest Ranch Association, P.O. Drawer, Shawnee, CO 80475, (866) 942-3472; www.coloradoranch .com. Each of the participating ranches is regularly inspected for cleanliness, facilities, hospitality, and honest representation. Phone for a brochure describing member ranches.

Grand Lake Chamber of Commerce, 14700 Highway 34; P.O. Box 429, Grand Lake, CO 80447; (970) 627-3402 or (800) 531-1019; www.grandlakechamber.com.

Granby

The hamlet of Granby lies along US 40 northwest of Fraser.

Drowsy Water Ranch (all ages)
County Road 2; (970) 725-3456 or (800) 845-2292; www.drowsywater.com. Open from early June to mid-Sept. $$$–$$$$.

Snuggled in a lush valley along Drowsy Water Creek, on the western side of the Continental Divide, this ranch is a family-run operation whose aim is to provide a memorable dude ranch experience. Owners Ken and Randy Sue Fosha welcome you to their home and vow to "treat your children as we do our own: with understanding, patience, love, and respect. Our ranch is for children. Our counselors and program supervisors are college students selected for their attentiveness, experience, and interest in child development and recreation."

Kids aren't likely to linger over breakfast at the Drowsy Water Ranch. Too many ways to have fun await them. Programs and activities abound for little ones, age 5 and under, and for older youngsters age 6 through teens. Families can spend the day together swimming in the heated outdoor swimming pool or enjoying ranch activities, or they can go their separate ways. While parents take to the trail on the back of a trusty steed or read a book under a shady tree, kids are receiving riding instruction, going on nature hikes, taking part in arena activities, making crafts, listening to storytellers, and fishing the stocked ponds. They participate in their own hayride and campfire cookout and then join parents in the Tepee Dancehall for an evening of down-home square dancing. Rates include accommodations in attractive log cabins, all meals, and all activities.

Kremmling

Kremmling is located approximately 100 miles northwest of Denver, off US 40.

Latigo Ranch (all ages)
P.O. Box 237, Kremmling, CO 80459; (970) 724-9008 or (800) 227-9655; www.latigotrails .com. Open early June through Sept and mid-Dec through Mar. $$$–$$$$.

Latigo Ranch encompasses 450 acres and has access to more than 50,000 acres of the Arapahoe and Routt National Forests. Horsemanship is taken seriously here, and careful instruction is provided by experienced wranglers. Novices may choose walk-only rides, while more accomplished equestrians may engage in trotting and cantering. Little cowpokes new to the sport are carefully guided along level paths by qualified wranglers.

Guests at Latigo Ranch can participate in cookouts, hayrides, nature walks, fly-fishing, and volleyball. They can dance to lively country-western music (kids are encouraged to join in), play table tennis, shoot a game of pool, swim in the outdoor swimming pool, and go on wiener roasts. Family rides are arranged so that all members of your family ride together, sometimes joining up with other moms and dads and their kids.

Six- to 7-year-olds ride as frequently as older children, but their treks are shorter in duration. Counselors also take them swimming, fishing, and hiking and play educational games with them.

Three- to 5-year-olds are supervised while parents are horseback riding. They learn about mountain animals, plants, and rocks; hear stories about Native Americans and horses; create crafts; and feed ranch pets Charlie the lamb, Charcoal and Smokey the rabbits, and Wilbur the pig. They ride Papoose the Shetland pony and play stick-toss with Stormy the dog.

Winter activities at Latigo Ranch include cross-country skiing on 60 kilometers of groomed track, sliding down a tubing hill, snowshoeing, and wildlife viewing.

Rates include accommodations in nicely appointed log cabins, all meals, and all activities. Cost varies with season. Babysitting for infants is available at extra charge if arranged at the time you make your reservations.

Walden

The small town of Walden, located in what is referred to as the North Park region of Colorado, about 150 miles northwest of Denver, is surrounded by unequaled wildlife-viewing possibilities. In 1995 the Colorado Senate designated tiny Walden (population 1,000) as the "Moose-Viewing Capital of Colorado." You are most likely to see moose in the early morning or late afternoon and early evening. Because other wildlife is also abundant, you may see more furry and feathered critters in these parts than people.

The moose are here year-round, but the roads are often impassable during late fall, winter, and spring. The best time to go is from Memorial Day through mid-Oct. And it's always a good idea to call (303) 639-1111 or check www.cotrip.org for road conditions.

Colorado State Forest (all ages)

If seeing and photographing a 7-foot-tall, 1,400-pound bull moose sounds exciting, take CO 14 south from Walden 20 miles to County Road 41 near the KOA Campground, and then go north on CR 41 for approximately 7 miles to the viewing platform. The deck overlooks a prime moose habitat, and moose are regularly seen in the creek bottom below. A wildlife interpretive trail is across the road from the platform.

State Park Moose Viewing Site (all ages)

Moose—along with deer, elk, coyotes, small game, and birds—are frequently seen at this site, located at mile marker 58, which is 24 miles southeast of Walden on CO 14. From the parking lot walk about 300 feet to the edge of a large meadow; the Nokhu Crags in the distance provide an outstanding backdrop for your photos. http://parks.state.co.us/parks/stateforest/visitorcenter.

Arapaho Wildlife Refuge Nature Trail (all ages)

This is another significant spot for wildlife viewing. Take CO 125 south from Walden for 8 miles, turn east on County Road 32, proceed for about ½ mile, and turn south to the trailhead parking lot. This ½-mile trail, accessible to strollers, wheelchairs, and the physically challenged, loops through a variety of wildlife habitats where you are apt to see a combination of moose, deer, beavers, porcupines, songbirds, and waterfowl. Interpretive stations along the way provide information and suggest what to watch for. The trail is open from early Apr to late Oct, weather permitting. Parking and restrooms are located at the trailhead. For more information call (970) 723-8202.

North Park Pioneer Museum (ages 3 and up)

365 Logan St. (in back of the Jackson County Court House); (970) 723- 8371 (phone in use only during summer open hours). Open mid-June through mid-Sept, Thurs through Tues 10 a.m. to 4 p.m.; closed Wed. Free. Donations are greatly appreciated.

"Everybody is welcome, and bring the kids," is the motto of this museum, opened in 1963 in a three-room ranch house built in 1882. Today the complex encompasses twenty-seven rooms packed with treasures. The kitchen has a coal range, a hand-operated dishwasher, and a "square skillet to cook a square meal." Other chambers include the Country Store and the Post Office, the Laundry Room with old-time washing machines and hand irons, an Army Room with Red Cross and U.S. Army and Navy uniforms from World Wars I and II, and the Buggy Shed, sporting a buggy and a mint-condition 1936 Dodge.

Your children will especially like the Toy Room, with old-fashioned dolls, games, and toys; and the School Room, showcasing antique desks along with old books, slates, sewing cards, lunch pails, and report cards.

Steamboat Springs

Steamboat Springs, located in the Yampa Valley 166 miles northwest of Denver along US 40, skillfully blends an Old West influence with a ski resort ambience, resulting in a compatible mix of down-home hospitality and exuberant vitality.

In 1913 Norwegian Carl Howelsen introduced recreational skiing to this valley. The Steamboat Springs Ski Resort continues to attract skiers, novice to Olympic-caliber, with ideal "Champagne Powder" and world-class facilities. Lodging, dining, shopping, and four-season recreation and festivals draw visitors to Mt. Werner year-round.

Cowboys have always played an important role in Steamboat Springs. Long ago the downtown streets were built wide enough to handle large herds of cattle, driven north from Texas. These days cowhands continue to drive their cattle, sheep, and horses to the high meadows for summer grazing, and ranching, farming, and coal mining are still practiced by area residents. According to a chamber of commerce resource, "It oughta have a Western mystique. It's been a cowboy town for more than one hundred years."

Howelsen Hill (ages 4 and up)

245 Howelsen Parkway; (970) 879-8499. Open daily during winter months, weather permitting. $$ to ski; watching is free.

Skiing was a necessary mode of travel for the early settlers due to heavy snowfall in this mountainous region. Then in 1913, when Carl Howelsen built a ski jump and proceeded to hurl himself 100 feet into the air, the Steamboat Springs townsfolk realized that skiing could be fun, too. These days, Howelsen Hill, in downtown Steamboat Springs, maintains 15-, 20-, 30-, 70-, and 90-meter jumps and "bump jumps" used by future Olympians as a training site.

Downtown

A pleasant mix of restaurants, shops, galleries, and historic buildings line the streets of downtown. You'll enjoy the small-town ambience. Here are a few standouts for families. Hours vary by season.

Off the Beaten Path (all ages)

68 9th St.; (970) 879-6830; www.steamboatbooks.com. Open daily year-round from 8 a.m. to 7 p.m.

A great bookstore with an in-house bakery—what a terrific combination! Your whole family will love the books, magazines, puzzles, games, and pastries. The kids will especially appreciate the tree house reading area. The selection is terrific. The small coffeehouse

Pretty Neat **Playgrounds**

Some playgrounds are definitely better than others. Steamboat Springs has two great play places, both the work of community volunteers. Located at elementary schools, they are unsupervised but open to the public until dark. You'll find them next to Steamboat Springs' Strawberry Park and Soda Creek Elementary Schools.

offers breakfast, lunch, and snacks. Their decadent desserts and gourmet coffee drinks are difficult to resist. Why try?

F. M. Light & Sons

830 Lincoln Ave.; (970) 879-1822. www.fmlight.com. Open daily, but hours change with the seasons. Call ahead.

Remember all those signs leading to South Dakota's Wall Drug Store? You see advertisements for F. M. Light & Sons long before you get here; there are more than 250 signs within a 150-mile radius. This western-wear store has been in business since 1905, and the fifth generation of the founding family operates it now. Kids love to have their picture taken next to the life-size plastic horse out front. Inside, there are $4.98 straw cowboy hats and lots of authentic western gear. For $3.98 youngsters can scoop a bag full of polished rocks: "You must be able to close the bag." Get discount tickets to the rodeo while you're here.

Steamboat Springs PRCA Summer Prorodeo Series (all ages)

Howelsen Hill Rodeo grounds, 501 Howelsen Parkway; (970) 879-1818; www.steamboat rodeo.com. Mid-June through Aug, Fri and Sat 7:30 p.m. $, kids under 6 free.

Bareback riding, steer wrestling, calf roping, barrel racing, and bull riding: It's big-time rodeo with a small-town feel. Your kids can even get in the act—the Calf Scramble challenges 6- to 12-year-olds, and even younger cowpokes can attempt the Ram Scramble. This rodeo is a great combination of serious sport and good fun.

Lyon's Corner Drug and Soda Fountain

9th Street and Lincoln Avenue; (970) 879-1114. Open daily; hours vary greatly according to season.

Everyone knows where Lyon's is—it's been on the same corner for more than seventy years. Drop in for a treat at their old-fashioned ice-cream fountain. You may have to wait—there are only ten stools. For a quarter, play golden oldies in the vintage jukebox.

Yampatika (all ages)

Outdoor activities in many locations. Store: U.S.F.S. Building, 925 Weiss Dr. (US 40 across from the Holiday Inn); (970) 871-9151; www.yampatika.org. Open Mon through Fri 8 a.m. to 5.p.m. Free.

Amazing
Steamboat Springs Facts

The name Steamboat Springs is said to have been chosen for the town in 1865 when three French fur trappers were traveling down the Yampa River. One of the men heard a chug-chug sound like that of a paddle-wheel steamer. Excited, the men rushed toward the rhythmic noise they perceived to be a steamboat and discovered instead a bubbling mineral spring. The town was named for the nonexistent steamboat.

The snow here is so special that it has a trademarked name. "Champagne Powder" describes incredibly light and fluffy snow for exceptional skiing. The term originated in Steamboat Springs.

Their motto is "Leave town with more than a T-shirt." This nonprofit group leads enjoyable, educational hikes—wildflower hikes, bird walks, history walks through downtown—and holds campfire programs in state parks and at the ski area. Programs are designed to encourage family participation. Check out the various Yampatykes Kids camps for 5 and 6 year olds, and the Junior Naturalists' Camp for 9 and 10 year olds. During the winter they offer "Ski with a Naturalist," a one-hour educational run down the mountain.

Call for a current schedule or visit their store where books, puzzles, games, posters, maps, and all other items have a cultural or natural history theme. Programs available for those with special needs.

Old Town Hot Springs (all ages)

3rd Street and Lincoln Avenue (west of downtown on right side of US 40 at 3rd Street across from the Rabbit Ears Motel); (970) 879-1828; www.sshra.org. Open daily year-round, Mon through Fri 5:30 a.m. to 9:45 p.m., Sat 7 a.m. to 8:45 p.m., and Sun 8 a.m. to 8:45 p.m. $–$$.

A family swim in the pool or a soak in the hot mineral pools that range in temperature from 98 to 102 degrees is a great way to end a day of outdoor adventure. If you crave more exercise, there is an Olympic-size lap pool. And your kids are sure to love their water slide. The facility also offers massages, a fitness center, and exercise classes.

Steamboat Springs Transit (all ages)

Look for white metal signs designating the route; (970) 879-3717. Operates daily, at least every thirty minutes. Schedule available at www.steamboatsprings.net. Free.

Enjoy the scenery; leave driving to the locals. The SST bus line runs through downtown, out to the ski area, and back. Buses are marked Condos or Downtown. Ask the driver for a complete schedule. Don't worry about having correct change—it's always **free.**

River Tubing (ages 2 and up)

On the Yampa River through town. Rentals $$.

The minute they see all those tubers floating down the river, your kids will want to jump right in. The gentle Yampa flows right through town with easy access from many spots. You'll discover a multitude of outfitters who rent tubes and include drop-off and pick-up services in their modest fees. The big black inner tubes have mesh across the middle so that no one falls through. Toddlers can ride double with an adult. Tubing companies require footwear for this activity. Call Steamboat Springs Parks, Open Space and Recreational Services at (970) 879-4300 for more information.

Perry–Mansfield Performing Arts Camp (ages 8 and up)

40755 Routt County Rd. 36; (800) 430-2787 for a brochure, rates, and seminar and performance dates; www.perry-mansfield.org. One- to six-week courses run from mid-June to late Aug. $$$–$$$$.

For the creative members of your family—would-be thespians; ballet, modern, and jazz dancers; musical theater and voice aspirants; creative writers; and those interested in stage management and production—this camp may be just the incentive needed to start a career in the arts.

Established in 1913 by Charlotte Perry and Portia Mansfield, this unique institution is the oldest performing arts school and camp in the country. Agnes de Mille choreographed her Rodeo ballet after attending a local square dance nearby. Dustin Hoffman helped perfect his acting in the studios and theaters at Perry–Mansfield. Other distinguished alumni include Julie Harris, John Cage, and Lee Remick. A limited number of scholarships are available by audition each year.

The Perry–Mansfield Performing Arts Camp presents several performances each season open to the public at nominal cost.

Off-season, the Perry–Mansfield Performing Arts Camp offers seven winterized cabins for rent in the hills of Strawberry Park ($$). Available from early Sept through mid-May, the cottages range in size from one to five bedrooms. For information and reservations, call (970) 879-1060 or (970) 879-0342.

Fish Creek Falls (all ages)

North on 3rd Street from Lincoln Avenue to Oak Street. Follow the signs; it's about 3 miles from town. Open dawn to dusk. $ for parking. Free admission.

Taller than Niagara, Fish Creek Falls impresses visitors—more than 250,000 of them each year. It's an easy, scenic ⅓-mile walk to the overlook. Or take the ¼-mile path down to the base of the falls. From here you can continue hiking 3 miles to Upper Fish Creek Falls. But remember, it's 3 miles back again!

The falls got its name because homesteaders around 1900 caught their winter's supply of fish here, using pitchforks, hooks, and gunnysacks.

Mountain Sports Kayak School (ages 6 and up)

800 South Lincoln Ave.; (970) 879-8794; www.mountainsportskayak.com. **Morning and afternoon sessions daily, weekend evening sessions. $$$$.**

This is the kind of experience that families fondly remember long after their vacation is over. Try kayaking together in a beautiful mountain setting. All equipment and kayaks are provided. The half-day "Never-Ever" class begins on shore, moves to ponds, and closes with a paddle down a gentle stretch of the Yampa River. Owner Barry Smith is an expert at instilling confidence as he teaches. Half-day to five-day intermediate and advanced classes also are available. If you have 3- to 5-year-olds, they ride in the kayak with you. Children 9 and older can take the lesson without you, but you don't want to miss this.

Steamboat Lake State Park (all ages)

1475 South Lincoln Ave. (north of Steamboat Springs, 26 miles on County Road 129); (970) 879-3922; camping reservations can be make online; http://parks.state.co.us/parks/steam boatlake. **Open year-round. $ per car.**

Sunset magazine includes the campgrounds here on their list of "The West's Top Ten." With many sites near the shoreline and most shaded by aspen or lodgepole pine, it's no wonder. Summer reservations for campsites or cabins are strongly advised.

There's a sandy swim beach, not easy to find in Colorado. The park boasts premier fishing—anglers catch rainbow and cutthroat trout year-round. Water-skiers and boaters also enjoy the reservoir and full-service marina. Picnic areas are located throughout the park. In the winter activities change to ice fishing and cross-country skiing. With more than 100 miles of trails nearby, snowmobiling attracts many enthusiasts.

On Mt. Werner—Summer Season

Silver Bullet Gondola (all ages)

(970) 871-5252; www.steamboat.com. **Open daily mid-June through Labor Day, 10 a.m. to 4 p.m.; early June through Sept, open weekends only; reopens for winter season the Wed before Thanksgiving. $$–$$$, one free child under age 5 with each paying adult.**

Enjoy spectacular scenery as the eight-passenger gondola carries your family up to Thunderhead Peak, elevation 9,080 feet. Get a snack or a meal and spend some time shopping for souvenirs at the Top Shop. Soak up some rays while you take in the view from the sundeck. You can hike back to the base, rent a mountain bike and glide down, or catch the gondola for the return trip.

Hiking (all ages)

More than 50 miles of trails on Mt. Werner offer something just right for everyone. Here are two good routes for families, both from the top of Thunderhead.

Vista Nature Trail. This 1-mile trail starts and ends at Thunderhead. Along the way you'll find signs about wildlife and native vegetation. The scenery is fantastic, and there are picnic areas along the route. Guided nature walks are scheduled here throughout the summer.

Thunderhead Hiking Trail. This 3-mile route takes you back down to the base on roads and trails. Allow one and a half hours hiking time, and be sure you all have water bottles and proper shoes. Remember that weather changes rapidly in the Colorado mountains, so bring a jacket.

Kids' Vacation Center (ages 3 to 12)

(970) 879-0740 or (877) 237-2628. Open early June through the first weekend in Sept, Mon through Fri 9 a.m. to 4 p.m. Reservations are a must. $$$$.

Need a little break from one another? Give your kids a chance to meet new friends and enjoy some Steamboat activities without you. Short hikes, outdoor games, arts and crafts, picnics, and water activities engage 3- and 4-year-olds. Older campers enjoy those activities plus mountain biking, kayaking, swimming, scavenger hunts, and tennis. Single- or multiple-day rates are available. This is a very popular program with Steamboat residents and visitors. Necessities include sunscreen, a swimsuit and towel, and a raincoat.

Gondola Square Adventure Zone (age 3 and up)

(970) 879-0740; www.steamboat.com. Open early June through first weekend in Sept, Mon through Sat 10 a.m. to 4 p.m.; Sun 9:30 a.m. to 4 p.m. $$$$.

Be sure to check out the thrills and adventures located at the base of the ski area in Gondola Square. The kids will love the variety of activities, such as the Children's Mini-Bounce, Human Gyro, Shoot 'n' Shower, Mechanical Bull, Ropes Course, East Face Climbing Wall, and Sling Shot Bungee Jump. Age and size restrictions are required for some activities.

Mountain Biking

(970) 879-0880. Open daily mid-June through Labor Day, 10 a.m. to 3:45 p.m. Hours may vary so call first. $$–$$$$.

Bikes are permitted on the gondola, so you can ride downhill all day. Fifty miles of trails challenge all levels with varying elevation changes. Bring your own bike and helmet, or rent at the base or top of the gondola. Helmets are required on the mountain—they're included with rentals.

An easier option for casual riders is the Yampa River Core Trail, a 4-mile paved path along the river that connects the ski area with town. Stop along the way to watch tubers and kayakers or visit the Yampa River Botanic Park.

On Mt. Werner—Winter Season

Ski Program for Kids

Steamboat offers a full range of child care, lessons, and facilities for kids 6 months to 18 years; $$$$. Reservations are required for all programs; (800) 299-5017. Here are a couple of standouts:

Buckaroos. All ski resorts offer child care, but not many offer ski lessons for 2-year-olds! Buckaroos combines all-day or half-day child care with a one-hour private ski clinic for children ages 2½ years old through kindergarten.

Kids' Ski Facilities. Rough Rider Basin is a kids-only zone—adults are not allowed unless they're with a child. This Wild West area with tepees, log cabin playhouse, mine shaft, and picnic spot has its own lift. Beehive Terrain Park is a kids-only zone for pint-size snowboarders. Kids-only beginner lifts include three magic-carpet conveyor lifts.

Billy Kidd Performance Center (ages 6 and up)

(800) 299-5017. One- and three-day programs. $$$$.

Top-notch coaches provide personalized, intensive clinics that challenge youngsters ages 6 to 12 with moguls and racing; includes video analysis.

Snow Tubing (ages 5 and up)

Howelsen Hill in downtown Steamboat Springs. On Tues, Wed, Fri, and Sat: 1:30 p.m., 2:30 p.m., 3:30 p.m., 4:30 p.m., 5:30 p.m., 6:30 p.m., 7:30 p.m., and 8:30 p.m. Tubing sessions are one hour in length. $$.

If you're at least 36 inches tall, you are eligible to participate in this old-fashioned winter fun.

Where to Eat

Giovanni's Ristorante, 127 11th St.; (970) 879-4141; www.giovanni's-steamboat.com. Open Wed through Sat at 5:30 p.m. for dinner. Linguine, scampi, veal piccata—Giovanni's serves fine Italian cuisine, as well as steak and seafood. $$

The Shack Cafe, 740 Lincoln Ave.; (970) 879-9975. Open daily for breakfast and lunch until 2 p.m. Wait in line along with the locals for hearty food in a casual log cabin atmosphere. Breakfast is served all day. Enjoy homemade soups and fresh-baked pies. $

Steamboat Yacht Club, 811 Yampa St.; (970) 879-4774. Open daily for lunch and dinner Dec through Sept. In the summer dine outside on the large deck overlooking the river. Your children will be entertained watching the tubers slide by. On winter evenings the dining room has a great view of ski jumpers at Howelsen Hill. The menu includes, soups, salads, sandwiches, meat entrées and seafood dishes—all delicious. This is one of those places where other diners may be celebrating very special occasions so, perhaps, talking about table manners before you arrive may be in order. If not needed, then it will be an excellent opportunity to show off (and later compliment) your children's superb social behavior. $–$$$

Winona's, 617 Lincoln Ave.; (970) 879-2483. Open daily for breakfast; lunch Mon through Sat. Here you'll find healthful and delicious food at a reasonable price. Peruse the bakery case of homemade treats. The cinnamon rolls are hard to ignore, and the cheerful atmosphere is just right for families. There are outdoor tables, too. $

Where to Stay

Best Western Ptarmigan Inn, 2304 Apres Ski Way; (970) 879-1730; www.steamboat-lodging.com. Located at the base of Mt. Werner. Complimentary ski storage, outdoor heated swimming pool, hot tub, and sauna. The Inn offers in-room refrigerators, cable TV, VCRs, and a slopeside restaurant. Roll-away beds available if requested when reservations are made. Small additional charge. Facilities for those with special needs are available. $$–$$$

Rabbit Ears Motel, 201 Lincoln Ave.; (970) 879-1150 or (800) 828-7702; www.rabbitears motel.com. You won't miss their neon sign! Owned and operated by the same family since 1959, this sixty-five-room motel offers lots of conveniences without a fancy price tag. Location, location, location—on the river, walking distance to town, directly across from the hot springs pool, next to the park. The **free** city bus stops right outside the door. Rooms vary in size and amenities, but most have microwaves and refrigerators. Discount passes to the pool and water slide and **free** continental breakfast make Rabbit Ears a real find. $$

Steamboat Grand Resort Hotel and Conference Center, 2300 Mt. Werner Circle; (970) 871- 5531 or (877) 269-2628; www .steamboatgrand.com. This grand hotel's use of native stone and natural woods, indoor streams, and two-story-high fireplaces creates a comfortable western-themed mountain lodge ambience. Located at the base of the ski mountain, it features beautifully appointed studios and one-, two-, and three-bedroom units; a state-of-the-art fitness center; an outdoor year-round heated swimming pool; and an on-site child care center. This resort was recently awarded the AAA Four Diamond Designation. $$$–$$$$

For More Information

Steamboat Springs Chamber Resort Association, 125 Anglers Dr.; (970) 879-0880; www.steamboatchamber.com or www .steamboatsummer.com.

Georgetown

Located 50 miles west of Denver on I-70, historic Georgetown is surrounded by the Arapahoe National Forest and spectacular mountain peaks. This small mountain town (population 900) is home to more than 200 Victorian structures that date back to the late 1800s and early 1900s.

You will find two parks in town with picnic tables and playground equipment. A marked nature trail (easy climb) leads from Georgetown Lake toward the Saxon Mine, with marvelous views of the valley. Boutiques, art galleries, historical museums, antiques shops, and cafes crowd the narrow streets.

"Tis the Season **to Be Jolly . . ."**

During the first two full weekends in Dec, Georgetown welcomes the Christmas season with its annual Christmas Market, an old-fashioned outdoor celebration in the European tradition.

At noon each day of the fest, a Swedish Santa Lucia processional, led by the Queen of Lights followed by local children, winds its way through the village streets. Craft and food booths provide Christmas gift ideas, strolling carolers add to the merriment, and an Old Country-style St. Nicholas hands out candies to the children. When you get chilled through and through, head for the bonfire, buy a bag of fresh-roasted chestnuts, and sip a cup of hot cider, guaranteed to warm your heart as well as your tummy. For more information call (303) 569-2840 or (800) 472-8230. **Free** admission.

Georgetown Loop Railroad (all ages)
Devil's Gate Station; (888) 456-6777; www.georgetownlooprr.com. Open daily late May through mid-Oct. $$$–$$$$.

It's difficult to say who loves trains more, children or grown-ups. It doesn't really matter—everyone aboard the Georgetown Loop Railroad can be a kid, at least for a day.

Powered by a steam, or sometimes diesel, locomotive, the excursion train huffs and puffs between the towns of Georgetown and Silver Plume, over the reconstructed, 95-foot-high Devil's Gate Bridge, and through spectacular vistas of forests and mountaintops. Inquire about special excursions such as the 4th of July Fireworks Train, the Dinner Train, the Pumpkin Festival Trains, and the Santa's Polar Adventure Trains.

Lebanon Silver Mine Tour (all ages)
Devil's Gate Station; (888) 456-6777. Open daily late May until early Sept. $. (This cost is for the tour. There is an additional charge for the train transportation to and from the mine.)

Accessible only via the Georgetown Loop Railroad, the abandoned Lebanon Silver Mine provides tours guided by members of the Georgetown Historical Society. You and your family will see the blacksmith shop, the tool shed, the manager's office, and the mine itself. This is a most enjoyable excursion and a memory-maker for kids.

Where to Eat

The Happy Cooker, 412 6th St.; (303) 569-3166. This casual cafe is an old standby in Georgetown, a favorite of locals and visitors in-the-know. They serve breakfast favorites such as quiches and Belgian waffles, and for lunch you might try their homemade soups and hot-from-the-oven breads.

During the summer months you can dine on the patio. $

For More Information

Gateway Visitor Center, 1491 Argentine St., Georgetown, CO 80444; (303) 569-2405; www.town.georgetown.co.us.

Summit County

Summit County's four major ski areas—Arapahoe Basin, Breckenridge, Copper Mountain, and Keystone—attract visitors from far and wide. Each area offers excellent family experiences year-round. During the summer season Lake Dillon provides a water playground.

To give you some idea of the scenery, the county's lowest town sits at 9,000 feet. Take advantage of Summit County's paved bike path system, more than 400 miles of off-road, paved trails connecting each town and resort.

Dillon

Located 26 miles west of Georgetown, just off I-70 on US 6.

Dillon Reservoir (all ages)

The main reason folks come to the tiny community of Dillon is to enjoy the outdoors. Here they can picnic beside the lake; rent a boat and fish for rainbow, cutthroat, and brook trout and kokanee salmon; and walk or ride the bike path that runs along the shoreline.

Frisco

Once a favorite camp of Ute Indians due to the large population of bison, elk, and deer and later a booming silver- and gold-mining community, the small town of Frisco is

Dillon **Down Under**

Dillon is quite a survivor. The original town was located at the bottom of the current Lake Dillon. This idyllic spot was at the confluence of three rivers, but in 1960 construction began on Dillon Dam and the entire town was forced to move. All the residents and some original buildings were relocated, including several restaurants that are still in business today.

perfectly located for an abundance of outdoor activities. The town is accessible from I-70 and lies west of Dillon.

Frisco Nordic Center (all ages)

18454 Highway 9, less than a mile south of Frisco on east side of CO 9; (970) 668-0866. $$–$$$.

During winter the Frisco Nordic Center provides cross-country ski rentals for adults and children and sleds for kids who would rather slide than glide. Forty kilometers of beginner, intermediate, and advanced trails are groomed daily, and 20 kilometers of packed snowshoe trails await. Group lessons are available in both cross-country skiing and snowshoeing.

Two Below Zero (all ages)

Rides leave from the Frisco Nordic Center; (970) 453-1520 or (800) 571-6853; www.dinner sleighrides.com. Open every day. They offer a winter dinner sleighride and a summer chuck wagon dinner and wild west show. Phone them or visit their Web site for dates and times. The "Cocoa Ride" begins at 5 p.m., and the "Dinner Ride" begins at 6:30 p.m. It is mandatory that participants arrive at least thirty minutes before departure time for check-in. Departures are always on time. Sleigh space is limited, so reservations are necessary. $$–$$$$.

Two Below Zero is a family-owned and -operated business providing dinner rides on mule-drawn sleighs. Three fourteen-passenger, hand-crafted red oak sleighs pulled by pairs of winsome mules (either, Bell and Bonnie, Mathew and Roy, Judy and Jane, or Agnes and Ada) will take you for a twenty-minute ride to a warm and comfortable dining tent with a wooden floor and two heating stoves. You will be served top sirloin steak and marinated chicken cooked on a gas grill and baked potato, French bread, fresh vegetables, and homemade dessert. Following dinner you will be entertained with live music.

Extra warm hats, gloves, scarves, shoes, and coats are a must for the ride to and from the camp during winter.

For More Information

Summit County Chamber of Commerce, P. O. Box 5450, Frisco, CO 80443; www.sum mitchamber.org.

Summit County Chamber of Commerce Information Center, (970) 468-5780 or (800) 530-3099.

Breckenridge

Breckenridge is 85 miles west of Denver, south from Frisco on CO 9. This pretty little mountain town began as a mining camp in 1859. Many a boom and bust followed until the early 1940s when, during World War II, the search for gold ceased and the town's

International Snow-Sculpture
Championships

This event attracts competitors from all over the world. Past participants have included artisans from China, Switzerland, Russia, Poland, Canada, England, Morocco, France, and, of course, the United States. Using only hand tools, four-person teams begin with identical twenty-ton blocks of tightly packed snow. After five days, including two evenings working until midnight and one around-the-clock stint, the snow sculptors will have transformed the mountain community into a glorious outdoor art gallery with works worthy of the best of museums (if only they wouldn't melt!).

Highly qualified artists, the likes of world-renowned Loveland, Colorado, sculptor George Lundeen—whose 16-foot bronze statue of aviation pioneer Elrey Jeppesen stands in the Jeppesen Terminal at Denver International Airport—serve as judges. Festivities take place in late Jan. Call (970) 453-6018 for exact dates and more details. **Free.**

population dwindled. Then in the 1960s "white gold" replaced the yellow kind, and the Breckenridge Ski Resort brought new life to the community.

Breckenridge is a picture-postcard-perfect Victorian-style village with more than 120 restored structures listed on the National Register of Historic Places. Six blocks of shops, boutiques, and restaurants adorn Main Street, while year-round activities for families vie for your attention.

In summer you can go white-water rafting, stream and lake fishing, hiking, horseback riding, mountain biking, and four-wheeling. You might try sledding on the Superslide or attempt to find your way out of the delightful Amaze'n Breckenridge labyrinth, Colorado's largest human maze (much like the one in Grand Lake). Your family can ride the Superchair, a four-person chairlift that takes passengers to an elevation of 12,000 feet for hiking, mountain biking, or lunch at the Vista House Restaurant.

Wintertime in Breckenridge brings Alpine and Nordic skiing, snowshoeing, ice fishing, dogsledding, snowboarding, snowmobiling, and ice-skating on Maggie Pond.

On the Mountain

Breckenridge Ski Resort boasts four interconnected mountains with 139 downhill trails serviced by twenty-two lifts. The vertical drop varies from 1,277 to 3,398 feet, and the average snowfall is 255 inches; www.breckenridge.com.

Professional snowboarders rave about Breckenridge's terrain garden known for its air, hits, slides, and gigantic half-pipes. The resort has a Pipe Dragon for building and maintaining the two half-pipes that meet Olympic specifications.

Ullr **Fest**

The weeklong, riotous Ullr (pronounced "OOO-lur") Fest is an annual wild-and-woolly event in which amateurs compete beside world-class athletes in what is known locally as the "Ullympics." While festivities include such wacky events as snowshoe volleyball, this is also the opportunity to see freestyle skiing experts perform daring inverted aerials and observe ballet and mogul disciplines. The zany, outrageous parade; the ice-skating party; and the kids' concert are sure to please. All this activity takes place in honor of Ullr, Norse god of winter. Festivities take place in Jan. Call (970) 453-6018 for more information. **Free.**

The children's ski school is located at both Peak 8 and Peak 9 Village Base areas. Alpine skiing lessons are available for those ages 3 and up, and snowboard instruction begins at age 6.

The Breckenridge Outdoor Education Center
524 Wellington Rd.; P.O. Box 697, Breckenridge, CO 80424; (970) 453-6422; www.boec.org.

This center provides daily half-day or full-day ski instruction for children and adults with disabilities or serious illnesses. Inquire about cost.

Where to Eat

Fatty's Pizzeria, 106 South Ridge St.; (970) 453-9802. Open daily for lunch and dinner. Fans of Fatty's say this casual pizza place puts out the best pizza pie in town. They also have daily specials such as pasta or Mexican dishes. $–$$

Where to Stay

Accommodations at Breckenridge range from bed-and-breakfasts to posh resort lodging.

Your best bet is to call the **Breckenridge Resort Chamber's Central Reservations System,** (970) 453-2918 or (888) 251-2417.

For More Information

Breckenridge Resort Chamber, 311 South Ridge St., P.O. Box 1909, Breckenridge, CO 80424; (970) 453-2913; www.gobreck .com.

Breckenridge Welcome Center, 203 South Main St., Breckenridge, CO 80424.

Fairplay

Gold was discovered in this area in 1859, and what is now the small town of Fairplay, with only about 450 year-round residents, was then a wild-and-woolly mining camp. Located south of Breckenridge, at the juncture of US 285 and CO 9, the hamlet boasts a few artisan shops, two historic hotels that have seen better days, a picturesque old church, and a wonderful outdoor museum.

South Park City Museum

Follow the signs from the center of town; (719) 836-2387; www.southparkcity.org. Open daily 9 a.m. to 7 p.m., Memorial Day through Labor Day; 9 a.m. to 5 p.m. Labor Day to mid-Oct. $, children 5 and younger **free.**

A visit to Fairplay's South Park City Museum reveals 19th-century life in a Colorado mining town. Seven structures stand on their original sites, and twenty-seven other weather-worn buildings that would have decayed and ultimately disappeared have been restored and moved to the museum location from abandoned mining camps and area ghost towns. Now filled to the rafters with more than 60,000 artifacts, the vintage structures represent life as it was between 1860 and 1900.

Your kids will delight in dashing from doorway to doorway to see the one-room schoolhouse; the general store filled with old-time canned goods, hardware, and clothing; and the stagecoach and wagon barn and livery. They may even appreciate their own dentist a little more after viewing the crude instruments used by the dentists of days long past. The museum has a railroad station and an old narrow-gauge train engine with a bell kids can clang.

Como

The hamlet of Como lies a few miles northeast of Fairplay, just off US 285. Once a major railroad terminus, the area is steeped in rail and mining history.

Wilderness on Wheels Foundation

On US 285 along Kenosha Creek, 60 miles southwest of Denver, 15 miles west of Bailey; (303) 403-1110; www.wildernessonwheels.org. Open mid-Apr to mid-Oct, weather permitting. **Free.** Donations appreciated.

The Wilderness on Wheels Foundation, with volunteer help and donated materials, has built a wonderful wilderness facility. A little more than 1 mile of boardwalk on twenty acres of land offers wheelchair access to campsites and stocked fishing ponds. In addition to the ponds, Kenosha Creek provides anglers with rainbow and brook trout. This facility also works well for families with small children. There's easy walking for little tykes and the boardwalk is stroller friendly, so you can go for a family hike without packing your baby on your back.

Reservations are suggested for the campsites. Disabled campers are welcome to bring along their able-bodied friends and relatives.

Helpful **Hints**

In resort and mountain towns, pick up **free** local papers, such as *Steamboat Today* or *Vail Trail*, for daily and weekly information on what to see and where to eat. You might even find discount coupons.

Leadville

From I-70 turn south on CO 91 at Copper Mountain; continue 24 miles to Leadville; www
.leadville.com.

Matchless Mine (ages 5 and up)

1¼ miles east of Harrison Avenue on East 7th St.; (719) 486-1229. Open daily Apr through
late Sept, 9 a.m. to 5 p.m. $, children 6 and younger free.

Leadville's history is nearly as rich as the fortunes extracted from its gold, silver, and lead
mines during the 1800s. Horace Tabor and his wife, Augusta, dry goods merchants who
became millionaires through mining investments, and "Baby Doe" Tabor, for whom Horace divorced Augusta, thus creating a national scandal, are among the most colorful of
Leadville's former residents.

On his deathbed Horace bade Baby Doe never to sell or leave his Matchless Mine.
Thirty years later, penniless but faithful to her promise, she was found in the mine's ram-
shackle cabin, frozen to death. Today visitors can visit Baby Doe's cabin and the exterior
of the mine.

Tabor Opera House (ages 5 and up)

308 Harrison Ave.; (719) 486-8409; www.taboroperahouse.net. Open daily 10 a.m. to 5
p.m., Memorial Day through Labor Day. Inquire about occasional stage performances.
Tours, $; performances, $$–$$$.

You won't want to miss a tour of Leadville's historic Tabor Opera House. Built for Horace
Tabor in 1879, it is now a museum extraordinaire. Lillian Russell, Florenz Ziegfeld's Mam-
selle Napoleon, and Sousa's Marine Band played to packed audiences during the opera
house's prime. Here you will see the original cashier's cage, its counter worn from all
the silver dollars that passed over its surface, and the mint-condition, signed and framed
photographs of well-known actors and actresses that line the walls. You will be allowed
backstage and on the stage itself to gaze upon Horace and Baby Doe's private box seat
and the trapdoor used by Houdini. Then follow your guide down the dusty steps to the

Unsinkable Molly

One of Leadville's famous former residents was the "Unsinkable Molly
Brown." Molly married mine superintendent James Brown, who owned a one-
eighth interest in a mine that eventually made the couple extremely wealthy.
They then moved to Denver, where Molly tried unsuccessfully to fit into high
society. Her acts of heroism while a passenger on the ill-fated *Titanic*, how-
ever, won her international recognition, ultimately forcing the city's hoity-
toity crowd to include her in their social circle.

lower-level dressing rooms, still endowed with antique furniture, actors' trunks, and stage props.

The survival of the Tabor Opera House is solely due to Florence Hollister and her daughter, Evelyn Furman, who in 1955 pooled their life savings and rescued this irreplaceable piece of history from demolition. Evelyn Furman continues to cherish the old building and to share it with guests.

National Mining Hall of Fame & Museum (ages 4 and up)

120 West 9th St.; (719) 486-1229; www.leadville.com/miningmuseum. Open daily 9 a.m. to 5 p.m., May through Oct; 11 a.m. to 4 p.m., Nov through Apr. $, children 6 and younger **free.**

To discover the romance and excitement of the glory days of mining, stop in at this museum, located in an expanded ca. 1896 schoolhouse. Here you will see twenty-two miniature dioramas meticulously created by artist Hank Gentsch, the "Wheelchair Woodcarver." The Crystal Room showcases outstanding mineral specimens on loan from the Smithsonian Institute in Washington, D.C. The Gold Rush Room contains gold specimens, photographs, artifacts, and documents relating to the nation's most prominent gold rushes, from Alaska to the Carolinas. Kids delight in the simulated underground mine.

Leadville, Colorado & Southern Railroad (all ages)

326 East 7th St.; (719) 486-3936 or (866) 386-3936; www.leadville-train.com. Operates daily Memorial Day through Sept. Departures are always dependent on weather conditions. Always safest to phone for exact departure times. $$$$.

You won't find a more scenic railroad excursion than that aboard this train. In the shadow of spectacular Mt. Massive, the second-highest peak in Colorado at 14,421 feet, you will embark on a memorable two-and-a-half-hour journey, departing from the historic redbrick depot built in 1893. You will travel through aspen groves and pine and spruce forests, follow the headwaters of the Arkansas River, and stop at the French Gulch water tower for photos and a stretch.

Where to Stay

Historic Delaware Hotel, 700 Harrison Ave.; (719) 486-1418 or (800) 748-2004; www .delawarehotel.com. There are several motels on the edge of town, but for location and historical ambience, plan to spend the night at this more-than-a-century-old, redbrick masterpiece with an elegant Victorian lobby and thirty-six guest rooms, including four two-bedroom suites. All have private baths and cable TV. Breakfast included in room rate. $–$$$

For More Information

Greater Leadville Area Chamber of Commerce, 809 Harrison Ave., Leadville, CO 80461; (719) 486-3900 or (888) 532-3845; www.leadvilleusa.com.

Vail

A Tyrolean-inspired ski resort that's grown and grown and grown—that's Vail. In its nearly forty-year history, both town and ski amenities have become internationally known. Host to World Alpine Ski Championships, it was also part-time home to President Gerald Ford. A mecca for the rich and famous, Vail also attracts Front Range residents with world-class skiing and snowboarding. Summer activities draw loyal fans from around the globe.

Colorado Ski and Snowboard Museum and Hall of Fame

(ages 6 and up)

231 South Frontage Rd., in the Vail Village Transportation Center; (970) 476-1876; www .skimuseum.net. Open daily 10 a.m. to 6 p.m. Springtime hours (Apr and May) 10 a.m. to 5 p.m. Free.

Filled with memorabilia spanning 130 years of Colorado ski history, this museum includes among its treasures the largest collection of mementos from the famous Tenth Mountain

New in **Town**

Getting around Vail can be intimidating, especially if you have only a short time to stay. Here are a few hints to help you get oriented.

Parking
Many areas in the village are pedestrian only. Drive directly to a parking garage, east at Vail Transportation Center or west at Lionshead Parking Structure. There is a fee during the winter, $$$ per day, but in the summer it's **free.**

Information
Stop at one of the visitor centers near the parking structures. They have maps and lots of literature. If you're in the area for a few days, be sure to get the weekly calendar of events. **Free.**

Another choice is the Activities Desk operated by Vail Associates, also a **free** service. You'll find their office in Lionshead.

The Village
From the visitor center see Vail on foot. Walk through the village and follow the path along the creek to Lionshead, or start at Lionshead and walk east. Explore shops and eateries along the way.

Transportation
The City of Vail operates a **free** continuous shuttle bus through the village. Hop on when you've had all the walking you can handle.

Division, which trained alpine troops at nearby Camp Hale for European combat during World War II. The Hall of Fame recognizes those individuals who have contributed significantly to the sport of skiing and snowboarding.

Gondola and Chairlift Rides

The following days and times vary according to weather conditions. Please phone the Vail Activity Desk at (800) 525-2257 for current information before your departure. Single-ride or all-day passes are available for both lifts. $$$.

Eagle Bahn Gondola (all ages)

At Lionshead, kids ride free all summer (a maximum of 3 kids per paying adult). June 25 through Aug 30, open daily 10 a.m. to 4 p.m., except Thurs through Sat when they stay open later until 9 p.m. Free Scenic Twilight Rides after 4 p.m. Call the mountain Information Center at (970) 754-8245 for a list of additional mountain activities.

Enjoy an eagle-eye view of the Vail Valley and surrounding wilderness areas. At the top you'll find a restaurant, an outdoor eating area, bike rentals, and hiking trails. Walk the short path to the overlook. The vista makes a perfect backdrop for your Christmas card photo.

Vista Bahn Chairlift

At Vail Village. Open daily late June through Labor Day, 10 a.m. to 4 p.m.

This high-speed, four-person chairlift whisks you to mid-Vail and back. Other choices? Take a hiking trail that connects to the gondola or hike down to the village.

Hiking (all ages)

Set off on your own or join a group—finding a great hike for your family won't be difficult.

Hiking Maps. Pick up a hiking/biking map at the visitor center. Besides routes it gives descriptions of hiking trails on Vail Mountain and at Beaver Creek. Take an easy green trail (fifteen to thirty minutes) or a blue intermediate (one-and-a-half to three hours). Choose a designated hiking trail (closed to mountain bikes) rather than a multiuse trail.

Vail Nature Center Hikes

601 Vail Valley Dr.; (970) 479-2291. Open May through Sept; schedule varies. $.

Interpretive walks are scheduled daily and on several evenings. How about a Morning Bird Walk or Wildflower Walk?

Mountain Biking

Equipment for beginners, intermediates, and experts in adult and child sizes are available at rental shops throughout Vail Village and at the top of Eagle Bahn gondola.

On Vail Mountain. Mountain biking is not just for expert riders. Several trails are easy rides on gravel roads. For routes and descriptions pick up a map of Vail Mountain Biking Trails at the visitor center. Take bikes up the mountain on the gondola; $$$$, all-day pass.

Gore Trail. Paved trails weave throughout Vail Village, following Gore Creek east to the Alpine Garden, amphitheater, playground, Tennis Center, and Nature Center. Continue on this trail, which parallels I-70 for 20 miles to Copper Mountain and Frisco in Summit County. There you can connect to Breckenridge.

Betty Ford Alpine Garden

In Ford Park west of the amphitheater. Open spring through fall, dawn to dusk. Free.

For a respite from active days, stroll through this beautiful formal alpine garden, the highest botanical development in the nation. You'll all appreciate the colorful displays, which include more than 2,000 varieties of flora. If the kids tire of the beauty before you do, there's a great playground just up the hill.

Ford Amphitheater (all ages)

In Ford Park; (970) 476-2918. Free.

The Bud Light Summer Nights Series offers free weekly concerts featuring internationally renowned classical music and dance groups throughout the summer. There is some covered seating and plenty of lawn to spread out a blanket and enjoy a picnic. Kids love to dance to the music and scramble on the large rocks scattered throughout the grass.

Rainy-Day **Blues**

On a rainy day you might be happy curling up with a book in the condo, but that won't keep the kids content for long. Here are a few other ideas.

Indoor Climbing Wall

Vail Athletic Club (970-476-7960; www.vailathleticclub.com) has daily climbing programs for ages 5 to 99! Learn the ropes from experienced instructors. All equipment is provided.

Indoor Ice-Skating

Call Dobson Ice Arena (970-479-2271) for public skating hours. Hockey practice, clinics, and competitions also occur here.

Indoor Swimming

Avon Recreation Center (10 miles west of Vail; 970-748-4060), with three pools and a Jacuzzi, will entertain your whole family. Kids love the water slides, fountains, and lazy river.

Arrowhead

As the smallest, least resortlike area in the valley, Arrowhead, near Edwards, is a wonderful choice for families new to skiing. The lessons at Arrowhead are the same as those you will get at Vail and Beaver Creek. The runs are just right for parents who want to ski together with young children. If you decide you want more of a challenge, ski from Arrowhead to Beaver Creek. Your lift tickets are good there, too. One more plus: Parking is free at Arrowhead.

Vail Nature Center (all ages)
601 Vail Valley Dr.; (970) 479-2291. Open daily Memorial Day through Labor Day. $.

A short trail along Gore Creek leads to an interpretive center/natural history museum. Informal hands-on displays teach about local plants and animals. The center offers a variety of programs for families, such as morning bird walks, wildflower walks, star gazing, and beaver pond tours. Children age 4 to 12 sign up for a day camp designed to familiarize them with the area's alpine environment. Older children can participate in art, photography, and hiking programs. For Vail winter activities, Vail Resorts' Web site offers up-to-date snow conditions, information on all programs, and "Cool Deals"—last-minute specials on lodging and other promotions: www.snow.com.

Golden Peak Nursery Child Care (age 2 months to 6 years old)
(970) 754-3285. Open daily 8 a.m. to 4:30 p.m. throughout winter ski season. Separate playrooms for infants (age 2 to 15 months), toddlers (16 to 29 months, and pre-schoolers (30 months to 6 years). Reservations required.

Kids' Mountain Adventure Zones
Free with lift ticket.

Ski-through attractions in several locations on the mountain that delight kids with bumps, jumps, and tunnels. Thunder Cat Cave, Chaos Canyon, and Dragon's Breath Mine—some are animated and educational; all are fun.

Adventure Ridge
On Vail Mountain at the top of Eagle Bahn gondola; some activities open at noon, others later in the afternoon. (970) 754-8245. Free gondola access to Adventure Ridge for non-skiers after 2 p.m. Activity fees, $$–$$$.

Vail's winter playground is a family delight. Start with the eight-lane tubing hill, complete with tow rope. Find out about sled dogging (a fast slide down the mountain on special footwear) and give it a try. Take a guided snow-bike tour (for kids age 14 and up). And encourage your youngsters to experience snowshoeing, a ride on a kids snowmobile, and being nearly weightless on a bungee trampoline. All this activity is bound to bring on the hungries. Not to worry. There are also five restaurants.

Hot Winter Nights

On Golden Peak. Weekly during ski season; check schedule at visitor center. Free.

A synchronized skiing demonstration choreographed to music lights up the night. The show ends with a spectacular fireworks display.

Where to Eat

Blizzard's Mountain Deli, 304 Hanson Ranch Rd.; (970) 476-1755. Known for their great sandwiches, this deli provides plenty of choices perfect for putting together a picnic for beside Gore Creek or up on the mountain. $

Blu's, 193 East Gore Creek (located in Vail Village); (970) 476-3113; www.blusrestaurant .com. Here you will find family dining and an eclectic menu with reasonable prices. $$

D.J. MacAdams, located in LionsHead Concert Hall Plaza; look for a tiny diner that's open 24 hours a day, Tues from 7 a.m. until Sun midnight. Locals will tell you they offer the "best breakfast deal in town." $–$$

Where to Stay

Sonnenalp Resort of Vail, 20 Vail Rd.; (970) 476-5656 or (866) 284-4411; www .sonnenalp.com. In the heart of Vail Village, this elegant yet comfortable resort can't be missed in summer when the window boxes overflow with blooms—they're award winners. Attention to detail applies to all facets of your stay at Sonnenalp. Rates include a full breakfast at Ludwigs restaurant. All-inclusive packages include coupons for KidVentures day-camp programs. There's

also an indoor/outdoor pool, a rarity in the area. $$$$

For More Information

For information on activities, lodging, and dining in Vail, there are two major resources:

Vail Valley Chamber & Tourism Bureau, 101 Fawcett Rd. Suite 240, Avon, CO 81620; (970) 476-1000; www.visitvailvalley.com.

Vail Activities Desk, (800) 525-2257; www .snow.com. Vail Associates provides **free** information on lodging, dining, and activities in the valley, including places not owned by the corporation. They describe themselves as a "concierge service to the whole valley." You are welcome to use their help even if you are not staying in Vail.

Vail Valley

Stretching for 15 miles west of Vail, known to locals as "Down Valley," the communities of Avon, Beaver Creek, and Edwards offer summer and winter activities geared to families. From the very commercial to totally natural, ultra expensive to **free,** it's all here.

AVON

Avon Recreation Center (all ages)

90 Lake St.; (970) 748-4060; www.avon.org. Open Mon through Fri 6 a.m. to 9 p.m.; Sat 8 a.m. to 9 p.m., and Sun noon to 7 p.m. $$.

A lap pool, slide pool, leisure pool, and whirlpool fit the bill for families. Kids will love the slide, sprays, fountains, and lazy river. Fitness and conditioning equipment are also available.

Nottingham Park

In Avon, west of the Recreation Center; (970) 748-4086; www.avon.org. Water activities open late May through Labor Day.

Kids are delighted by the amenities in this forty-eight-acre open-space park. They'll enjoy running off steam and playing at the playground if this is just a quick stop. But if you can stay longer, there are paddleboats and canoes, or you can rent a mountain bike (adult, child, and trailers) for a half hour or more. If you're not prepared for some croquet, volleyball, soccer, basketball, or in-line skating, equipment is for rent in the log cabin. Or, if you haven't attempted disc golf, give it a try on the nine-hole disc golf course. It's **free;** disc rental is $2. Keep this park in mind when you need an after-dinner activity. Winter at the lake brings ice-skaters, from twirling ballerinas to hockey players.

BEAVER CREEK

Self-described as sophisticated, Beaver Creek exudes resort atmosphere. Upscale lodging, dining, and shopping cluster at the base of the ski area. Among the ultraposh amenities, you'll find a few family-oriented treasures, and you may enjoy browsing a bit—looking is **free!**

Beaver Creek is a full-service ski area with ski school, child care, and rental facilities. It's owned and operated by Vail Associates.

To drive to Beaver Creek, you must first stop at the security gate at the base of the mountain to obtain a day pass. During ski season visitors must park in Avon and take a **free** shuttle.

Beaver Creek Children's Museum (all ages)

In Beaver Creek village; (970) 926-5855. Open late June through Labor Day, Wed through Sun 10 a.m. to 4 p.m. **Free.**

Just the spot for some indoor fun, the Children's Museum entertains kids with hands-on interactive exhibits. Fun at One, special events, and Friday workshops at 1 p.m. are **free,** but advance registration is required.

Beaver Creek Ice-Skating (ages 4 and up)

Outside in the center of the village; (970) 845-0438. Open daily year-round, weather permitting, 6 p.m. to 10 p.m. $$ for skating and rental.

This experience might go in your family record book—there are not many places where you can ice-skate outside in the summertime! It's also fun in the winter.

Five Senses Trail (all ages)

Wander at your own pace along this 1½-mile self-guided trail beginning at Beaver Creek Chapel and ending at Flood's Ponds. **Free.**

Where to Eat

There are hundreds of restaurants, delis, markets, and snack stops in the Vail Valley. Those in Vail and Beaver Creek tend to be quite pricey—okay for that special meal but cost-prohibitive for three meals a day. Also, crowded restaurants with leisurely paced dining can be one frustration too many for worn-out youngsters. To save both time and dollars, consider arranging lodging that includes some kitchen facilities. And remember, there's always takeout.

Here are a couple of suggestions away from the main resort areas in the small town of Edwards, fifteen minutes west of Vail.

Fiesta's, in Edwards Plaza; (970) 926-2121. Open daily for lunch and dinner; also open for weekend breakfast. The Marquez sisters share their family secrets here—their great-grandparents' recipes from New Mexico. Fiesta's continually earns the Best Mexican Food award from Vail Valley residents, so count on a crowd. $–$$

Markos, in Edwards Plaza; (970) 926-7003. Open daily for lunch and dinner. Tasty Italian food in a relaxed atmosphere makes Markos appealing. Choose from grinders to made-to-order Fettuccine Royale. And there's always pizza. $–$$$

For More Information

Beaver Creek Information Center, (970) 754-4636; www.beavercreek.com.

Vail Valley Chamber & Tourism Bureau, 101 Fawcett Rd., Suite 240, Avon, CO 81620; (970) 476-1000; www.visitvailvalley.com.

Glenwood Springs

Glenwood Springs was fated to become a popular destination for travelers. Drawn to the mineral-rich springs, the Ute Indians were the first to come to the area. Considering the springs to be sacred, they took to the waters for spiritual cleansing and physical healing. When white settlers came, the Ute moved on, and soon weary miners were soaking away their aches and pains in the warm revitalizing waters. The word spread quickly, bringing notables such as Presidents Theodore Roosevelt and William Taft, followed by members of high society.

Glenwood Springs is situated at the confluence of the Colorado and Roaring Fork Rivers, thus creating excellent rafting, kayaking, and canoeing. Diverse river conditions

allow adventurers to float peacefully past scenic vistas or shoot white-water rapids with names like "Man-eater" and "Panic Alley."

Glenwood Springs Hot Springs Pool (all ages)

415 East 6th St.; (970) 945-6571 or (800) 537-7946; www.hotspringspool.com. Open daily, 7:30 a.m. to 10 p.m. during summer, 9 a.m. to 10 p.m. during winter. All-day pass to pool, $$; water slide, $–$$.

With water kept at a comfortable 90 degrees, the Glenwood Springs Hot Springs Pool is the largest outdoor hot springs swimming pool in the world. Measuring 405 feet long and 100 feet wide, it contains 1,071,000 gallons of constantly filtered water. An adjacent 100-foot therapy pool is kept at 104 degrees. The lap lanes, diving boards, and especially the water slide appeal to all ages.

If you visit in winter, brave the run from the dressing rooms to the pool, hop in, and hope for a snowstorm. Could anything be more invigorating than to soak in the toasty water while watching feathery snowflakes sifting down from the sky?

The complex features parklike grounds, a full-service restaurant, a snack pavilion, swimsuit and towel rentals, lockers, showers, a health and fitness center, and minigolf.

Glenwood Caverns Adventure Park (ages 6 and up)

51000 Two Rivers Plaza Rd.; (970) 945-4228 or (800) 530-1635; www.glenwoodcaverns.com. Open daily throughout the year, weather permitting, but days and hours may vary due to inclement weather conditions. Call ahead for dates and times, and for cave tour times and reservations. (Reservations for cave tours are not required but are highly recommended.) Children age 3 and younger are free when accompanied by an adult. $$–$$$$.

This Adventure Park just keeps getting better and better as new attractions are added. It's the kind of place you want to return to over and over again in order to participate in the activities you liked best the last time you were here and to try out the latest additions.

Whimsically called the Fairy Caves, these caverns are surrounded by mystery. No one seems to know exactly who discovered them or when they were first found.

Formed in limestone deposited approximately 325 million years ago, the caves are located on top of Iron Mountain, just north of Glenwood Springs. The property on which

Seeking Doc **Holliday**

Both Wyatt Earp and Doc Holliday eventually made their way to Glenwood Springs, where Holliday hoped that the healing waters of the mineral springs would eradicate his advanced tuberculosis. A short hike from the Glenwood Springs Chamber of Commerce office, at Grand Avenue and 11th Street, takes the curious to Linwood Cemetery and Holliday's gravestone, which reads simply, HE DIED IN BED; 1852–1887.

they dwell was homesteaded in the 1800s by the C. W. Darrow family, who opened the caves for public tours around 1886. A pathway providing access via horseback, horse and carriage, or foot was formed; electric lights were installed; and a tunnel was blasted through the rock to expose a spectacular view of Glenwood Canyon. Even though the caves were eventually closed, private expeditions discovered more caves over the years.

Reopened to the public in May 1999, and almost immediately honored by being designated as "One of the Top Ten Caves in the U.S." by USA Today, the caves offer several levels of touring. The Family Tour covers a distance of half a mile and takes approximately two hours. Participants make their way through subterranean caverns, grottos, and a maze of corridors; visit a cliffside balcony with panoramic views of Glenwood Canyon; and stare in wonder at newly discovered areas where formations remain untouched by man. Unusual crystalline formations, unique cave bacon, and fragile soda straws enhance the Barn, a towering, five-story chamber. "Oohs" and "aahs" accent the culmination of the tour as viewers exclaim in delight at the glittering stalactites and gleaming stalagmites that line the entire length of the Kings Row cavern.

For those in your family who crave adventure, there is the Wild Tour, consisting of a three- to four-hour journey to rarely visited areas deep within the caves. Cavers are provided with necessary equipment, including lighted helmets. Participants must be age 13 or older. This is a challenging undertaking, and a previous tour of the Fairy Caves to observe how your children react to caving is highly recommended before venturing on this one.

Besides the cave tours, many activities have been added. First, there's the thrill of riding the Iron Mountain Tramway up to the top of Iron Mountain. The ride takes about ten minutes and, during the summer, there is often a line, so allow extra time for a wait. Kids can test a variety of interactive learning experiences at Discovery Rock, and some or all probably will be tempted to try out the Climbing Wall and the Alpine Coaster, Zip Line, and Giant Swing thrill rides. The younger kids can pal up with Mom, Dad, or an older sibling if they are a bit reticent about going it alone.

Who could resist the Bungee Trampoline and the opportunity to flip, flop, fly, soar and somersault like an expert gymnast before being brought back to safety via the bungee cord?

The very day it opened, the 4-D Theater, became an instant hit. Special effects, interactive seats and surround sound make viewers feel as though they are actually part of the movie. The films are terrific for all ages. You and your kids will travel along with an endearing little turtle on his epic journey from the freezing Antarctic to warm tropic waters, plunge headfirst into the depths of a haunted gold mine, and take a thrilling ride over snow-blanketed mountains and across rickety, dilapidated bridges.

The Lookout Grille, providing fantastic panoramic views serves items ranging from hamburgers to quesadillas and fish and chips. There's a kid's menu, too.

Bring caps, sweaters, and jackets. The cave temperature consistently remains at fifty-two degrees Fahrenheit. Elevation is 7,100 feet.

Canyon Bikes (all ages)

125 Center Dr., #2; (800) 439-3043; www.canyonbikes.com. Open Memorial Day through Labor Day, 8 a.m. to 8 p.m.; off-season, 9 a.m. to 5 p.m. $$$–$$$$.

These folks specialize in rental bikes for self-guided rides along the Glenwood Canyon bike trail that include a detailed, printed map to the route, bike locks, helmets, and packs. If your children are small, you can rent Burley trailers and trailer bikes here, too.

Where to Eat

Daily Bread, 729 Grand Ave., downtown; (970) 945-6253. Open Mon through Fri 7 a.m. to 2 p.m., Sat 8 a.m. to 2 p.m., Sun 8 a.m. to noon. Closed Mon during winter. Nine varieties of bread, puffy fragrant cinnamon rolls, and fantastic granola—all made here—are just a few reasons why Daily Bread has such loyal customers. There are always lots of families. Count on a crowd on weekends. $

Where to Stay

Because the Hot Springs Pool is such a draw, Glenwood Springs hotels, especially those nearest the pool, fill quickly during summer. Many Colorado families return year after year. Make reservations early.

Caravan Inn, 1826 Grand Ave. (CO 82); (970) 945-7451 or (800) 945-5495; www .caravaninn.com. Located only one mile from the Hot Springs Pool and close to many restaurants and shops, this motel is ideal for families. Amenities include suites with kitchenettes, rooms with microwave ovens and refrigerators, cable TV with HBO, a hot tub and outdoor swimming pool during summer months, a guest laundry, e-mail and high-speed Internet, and **free** deluxe continental breakfasts. Children age 12 and under stay **free.** $–$$$

Hot Springs Lodge, 415 East 6th St.; (970) 945-6571 or (800) 537-7946; www.hotsprings pool.com. If you're planning to spend your time in the Hot Springs Pool, the Lodge can't

be beat for location. Right across the street from the pool, you can walk back and forth easily; no need to join the parade looking for a parking place. Another bonus—Lodge guests receive passes for the pool, unlimited access to the therapeutic mineral pools, and a continental breakfast.

Many rooms have refrigerators, and there are laundry facilities—always appreciated by those with kids. $$$–$$$$

Hotel Colorado, 526 Pine St.; (970) 945-6511 or (800) 544-3998; www.hotelcolorado .com. Sleep where U.S. presidents have slept! Theodore Roosevelt and William Taft were guests here. So was Al Capone. In business more than a hundred years and now a National Historic Landmark, the Hotel Colorado is a good stop whether you stay here or not. Walk through the grand lobby and check out the legendary birthplace of the "Teddy Bear." Gift shop, restaurant, and Legends Trading Company are open to the public. If you plan to spend the night, perhaps you'd like to call ahead to reserve a family room: two bedrooms connected by a bathroom. $$$–$$$$

For More Information

Glenwood Springs Chamber Resort Association, 1102 Grand Ave.; (970) 945-6589; www.glenwoodchamber.com.

Aspen

The well-known resort community of Aspen is located on CO 82, 40 miles southeast of Glenwood Springs.

Walk down Main Street in Aspen and you are apt to glimpse at least one celebrity. Stay in one of the luxury hotels and frequent the ski slopes, and you will run into several. Stroll out of the main shopping area just a few blocks, however, and you'll be in a small-town neighborhood of mining-era Victorian houses.

Once a rowdy silver-producing town, Aspen fell into near ruin with the crash of the silver market in 1893. The present-day glitz and glamour are still tinged with a bit of the town's rough-and-tumble past—and that's the charm of Aspen.

Aspen in Summer

Although Aspen may be best known for its stellar ski slopes and winter beauty, its summer season also has lots to offer outdoor enthusiasts—hiking, fishing, mountain biking, rafting, backpacking, llama trekking, golfing, tennis, jeep tours, and music festivals, to mention a few.

On the Mountain

The town is surrounded by four outstanding ski mountains: Aspen Mountain, Aspen Highlands, Tieback/Buttermilk, and Snowmass; www.aspenchamber.org. Besides world-class downhill skiing, the resort community offers outstanding cross-country skiing, snowshoeing, dogsledding, and sleigh rides. And then there are Sno-Cat tours, snowmobiling, ice climbing, ice-skating, and ice fishing. The ski schools provide lessons for all skill levels. The Camp Aspen/Snowmass group lessons program offers instruction for children as young as 3 years old. Nursery care is available for those age 8 weeks to 4 years old. Children as young as age 3 can participate in snowboarding group lessons.

Where to Eat

Boogie's Diner, 534 East Cooper Ave.; (970) 925-6610. Open for lunch and dinner. This casual restaurant features generous portions at affordable prices. $–$$

Art on the **Corner**

This unique outdoor art show, located in Grand Junction's Downtown Shopping Park, hosts a variety of sculptures from many artistic approaches. Sculptors loan their work for one year. All pieces, featuring some of the country's best artisans, are for sale. The city purchases one piece each year for its own collection. **Free.**

Dinosaur **Hiking Trail**

Rabbit Valley (970-244-3000), located 30 miles west of Grand Junction on I-70, features a 1½-mile "Trail through Time," a self-guided walking tour rich in fossils. Several species of dinosaurs, including Apatosaurus, diplodocus, and brachiosaurus, have been found in Rabbit Valley.

Scientific research is ongoing here, and you can see paleontologists at work during the summer months (best to phone to confirm days and times). The iguanodon fossils discovered here in 1982 are considered the oldest of this type ever found.

Main Street Bakery Café, 201 East Main St.; (970) 925-6446. Good, inexpensive meals. Great bakery for picking up snack items for later. $

Where to Stay

Stay Aspen–Snowmass Central Reservations, (888) 649-5982; www.stayaspen snowmass.com.

For More Information

Aspen Chamber Resort Association, 425 Rio Grande Place; (970) 925-1940 or (800) 670-0792; www.aspenchamber.org.

Aspen Skiing Company, (800) 908-5000; www.ski.com.

Grand Junction

Grand Junction is located toward the western edge of the state along I-70, southwest of Glenwood Springs. With a population of approximately 33,000, the town is family friendly, and the area is teeming with wonderful attractions and activities. The streets are easily maneuvered; a downtown, outdoor pedestrian mall makes shopping a pleasure; and tree-shaded residential neighborhoods lend a comfortable, down-home atmosphere to the city.

Lincoln Park (all ages)

North Avenue and 12th Street; (970) 254-3842. Pool is open daily late May through Labor Day. Call for "open swim" hours. $–$$.

If the kids need a break from car travel, this city park is a great place to get rid of the wiggles. It has picnic tables under shade trees and an outdoor pool with a 351-foot water slide.

Cross Orchards Historic Site (all ages)

3073 F Rd.; (970) 434-9814; www.museumofwesternco.com. Open mid-Apr through mid-Oct, Tues through Sat, 9 a.m. to 4 p.m. $.

Once one of the largest apple orchards in the state, from 1896 to 1923, this farm features self-guided tours through the remaining orchard to the six-sided summer house and through the pantry, kitchen, dining room, and sleeping quarters of the workers' bunkhouse. Meander over to the old barn and you are likely to see brown-eyed mules, pigs, and a few turkeys, chickens, and ducks. Docents in period clothing answer questions and explain the history of the farm. Sit for a while under a shade tree or on the bunkhouse porch, try one of the cook's hot-from-the-oven cookies, visit the blacksmith in his work shed, and stop by to watch as the carpenter creates simple old-fashioned wooden toys. Lovely flower beds grace the grounds, and a picnic area is perfect for those who choose to bring along their lunch. And don't forget the Country Store for gift items and locally produced food products.

Where to Eat

Fiesta Guadalajara, 710 North Ave., Grand Junction; (970) 255-6609. Open Mon through Thurs 10 a.m. to 11 p.m.; Fri and Sat 11 a.m. to 11 p.m.; Sun 11 a.m. to 9:30 p.m. Taking into account that authentic Mexican cuisine combines the exotic and satisfying flavors of Spanish and Native-American cultures, Fiesta Guadalajara serves its guests creative, tasty dishes by incorporating regional ingredients with traditional techniques. The service is friendly and the atmosphere is definitely "south of the border." $–$$

Where to Stay

Country Inns of America, 718 Horizon Dr., Grand Junction; (970) 243-5080 or (800) 990-1143; www.countryinnsgj.com. Guest laundry, a swimming pool, and a wading pool make these accommodations popular with families. Apartment-style rooms with one, two, and three bedrooms available. $$–$$$$

For More Information

Grand Junction Visitor and Convention Bureau, 740 Horizon Dr.; (800) 962-2547; www.visitgrandjunction.com.

Colorado National Monument Visitor Center and Bookstore, (970) 858-3617; www.nps.gov/colm/supportyourpark/book store.htm. Open every day except Christmas 9 a.m. to 5 p.m.; Memorial Day through Labor Day 8 a.m. to 6 p.m. **Free** audiovisual program shown continuously.

Grand Mesa

Billed as "The World's Largest Flat-Topped Mountain," the Grand Mesa encompasses 300 lakes stocked with rainbow, lake, and brook trout; mile upon mile of hiking trails; and bear, deer, and elk viewing. The 10,000-foot-high plateau comprises 53 square miles of aspen groves, pine forests, and spectacular valley views. Located 23 miles east of Grand Junction off I-70, the **Grand Mesa Visitor Center** (970-856-4153) or (970-874-6600) is open from 9 a.m. to 5 p.m. most days throughout the summer.

Fruita

Located just west of Grand Junction, off I-70.

Dinosaur Journey (ages 4 and up)

On CO 340, just south of I-70 at exit 19, (550 Jurassic Ct.); (970) 858-7282 or (888) 488-3466; www.museumofwesternco.com. Open daily year-round, summer: 9 a.m. to 5 p.m. daily; winter: Mon through Sat 10 a.m. to 4 p.m.; Sun noon to 4 p.m. $–$$.

If you come anywhere close to Grand Junction, a stop at this fascinating museum is an absolute must. This is one of those attractions that is worth going out of your way to experience.

Prepare your littlest ones by telling them to expect growls and roars and giant (some are full-size) moving dinosaurs with big teeth and huge claws. Then turn them loose and anticipate an argument when it's time to leave.

Kids love this place. The 22,000-square-foot museum encompasses remarkably realistic, robotic reproductions of dinosaurs, including a Utah raptor called "The Super Slasher" in the process of eating another dinosaur and a gigantic, fuzzy, long-furred, long-tusked woolly mammoth. Perhaps the most popular with kids is the dilophosaurus from the early Jurassic Period that periodically spits a stream of "venom" toward squealing kids. Children can make dinosaur footprints in wet sand with plastic dino feet, trace shapes of prehistoric beasts onto paper with crayons, watch as little plastic dino babies hatch from their eggs (all the while chirping and looking anxiously from side to side), and sweep away sand to expose simulated bones hidden in a large tray. Also a big hit with kids is the earthquake simulator, where they stand on a surface that shakes and quakes while the sounds of an earthquake rumble around them.

Colorado National Monument

Take the Fruita exit off I-70 and follow the signs leading to the west entrance; (970) 858-3617; www.nps.gov/colm/index.htm. $$.

This 20,000-acre natural museum of geologic splendor—featuring sheer-walled canyons, arched windows, rock spires, massive domes, and natural monoliths—provides peaceful

Dino **Find**

In 1993, during a Family Dino Camp session sponsored by Dinosaur Journey, a 14-year-old resident of Boulder, Colorado, discovered an egg from an armored *Mymoorapelta maysi*. It was the first egg ever found in the Mygatt–Moore Quarry. The egg was thoroughly studied by the world's foremost expert on dinosaur eggs, Dr. Karl Hirsch, at the University of Colorado–Denver.

sanctuaries for visitors. Desert bighorn sheep, coyotes, bobcats, mountain lions, mule deer, antelope, squirrels, and rabbits call this majestic place home. You are likely to see canyon wrens, turkey vultures, ravens, and, hopefully, the magnificent golden eagle.

Two good hikes for families with younger children are the Window Rock Trail, an easy, ½-mile round-trip ramble over level ground; and Otto's Trail, a gently sloping, 1-mile round-trip walk. Use caution at overlooks and steep drop-offs.

Annual Events

JANUARY

International Snow-Sculpture Championships, Breckenridge, late Jan; (888) 251-2417; www.gobreck.com/townevents. Skilled artisans come from around the world to compete in this event. Plan to stay for several days so that you can see the sculptures in the making and in their magnificent finished state. **Free.**

JUNE

Strawberry Days, Glenwood Springs, mid-June; (970) 376-3756; www.strawberry daysfestival.com. Colorado's longest running civic celebration began as a one-day picnic and developed over the years into an almost weeklong celebration. There's a Kidsfest, a parade, live music, craft and food booths, and a carnival. Reserve lodging far in advance for this one.

JULY

Steamboat Springs Cowboy Roundup Days, Steamboat Springs, early July; (970) 879-1818. This family-friendly event has been an ongoing tradition since 1876, when only a few settlers and Native Americans attended. The festival includes an all-you-can-eat flapjack feed, footraces, a small-town-style parade, a PRCA ProRodeo, and a grandiose fireworks display.

Dinosaur Days, Grand Junction, mid-July; (970) 242-0971 or (800) 962-2547. This celebration includes a "Kids' Day at the Dinosaur Quarry" when youngsters can dig for replica fossils. Other events include a parade with floats depicting a prehistoric theme, the Stegosaurus Stomp Street Dance, and a Shoppasaurus Sidewalk Sale. Some events **free.**

DECEMBER

Christmas Market, Georgetown, early Dec; (303) 569-2840. During the first two full weekends in Dec, Georgetown welcomes the Christmas season with an old-fashioned outdoor celebration in the European tradition. This traditional Christmas celebration includes appearances by St. Nicolas, horse-drawn wagon rides, High Tea at Grace Hall, Santa Lucia Children's Procession, Christmas historic museum tours, **free** holiday entertainment, and hot roasted chestnuts. **Free.**

Southwestern Colorado

I n southwestern Colorado you will find the state's highest concentration of ancient Native American ruins, an abundance of small, friendly towns, and superb wilderness areas for outdoor recreation. This region also boasts excellent skiing, premium rafting, and legendary excursion trains.

Buena Vista

This small town, a favorite of outdoor enthusiasts, is located on US 24, north of US 50, about a two-hour drive southwest of Denver.

TopPicks in Southwestern Colorado

- **Bachelor–Syracuse Mine Tour,** Ouray
- **Cumbres & Toltec Scenic Railroad,** Antonito
- **Durango & Silverton Narrow Gauge Railroad,** Durango and Silverton
- **Great Sand Dunes,** Alamosa
- **Hiking, picnicking, skiing,** Crested Butte
- **Jeeping,** Ouray
- **Mesa Verde National Park,** Cortez
- **Ouray Hot Springs Pool,** Ouray
- **Trimble Hot Springs (pool and park),** Durango
- **Vallecito Lake,** Bayfield

SOUTHWESTERN COLORADO

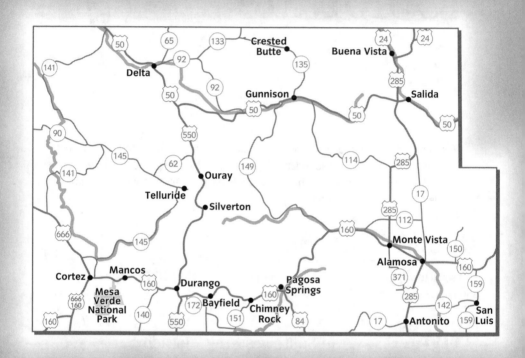

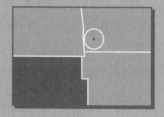

River Rafting

According to Mark Twain's *Huckleberry Finn*, "We said there weren't no home like a raft, after all. Other places seem so cramped and smothery, but a raft don't. You feel mighty free and easy and comfortable on a raft."

A great way to share in Huck's enthusiasm for rafting would be to run the Arkansas River, and the very best place to access the river is at Buena Vista. From exhilarating, wild white-water rafting to leisurely float fishing, you will "feel mighty free and easy and comfortable" on the Arkansas.

The Buena Vista area is home to numerous rafting outfitters. It is important, however, to choose your outfitter carefully. Inquire about the experience of the guides. Ask how long the operation has been in business and if the company is licensed with a government agency. Do those in charge seem to take passenger safety seriously, and are your questions being answered carefully? Call the **Colorado River Outfitters Association** at (303) 229-6075 for advice and more information or visit www.croa.org.

Where to Eat

K's Dairy Delite, 223 South US 24; (719) 395-8695. Open Mar to mid-Nov. "People live for K's to open in the spring." That's what residents say about this Buena Vista favorite. Stop in for a cone—vanilla, chocolate, or twist. There's also a fast-food menu and plenty of local flavor. $

Casa del Sol, 303 North US 24; (719) 395-8810. Open daily, May through Sept, for lunch and dinner. Also open Thurs through Mon for lunch and dinner through winter months. Traditional Mexican cuisine served in a charming setting attracts a loyal crowd, so reservations are advised. Dine inside or in the courtyard. $–$$$

Salida

South of Buena Vista, US 24 and CO 291 lead to the small town of Salida.

Mount Shavano Fish Hatchery and Rearing Unit (all ages)

7725 County Rd. 154 (½ mile northwest of Salida); (719) 539-6877. Open daily 7:30 a.m. to 4 p.m. Guided tours during the summer; self-guided tours during the winter. Free.

If you've ever wondered where all those kokanee salmon and rainbow, cutthroat, brook, and brown trout that you keep pulling out of Colorado's rivers, lakes, and streams come from, you might want to visit this hatchery. One of sixteen propagation units maintained by the Colorado Division of Wildlife, it hatches more than six million trout and salmon eggs each year and produces approximately 375,000 pounds of fish annually.

Kids can buy packets of fish food to feed the fish and obtain **free** posters and pamphlets here. Wildlife books and videos are available for purchase. There are self-guided tours (or guided tours upon request).

Centennial Park and Salida Hot Springs (all ages)

410 West Highway 50; (719) 539-6738; www.salidarec.com. Open Mon through Fri 6 a.m. to 9 p.m.; Sat 10 a.m. to 9 p.m.; Sun noon to 9 p.m. $–$$.

Centennial Park is home to the Salida Hot Springs, featuring a wading pool, a shallow pool, and a 4- to 10-foot-deep, 25-meter pool with two lap lanes. Collected underground and piped in from the mountains 5 miles away, the odorless, hot mineral water flows continuously into the various pools. Centennial Park also has tennis, volleyball, and basketball courts; horseshoe pits; a playground; and picnic tables.

Gunnison

Located west of Salida on US 50, the town of Gunnison, home to Colorado's Western State College, is surrounded by 1,600,000 acres of the Gunnison National Park, with more than 700 miles of trout streams.

Jorgensen Park and PacMan Lake (ages 3 and up)

Open daily. Free.

Jorgensen Park's PacMan Lake allows kids age 14 or younger to fish free without a fishing license, and they may keep as many as four fish. The lake is stocked during the first week in June every year. Also at the park are two half-pipes for the skateboarders in your family.

Gunnison Pioneer Museum (ages 4 and up)

At the east end of Gunnison, on US 50; (970) 641-4530; www.gunnisoncrestedbutte.com/activity/pioneer-museum. Open Mon through Sat 9 a.m. to 5 p.m. and Sun 1 to 5 p.m., Memorial Day through Sept. $–$$, children 5 and younger free.

Your children are sure to enjoy traipsing through the ca. 1905 schoolhouse, the old post office, antique car museum, and the dairy barn with a hayloft. They can see a vintage narrow-gauge train engine, gondola, boxcar, livestock car, and caboose.

Curecanti National Recreation Area (all ages)

Along concurrently running US 50 and CO 92, between Gunnison and Montrose; (970) 641-2337; www.nps.gov/cure. $$$.

The Curecanti National Recreation Area encompasses 53 miles of the Black Canyon of the Gunnison and the 12-mile-long Black Canyon of the Gunnison National Monument, a spectacular gorge cut deep into the landscape over a two-million-year period of time by the raging Gunnison River.

Within the recreation area, 20-mile-long Blue Mesa Lake provides excellent fishing for kokanee salmon and brown, rainbow, Mackinaw, and brook trout. Those who fish these waters regularly say that the prime fishing times are early morning and late evening, when the fish are feeding, and that flies usually bring good results in the evening. Shore fishing is best in late spring and summer, when the lake levels are at their lowest. When the lake rises the fish are found in the deeper middle portion of the lake. A Colorado fishing license is required for all persons age 16 or older. You can purchase a license at the marina or at area sporting-goods stores.

Many opportunities exist in the Curecanti National Recreation Area for hiking, camping, picnicking, and boating. Kids can earn Junior Ranger status by completing an activities booklet and interviewing a park ranger. They will receive an award certificate and a Junior Ranger badge.

For brochures and more information about the Curecanti National Recreation Area, write to or phone **National Park Service,** 102 Elk Creek, Gunnison, CO 81230; (970) 641-2337.

Crested Butte

Approximately 28 miles north of Gunnison, CO 135 dead-ends in the middle of Gunnison National Park at the historic town of Crested Butte and the ultramodern Crested Butte Mountain Resort. Located only 3 miles apart, the two communities are complete opposites. Crested Butte is an enchanting, ca. 1870 former coal-mining camp with Victorian storefronts, art galleries, excellent restaurants, and charming boutiques. Crested Butte Mountain Resort boasts state-of-the-art skiing, luxury accommodations, and first-class amenities.

Summertime in Crested Butte

During summer Crested Butte blossoms with exceptional hiking along paths bordered by acres of more than 300 species of wildflowers. The Colorado state legislature has proclaimed Crested Butte the official Wildflower Capital of the state.

If your family enjoys mountain biking, there is bound to be a trail exactly right for your combined expertise levels. No need to transport your bikes to a trailhead, though, because you can take off in just about any direction from the center of town and find historic, scenic, easy, or challenging biking trails at the end of the street.

Other warm-weather activities include white-water rafting, horseback riding, four-wheeling, ghost-town exploring, hot-air ballooning, and horse-drawn carriage rides. Crested Butte is home to the Mountain Bike Hall of Fame.

Chairlift Rides (all ages)
Daily, mid-June through Aug, 9:30 a.m. to 2:30 p.m. $$$ for an all-day pass; children under 6 free.

Two high-speed quad lifts whisk summer guests up the mountain. The Keystone Lift will also take your bikes. At the top you'll find hiking/biking trails and picnic areas. Or just ride round-trip, enjoying the spectacular scenery.

High-Altitude **Hints**

Parents are reminded that in Colorado, altitude will play an important part in your vacation. At Crested Butte you are at an elevation of more than 9,000 feet, and it may take a little time for your children to adjust. Recommendations include drinking much more water than usual, wearing sunscreen and sunglasses, and taking it easy the first day.

Hiking (all ages)

For a list of more than 20 hiking trails, including directions, distance, and difficulty, check out Crested Butte's Web site at www.visitcrestedbutte.com. This Web site also gives some great guidelines you should know before heading out.

Mountain Biking (ages 8 and up)

Rent equipment at the base of the mountain to enjoy a day of riding for beginners and intermediates.

Winter on the Mountain

If summers are spectacular in Crested Butte, then winters would have to be considered divine. When frosty-white snow ladens the roofs and hems the windowsills of the town's winsome little Victorian cottages, the ski slopes at Crested Butte Mountain Resort beckon. With an elevation of 12,162 feet at the summit and 9,375 feet at the base and with fourteen lifts, including two high-speed detachable quads, the resort prides itself on tempting skiers of all levels. In fact, Crested Butte Mountain Resort leads the state in teaching first-time skiers.

An extensive children's program is maintained here. The nursery accommodates babies up to six months old and has an infant-to-teacher ratio of two-to-one. Those age 6 months to potty-trained are provided with appropriate activities supervised by highly qualified early-childhood professionals. For the potty-trained to age 7 years, a typical day includes snow play, structured activities, and rest time for those who require a nap. The learn-to-ski Mites program is for 2- to 3-year-olds, and the Miners program teaches kids ages 4 through 7 to ski through an innovative teaching system that lets your child move through a series of stations at his or her own pace while mastering the basics of balance and how to ride the lifts.

Where to Eat

Donita's Cantina, 330 Elk Ave.; (970) 349-6674; www.donitascantina.com. Donita's serves dinner only. Hours vary greatly according to weather conditions, seasons and holidays. Phone ahead. This is the best Mexican fare in town, perhaps for miles around. No reservations taken except for groups of ten or more, so it's best to plan to dine early to beat the crowd. $–$$

Bubba and Betty **Bear**

Your whole family will want to meet Bubba and Betty Bear. Fuzzy, huggable Bubba and Betty stand 7 feet tall and can ski like Olympic downhillers. Crested Butte's official mascots and comedians, Bubba and Betty live in an igloo near the Children's Ski Center. Kids are welcome to drop in to play with Bubba and Betty whenever the bears are at home. They also have a clubhouse on the deck of the Twister Warming House where they visit with children and fans during lunchtime.

Bubba and Betty love hanging out with kids and skiing Crested Butte Mountain Resort's slopes. Although they are a lovable, cuddly pair, it's not easy to keep up with them when they decide to hit the "Extreme Limits." On the steeps, Bubba and Betty are two very "extreme bears."

If you spend your Christmas holidays at the resort, you'll see Bubba and Betty in their Santa and Mrs. Claus suits handing out candy canes to all skiers. You also will find them in the gift shops on T-shirts and as cloned stuffed animals.

Bubba and Betty's beginnings are somewhat of a mystery, but legend has it that during the installation of the Paradise high-speed quad lift, an engineer came upon a massive piece of ice. Being a conservative soul, he decided to drag the slab to the Paradise Warming House to be recycled into ice cubes for beverages.

As the ice began to melt, however, two magnificent polar bears slowly emerged, opened their eyes, and smiled from ear to ear when they spotted some children skiing nearby.

Bubba and Betty Bear make skiing fun for kids. Through fun, the resort hopes to entice more children to give skiing a try.

Where to Stay

Mt. Crested Butte Vacations, P.O. Box 5700, Mt. Crested Butte, CO 81225; (970) 349-2222 or (888) 945-3356; www.skicb.com. $$$–$$$$

For More Information

Crested Butte–Mt. Crested Butte Visitor Center, 601 Elk Ave.; P. O. Box 1288, Crested Butte, CO 81224; (970) 349-6438 or (800) 545-4505; www.cbchamber.com.

Gunnison–Crested Butte Tourism Association, 202 East Georgia, Suite B, Gunnison, CO 81230; (800) 852-2859; www.gunnison crestedbutte.com.

Delta

Known more for corn, potatoes, and onions than as a tourist destination, Delta is a relatively undiscovered stop for travelers. Located between Grand Mesa and the Uncompahgre Plateau are orchards, wineries, and miles of interesting back roads to explore. As you walk or drive around town, take note of the colorful murals depicting the area's history, ring bells from the collection at the Delta Museum, and stop for cinnamon rolls at the Amish bakery.

Confluence Park (all ages)

At US 50 and CO 92. Open daily, dawn to dusk.

You'll all enjoy this 265-acre multirecreational park. Confluence Lake is regularly stocked and has a wheelchair-accessible fishing dike. An island accessed by bridge, a sandy swim beach, an instructional pond for learning and practicing water sports, and picnic sites along the lake make this a popular summertime spot. Many come for the pageants, concerts, dances, and theater productions in the amphitheater.

Let your kids out of the car for a quick break at the skateboard park. Or try the 5 miles of trails (all wheelchair and stroller accessible) that wind through the park along the Gunnison and Uncompahgre Rivers and Confluence Lake. Interpretive signs highlight the wildlife—beavers, eagles, and blue herons—along the way.

Bill Heddles Recreation Center (all ages)

In Confluence Park; (970) 874-0923. Open daily year-round, Mon through Fri 6 a.m. to 9:30 p.m., Sat 8 a.m. to 8:30 p.m., and Sun noon to 5:30 p.m. $.

Indoor swimming pool, therapeutic pool, tot pool—all great family attractions after an active day or if less-than-perfect weather keeps you inside. There's also a sauna, weight room, two gyms, racquetball courts, and a snack bar.

Where to Eat

Daveto's, 520 Main St.; (970) 874-8277. Open Tues through Sat 11 a.m. to 9 p.m. for lunch and dinner. Nothing fancy here, but the home-cooked Italian dishes are worth a stop. Try the white pizza. $–$$

Where to Stay

The Fairlamb House Bed & Breakfast, 700 Leon St.; (970) 874-5158; www.fairlamb bb.com. John and Elizabeth graciously welcome families to their beautifully restored 1906 home. Enjoy cold lemonade, spicy salsa, and chips while your kids play in the fenced backyard. Resident dog Nori will want to join in. Breakfast includes just-out-of-the-oven muffins, fresh fruit, and Elizabeth's special pancakes. $–$$

Telluride

The mountain town of Telluride, on CO 145, is a National Historic District and has a reputation for having a festival of some sort nearly every weekend throughout the summer. From bluegrass to jazz, hot-air ballooning to mountain biking, and wine to mushrooms, there always seems to be something to celebrate in Telluride. And for those who can find nothing to pay homage to, there is an annual "Nothing Festival" held in mid-July.

The Telluride Gondola (all ages)
(970) 728-2711. Open daily 7 a.m. to 12 p.m. Free.

"The g" is the only transportation system of its kind in North America. This high-speed gondola links the town of Telluride with the Mountain Village. It operates year-round and is absolutely **free** to foot passengers. Ride it for transportation or ride just for fun—it takes fourteen minutes. Some cars are wheelchair accessible and welcome four-footed friends as well.

Historic Walking Tour (all ages)
Downtown. Free.

Not as boring as it sounds, this is a self-guided walk through town. The walking tour is printed in the *Official Visitor's Guide*, available at the visitor center. Learn some history of this Victorian mining town and get oriented to today's Telluride. Along the way you'll pass the old town jail, which is now the library (stop in for story hour), and the infamous Butch Cassidy Robbery Site. Too bad it doesn't include Robert Redford!

Town Park (all ages)
At the east end of Pacific Avenue; (970) 728-2173; www.telluride.com. Free.

Everything you'd ever want in a park and more! It's worth a stop for the playground alone, but there's also a stocked fishing pond; a skateboard ramp; tennis, volleyball, and basketball courts; and a nine-hole disc golf course. Two great hikes, the San Miguel River Trail and Bear Creek Trail, start here.

If you want to stay longer at the park, there are forty-seven campsites. They're on a first-come, first-served basis; no reservations accepted.

Imagination Station. This outstanding community-built playground lives up to its name. Your kids will have a ball here on great climbing equipment and swings installed on a soft base of wood chips. The design is one of a kind.

Kids Base Camp. Kids 12 weeks to 12 years old can join in the arts and crafts, dancing, swimming, and playtime during this program which offers full-day, half-day, or hourly sessions. The camp is available during both summer and winter. For more information, call (970) 728-2514.

Just **Hop On**

Telluride operates a **free** shuttle bus down its main street (Pacific Avenue) to the town gondola station and back every fourteen minutes.

Swimming Pool (all ages)

In Town Park (970) 728-9919. Open Memorial Day through Labor Day, Tues through Fri 1 to 5:30 p.m.; weekends 10 a.m. to 6 p.m. $.

Lifeguards are on duty. Adult lap swim held twice daily.

Sledding and Tubing (all ages)

Town Park. Open daily, daytime only, weather permitting. Free.

Bring your own sled or tube to Firecracker Hill. If yours didn't fit in the suitcase, there's a hardware store in town that sells what you need.

Ice Skating (all ages)

In Town Park and on Mountain Village Pond; (970) 728-2173. Daily, until dark, Dec through Feb, weather permitting. Free.

Bring your own skates or rent them at local ski shops. There's a warming hut with a fireplace for those using the outdoor rink. Skating outside seems like more fun but when the temperature keeps falling lower and lower, the indoor rink looks better and better. Schedules are posted for evening hockey and broomball games.

Bridal Veil Falls (all ages)
East of downtown.

Its 450-foot drop makes Bridal Veil the highest unbroken waterfall in Colorado. You can hike or bike 2 miles on Bear Creek Trail or drive. Parking at the base of the falls is limited.

Hiking and Biking (all ages)

For information call Norwood Ranger Station, (970) 327-4261. Free.

Wildflowers in mid-July and fall colors at Sept's end are the high points. Many trails can be accessed right from town. Telluride Ski Area offers additional choices from the gondola at Station San Sophia. Maps are available at shops in town.

Bear Creek Preserve

Access the Bear Creek Trail here. At this 320-acre preserve, owned by the Town of Telluride, children ages 5 to 12 can earn their Junior Ranger Certificate. Take a hike with the Bear Creek Ranger, help with a project in the preserve, and complete the Bear Creek Activity Book.

San Miguel River Trail

This unpaved trail follows the San Miguel River through town and along the valley floor. The easy path is popular with walkers, runners, bikers, and in-line skaters. Beavers, musk-rats, and birds live along the willow-lined river.

Skiing (ages 3 and up)

565 Mountain Village Blvd.; (970) 728-7533 or (800) 801-4832; www.telski.com. $$$$.

Telluride is a full-service ski area. Children's ski lessons begin at 3 years old, snowboarding lessons at age 7. Child care (no skiing) is available for children two months to 3 years. All programs require reservations. Check on bargain family packages offered Jan through mid-Feb.

Where to Stay

Both the town and Mountain Village can accommodate families in hotels, inns, and condominiums, budget-minded to luxury. More than 95 percent are within 3 blocks of a lift or the gondola.

Central Reservations, 700 West Colorado Ave.; (970) 728-3041 or (888) 605-2578; www .visittelluride.com.

For more information

Telluride Visitors Services, (970) 728-3041; www.telluride.com. Telluride's official Web site. Visit for additional news on events, festivals, activities, and lodging.

Know the Skier's Responsibility Code

The National Ski Patrol, the Professional Ski Instructors of America, and the National Ski Areas Association officially endorse this list of rules.

Always stay in control in order to be able to stop or avoid other people or objects.

People ahead of you have the right of way. It is your responsibility to avoid them.

You must not stop where you obstruct a trail, or are not visible from above.

Whenever starting downhill or merging onto a trail, look uphill and yield to others.

Always use devises that help prevent runaway equipment.

Observe all posted signs and warnings. Keep off closed trails and out of closed areas.

Prior to using any lift, you must have the knowledge and ability to load, ride and unload safely.

Ouray

Ouray, on US 550 northeast of Telluride, prides itself on being a family town. Founded in 1876, it was settled by miners and prospectors but was never a tent city. By 1886 it had a school, several churches, a hospital, a four-star hotel, a smattering of restaurants, and several hardware and clothing stores. The focus was on families then, and it still is.

Affectionately called "Switzerland of the Rockies" by locals, and rightly so, this charismatic mountain town is flanked by the rugged San Juan Mountains. Deer, elk, bears, and rabbits inhabit these once-sacred hunting grounds of the Ute Indians.

There's a children's and beginner's ski hill with a **free** rope tow on 3rd Avenue, at the south end of town. A favorite spot of local kids, it is open daily after school and on weekends and holidays at no charge. There also is a **free** sledding hill on 5th Street.

Jeeping (age 4 and up)
(800) 228-1876 or (970) 325-4746; www.ouraycolorado.com. $$$–$$$$.

Excursions aboard roofless, sideless jeeps provide thrilling adventures along narrow gravel roads to ghost towns at elevations of 8,000 feet and above, and even to the crest of the Continental Divide.

Ouray Ice Park (ages 5 and up)
In town on the Camp Bird Mine Road. Phone for information, (970) 325-4288; www.ouray icepark.com. Free.

This park offers ice climbing and instruction, an advanced cross-country skiing course, hiking and snowshoeing trails, and wonderful wintertime photo opportunities.

Ironton Park X-Country Ski Park (ages 5 and up)
South of town on US 550. Free.

You can bring your kids here to teach them to cross-country ski on the beginner's trails. Trails for more advanced skiers also are available. All at no charge.

Ouray Hot Springs Pool and Park (all ages)
On US 550 at the north end of town; (970) 325-7073 or (800) 228-1876. Open daily 10 a.m. to 10 p.m. during summer; shorter hours during spring, fall, and winter. $–$$.

Once a gathering place for the Ute Indians, who enjoyed their revitalization and healing powers as early as the 14th century, Ouray's natural hot springs are still providing enjoyment to those who come to swim or just soak away stress and pamper themselves. Channeled from deep beneath the San Juan Mountains, the hot springs water now fills this beautiful 250-foot-by-150-foot oval, with lap lanes, diving area, children's splash pool, and a 104-degree "hot tub" soaking section.

The bathhouse contains showers, hair dryers, a playpen and changing table for infants, and secure lockers. You can purchase a sandwich and beverage at the SnackHaus and browse in the gift shop. The fitness center has workout equipment and offers weight training and aerobics classes. The adjacent park features a running track, a playground, tennis and basketball courts, and picnic tables.

Bachelor–Syracuse Mine Tour (ages 6 and up)

On County Road 14, about a fifteen-minute drive from Ouray; (970) 325-0220; (888) 227-4585; www.bachelorsyracusemine.com. Open daily from mid-May to mid-Sept, 9 a.m. to 4 p.m.; open longer hours during the middle of summer. $$–$$$.

If you've always wanted to go deep into a gold mine, here's your chance. You will board a mine train (called a "trammer") and travel a horizontal 1,800 feet into Gold Hill, accompanied by a thoroughly trained guide who more than likely once made his living mining at the Bachelor–Syracuse Mine. You will see rich veins of silver and other mineral deposits, visit the work areas to see how explosives are used (there are no explosives underground at this time), and hear the legends and lore of this very successful mine. Bring your camera (and your flash unit), because it's okay to take photographs. Take along a sweater or jacket, as the temperature within the mine is very cool.

Either before or after your mine tour, consider learning how to pan for gold and perhaps "strike it rich" in a stream that flows directly from the mine. An instructor will show you how the old-timers found many a gold nugget in this area. You can keep any gold that you find. The fee is $5 per person for a forty-five-minute session and includes use of a gold pan.

Treasure Chest Gift Shop. If your prospecting luck isn't so good, there are ore specimens from local mines and gold, silver, and gold-nugget jewelry for sale in the mine's Treasure Chest gift shop. Or if you want to strike out on your own following your gold-panning lesson and trial run, you can also purchase gold-panning supplies in the gift shop.

Outdoor Café. The Bachelor–Syracuse Mine's Outdoor Cafe serves reasonably priced, all-you-can-eat breakfasts, and barbecued lunch items. The cafe is open during mine-touring hours. $

Where to Eat

Bon Ton Restaurant, 426 Main St.; (970) 325-4951 or (866) 243-1502; www.stelmo hotel.com; (also number for St. Elmo Hotel). Open year-round for dinner. For that special night out, this is probably your very best choice. Terrific Italian and continental cuisine, wonderfully prepared and beautifully presented. This is the perfect place for your children to put into action those good manners they've worked so hard on. $–$$$

The Outlaw, (970) 325-4366; www.outlaw restaurant.com. Reservations required. Guests are picked up between 5:30 and 6 p.m. at their hotels and motels and transported by four-wheel-drive vehicles to the Outlaw campsite. Open nightly "from when the snow melts to when the snow flies," which loosely translates to early June to late Sept. For a memorable cookout, join the gang at the Outlaw for an evening of great food and congenial camaraderie beside a roaring canyon creek. Your twelve-ounce rib-eye steak will be cooked over coals just the way you like it and served with fried potatoes, corn on the cob, baked beans, salad, and fresh-baked brown bread. All the while, your watermelon will be chilling in the stream. Following dinner, enjoy a mug of camp coffee while your kids toast marshmallows over the campfire. $$–$$$$

Timberline Deli, 803 Main St.; (970) 325-4958. Open daily year-round for lunch and dinner. Serves sandwiches, soups, bagels, and desserts. They also prepare box lunches to go. $

Where to Stay

Alpenglow Condominiums, 215 5th Ave.; (970) 325-4664 or (866) 739-4917; www.alpen glowouray.com. Open year-round. Offers one-, two-, and three-bedroom units with fully equipped kitchens, private decks, fireplaces, and cable TV. Off-season rates and package deals available. $$–$$$$

Ouray Victorian Inn, 50 3rd Ave.; (970) 325-7222 or (800) 846-8729; www.victorian innouray.com. This motel-style lodging has spacious rooms, two hot tubs, and a playground. Guests receive a **free** buffet breakfast. $$–$$$$

For More Information

Ouray Chamber Resort Association, P.O. Box 145, Ouray, CO 81427; (970) 325-4746 or (800) 228-1876; www.ouraycolorado .com.

Silverton

Located south of Ouray on US 550 where it meets CO 110, the historic mining town of Silverton is so picturesque that it has been used as a setting for several motion pictures. Portions of *A Ticket to Tomahawk, Maverick Queen,* and *Across the Wide Missouri* were shot here. A walk through both the business and the residential districts reveals numerous structures and homes built in the 1880s.

Christ of the Mines Shrine

The route to the Christ of the Mines Shrine is an easy walk, perfect for a picnic lunch hike. Beginning at the end of West 15th Street, southwest of town, the path is a gradual uphill climb. From the shrine you will have a wonderful panoramic view of Silverton.

The statue was constructed in Italy of Carrara marble and stands as a tribute to all those who worked the area mines. It also serves as a reminder of the town's mining heritage. Local volunteers built the alcove that houses the beautifully carved, twelve-ton figure of Christ.

Old Hundred Gold Mine Tour (ages 6 and up)

From Silverton's courthouse turn right on County Road 2, and go east 4 miles to Howardsville. Turn right onto County Road 4 and go ¼ mile, then take the left fork up County Road 4-A for ¾ mile to the mine. Watch for blue-and-white mine-tour signs located along the way and at road forks starting ½ mile from Silverton on County Road 2; (800) 872-3009; www.minetour.com. Open daily mid-May through mid-Oct, 10 a.m. to 4 p.m. $$–$$$.

A tour of this mine takes participants approximately ⅓ mile into the heart of Galena Mountain via a mine tram. Visitors don yellow slickers and white hard hats, travel to the Main Level Station, and then walk on level, gravel paths through well-lighted tunnels into the center of an actual gold vein. You will see a drilling demonstration performed by a miner using a hammer and steel and a "jackleg" air drill.

With the purchase of a tour ticket, your kids can pan for gold at no extra charge at the sluice box. They get to keep any gold they happen to find. Bring a lunch to eat in the covered picnic area. Drinks and snacks are available on the premises. The gift shop sells mine souvenirs, crystals, minerals, books, and postcards. The tour lasts approximately fifty minutes. Bring a jacket, because the underground temperature is a steady 48 degrees. Video and still cameras with flash are welcome. You'll no doubt want a photo of your children in their slickers and hard hats.

Where to Eat

Grand Imperial Hotel and Grumpy's Restaurant, 1219 Greene St.; (970) 387-5527; www.grandimperialhotel.com. This historic hotel, built in 1882, serves breakfast, lunch, and dinner year-round. A honky-tonk pianist entertains diners during summer months. $$–$$$

Where to Stay

Grand Imperial Hotel, 1219 Greene St.; (970) 387-5527; www.grandimperialhotel .com. Comfortable rooms in a variety of sizes; centrally located. $$–$$$

For More Information

Silverton Chamber, P.O. Box 565, Silverton, CO 81433; (970) 387-5654 or (800) 752-4494; www.silvertoncolorado.com.

Durango

US 550 runs south into US 160 at Durango. This friendly town, with a population of approximately 16,000, makes an ideal jumping-off point for an almost endless number of family-oriented activities.

Animas Valley Museum (all ages)

3065 West 2nd Ave.; (970) 259-2402; www.animasmusem.org. Open mid-May through Oct, Mon through Sat 10 a.m. to 6 p.m.; Nov to Apr Tues through Sat 10 a.m. to 4 p.m. Minimal charge for adults. Children age 7 through 12, $1; children age 6 and under are free.

Kids can see what going to school was like in the late 1800s and early 1900s at this museum. They can also view a large collection of stuffed animals from that same era.

Durango & Silverton Narrow Gauge Railroad (D&SNG) (all ages)

479 Main Ave.; (970) 247-2733 or (877) 872-4607; www.durangotrain.com. Excursions are available year-round (except during Nov, when they make repairs) with numerous schedules. Phone for a brochure describing the various dates, times, and rates. Reservations are highly recommended. $$$–$$$$.

During your stay in Durango be sure to allow a full day to ride this vintage train through the spectacular San Juan Mountains from Durango to Silverton. Climb aboard one of the open or closed coaches for a three-hour journey to Silverton, spend two hours in town, and then take a three-hour ride back to Durango. Small kids, rocked to sleep by the swaying train, often snooze all the way back. You also have the option of either staying over in Silverton for the night and returning to Durango the following day or riding the motorcoach to Silverton and returning to Durango the same day by train. During high season one train (with restroom) each day is equipped for wheelchairs. Keep in mind that this is a coal-fired steam train, so you are likely to obtain a few black smudges before the day is over. It's best to wear washable, dark clothing. If you choose to ride in the open cars, be sure everyone in your family has sunglasses, as much for protection from the occasional flying cinder as from the sun.

Soaring Tree Top Adventures (age 8 and up)

964 County Rd. 200; (970) 769-2357; www.soaringcolorado.com. Open daily, mid-May to mid-Oct. Price includes round-trip transportation from Durango to the soaring site in private, first-class passenger cars aboard the historic Durango & Silverton Narrow Gauge Railroad, lunch, a five and one-half-hour soaring experience, an eco-tour, equipment, guides and gear. $$$$.

Consisting of 24 spans, 34 platforms, and 1.2 miles of zip line, Soaring Tree Top Adventures is said to be the safest, highest, and largest treetop-touring course in the United States. Participants glide over and through aspen groves, and through old-growth ponderosa forest, and criss-cross over the Animas River on zip lines ranging in length from 56 to 1,400 feet. Unlike most courses that are made of 7–19 galvanized steel wrap cables, this one is constructed of helicopter-grade 19–7, reverse-wrap stainless steel (platforms, cables, turnbuckles, etc.) that will not rust. The smooth, stainless steel cables avoid the loud squealing noise emitted by the cheaper galvanized steel used by some other courses, thus making your flight through and above the trees the most thrilling, yet serene and peaceful, adventure one can imagine.

Great care was taken in designing the course to be completely eco-friendly. Old growth ponderosa pines support the platforms in such a way that no screws, bolts or hooks penetrate or harm any trees in any way.

"Sky Rangers" (guides with 40 hours of wilderness first-aid training and advanced rappelling and climbing skills) are on hand to assist zip liners with every need, always emphasizing safety. There is a Sky Ranger at every platform to receive guests and send them on to the next thrill.

If some members of your family plan to go zip lining and others would prefer to keep their feet on the ground, there are two less expensive options to consider: Option one

End of **the Trail**

North of Durango 3⁴⁄₁₀ miles, on the edge of the San Juan National Forest, is the Junction Creek Trailhead—official end of the Colorado Trail. For hikers completing the entire trek (more than 450 miles) from suburban Denver, it's a place for final pictures at the trail sign, crazed celebration, or retrospective contemplation.

allows Day Guests to travel with their group on the train, exit the train at the zip line course, follow along through the forest to take photos during the first spans, eat lunch with the group and walk along the river while enjoying their wilderness encounter. Option two participants can stay on the train when the others get off at the zip line site and continue on to the lovely western town of Silverton to shop and sightsee, returning to Durango later on the same train that will stop to pick up the other members of their party at the soaring site.

Guests who have thrilled to zip lining with Soaring Tree Top Adventures have ranged in age from 5 to 90 years old. Each one of us knows our own children better than anyone else. We have an obligation to determine for them if they would enjoy this activity and at what age each child would feel comfortable and ready to participate. Some kids would be ready at age 6; others would still not be ready at age 12. You must decide.

Outlaw Tours (all ages)
555 Main Ave.; (970) 259-1800 or (877) 259-1800; www.outlawtours.com. Open year-round. $$$$.

Enjoy superb mountain scenery while professional guides in specialized four-wheel-drive vehicles take you on a great adventure. Their combination jeep and train trip includes a van ride to the Silverton area, followed by four hours of jeeping to ghost towns and mines. They stop to do a little prospecting with the kids—"90 percent of the time we find rocks with silver or gold in them." Brunch is served along the way; then there's one-and-one-half hours of free time in Silverton before your return ride on the Durango & Silverton Narrow Gauge Railroad. Your kids may enjoy the train ride much more if it's only one-way.

Outlaw Tours rents bicycles and will deliver you and the bikes (adult size, child size, carriers, and tagalongs) to a location that ensures that your ride is both scenic and down-hill. Jeeps and all-terrain vehicles are also available for rent.

During winter months, take a sleigh ride or a tour on a snowmobile. They offer one-, two-, three-, and four-hour rides.

Durango ProRodeo Series (all ages)
At the La Plata County Fairgrounds, 25th Street and Main Avenue; (970) 247-2308. During June through July, days and times often vary. It would be best to call ahead for an up-to-date schedule. $–$$$.

For rootin' tootin' buckin' bronco action, consider attending one of Durango's weekly summer rodeos. The Durango ProRodeo Series, a professional event sanctioned by the PRCA and the WPRA, features clowns, bull riders, trick riders, and a Wild West show. A barbecue at 6 p.m. precedes the rodeo. Cost for the barbecue ($) depends on the items ordered.

Community Recreation Center (all ages)

2700 Main Ave.; (970) 375-7300. Open daily year-round, Mon through Fri 5:30 a.m. to 9:30 p.m., Sat 8 a.m. to 8 p.m., and Sun 8 a.m. to 6 p.m. $.

This recreation center has a family emphasis, with a gym, lap pool, indoor track, racquet-ball, game room, climbing wall, cafe, and babysitting.

Trimble Hot Springs (all ages)

6475 County Rd. 203 (off US 550 north); (970) 247-0111 or (877) 811-7111; www.trimblehot springs.com. Hours vary significantly, depending on the weather, time of year, and type of activity. Call or visit their Web site. Scheduling is kept up-to-date on the site. $$–$$$$.

For extensive swimming and spa facilities, head for the Trimble Hot Springs. Here you will find an Olympic-size outdoor pool; a second, jetted outdoor pool; private indoor tubs; toddler gymnastics classes, sauna, massage, yoga, t'ai chi, and a picnic area with nicely landscaped grounds, tables, and a volleyball court.

They usually stay open late, so keep this in mind as an after-dinner activity. You'll all sleep well.

Where to Eat

Carver's, 1022 Main Ave.; (970) 259-2545; www.carverbrewing.com. Open daily 6:30 a.m. to 10 p.m. Local vote says this is the best breakfast and bakery in town, and it's easy to agree. Bet you can't leave without buying a loaf of bread! Besides outstanding a.m. food, there's homemade soup, and Carver's is also a microbrewery. This is a good choice any time of the day. Weekend breakfast draws a crowd. Bring a back-up sack of toys to keep little ones busy in case there is a wait. $

Gazpacho, 431 East 2nd Ave.; (970) 259-9494; www.gazpachorestaurant.com. Open daily Mon through Sun 11:30 a.m. to 10 p.m. Brightly colored furniture and Mexican folk art decorate the rooms of this multilevel restaurant. Steaming hot platters of smothered burritos, enchiladas, and stuffed sopapillas satisfy even super-hungry teens. $

Ken and Sue's Place, 636 Main Ave.; (970) 385-1810; www.kenandsus.com. Open for lunch Mon through Fri 11 a.m. to 2:30 p.m. Open for dinner Sun through Thurs 5 a.m. to 9 p.m.; Fri and Sat 5 p.m. to 10 p.m. Ken and Sue understand what it's like dining with children—they have three. A graduate of the Culinary Institute of America, Ken dishes up New American cuisine with a flair—Aunt Lydia's meat loaf with red wine gravy, smashed potatoes, sautéed spinach, maple-mustard-glazed 12-ounce New York strip steak, giant onion rings, and red and bleu smashers with blistered asparagus. The shaded patio is a popular summertime dining spot. $$–$$$$

Olde Tymer's Cafe, 1000 Main Ave.; (970) 259-2990. Open for lunch and dinner. They never alter their menu much. "We're a locals' place, and we know the traditions of Olde

Tymer's should remain." Those traditions include Durango's best burger. You can also enjoy soups, salads, New Mexican green chili, and daily specials. $

Seasons Rotisserie and Grill, 764 Main Ave.; (970) 382-9790. Open daily for dinner, Mon through Fri for lunch. If your family is ready for a slightly more upscale dinner, Seasons is a great choice. Creative menu, delicious dining. The staff is very family friendly. $$

Serious Texas Bar-B-Q, 3535 North Main Ave.; (970) 247-2240; www.serioustexas.bbq .com. Open daily 11 a.m. to 9 p.m. Great barbecue items and lots of napkins for sticky little fingers. A relaxed and casual setting. $

Skinny's Grill, 1017 Main Ave.; (970) 382-2500; www.durango.travel/dining/skinnys-grill. Extensive menu, including vegetarian choices, children's menu, fresh baked bread, burgers, fajitas, and award-winning buffalo burgers. $

Where to Stay

Leland House, 721 East 2nd Ave.; (800) 664-1920; www.rochesterhotel.com. This inn nicely accommodates families. Its six attractive suites with small kitchens, private baths, bedrooms for parents, and living rooms with sofa sleepers for children are perfect for families that want to pack picnic lunches, heat baby bottles, and indulge in bedtime snacks. The Leland House is conveniently located close to shopping, restaurants, and the Durango & Silverton Narrow Gauge Railroad station. A complimentary breakfast is served across the street at the Leland House's sister inn, the Rochester Hotel. $$$–$$$$

Strater Hotel, 699 Main Ave.; (970) 247-4431 or (800) 247-4431; www.strater.com. You'll get an automatic history lesson along with comfortable rooms in a great location. This Victorian-era hotel combines period decor with modern amenities. Be sure to check out the saloon. $$–$$$$

For More Information

Durango Area Chamber of Commerce and Durango Area Tourism Office & Visitor Center, 111 South Camino del Rio; P.O. Box 2321, Durango, CO 81302; (970) 247-3500 or (800) 525-8855; www.durango .org. Open 8 a.m. to 5 p.m. Mon through Fri.

Purgatory/Durango Ski Area

Located 25 miles north of Durango, this ski area offers both summer and winter activities. Before the snow flies, your children can engage in a wide range of attractions, including chairlift rides, minigolf, an alpine slide, diggler mountain scooters, disc golf, a bounce castle, guided nature hikes, a climbing wall, a bungee trampoline, horseback riding, a hike with a llama, a mechanical bull, and a Durango Mining Company Adventure. For a complete description and the cost of each activity, visit their Web site at www.durango mountainresort.com and click on summer activities/village.

During the winter months this ski resort doesn't attract many glitzy, designer-tog types. Perhaps that's because it is so down-home friendly. The family-oriented resort receives an average of 300 inches of dry powder snow and many days of sunshine each year, resulting in outstanding skiing. It has a vertical drop of 2,029 feet and a good mix of novice, intermediate, and expert runs. You will find child care for youngsters ages 2 through 12. Ski lessons are available for children ages 3 or older.

The **Nordic Center at Purgatory,** located across the street from the resort, features touring and telemark lessons on more than 15 kilometers of groomed trails. Rental equipment is available. There is a nominal trail fee, call (970) 385-2114 for additional information.

For More Information

Purgatory/Durango Ski Area, #1 Skier Place, Durango, CO 81301; (970) 247-9000 or (800) 982-6103; www.durangomountain resort.com.

Mancos

Rimrock Outfitters (ages 5 and up)
12175 County Rd. 44; (970) 533-7588; www.rimrockoutfitters.com. $$$–$$$$.

This is the place to do cowboy things—breakfast rides or dinner rides on horseback or horse-drawn wagon, one- to four-hour rides, or all-day trail rides. Perry and Lynne Lewis and their Rimrock Outfitters also offer one- to five-night pack trips. Gentle horses, good grub, singing around a campfire. And when the snow flakes fall, bundle up in your hats, coats, scarves, and snuggies, and hop aboard one of the ranch's nifty sleighs.

For More Information

Mancos Valley Information Center, 235 Main St., Mancos, CO 81328; (970) 533-7434; www.mancosvalley.com.

Town of Mancos, 117 North Main Ave.; P. O. Box 487, Mancos, CO 81328; (970) 533-7725.

Cortez

Continue west 17 miles from Mancos on US 160 to its junction with US 666 to reach the historic city of Cortez.

Known as the "Archaeological Center of the United States," Cortez sits on the edge of the high Sonoran Desert surrounded by villages once occupied by the Ancestral Puebloan People, who dominated the Four Corners area (where Colorado, Utah, Arizona, and New Mexico meet).

Long before the Spanish explorers discovered this region, the Ancestral Puebloans carved entire communities into the sandstone cliffs and along the mesas. Their culture

Read 'em **Cowpoke**

Here's an entertaining, educational children's book that both sons and daughters can relate to: *Yipee-Yay: A Book about Cowboys and Cowgirls* by Gail Gibbons.

was present until about the year A.D. 1300, when the Ancient Pueblo People suddenly disappeared from the area.

Mesa Verde National Park (all ages)

Off US 160, 7 miles east of Cortez; (970) 529-4465 or (800) 449-2288; www.nps.gov/meve. Open daily year-round; camping, lodging, and gasoline available seasonally. Most of the ruins are inaccessible during winter months. Phone for information regarding current road conditions, schedules, rates, and weather. $$ per car. Balcony House and Cliff Palace tours, $.

At Mesa Verde National Park, a designated World Heritage Site, you can see some of the world's largest, best-preserved cliff dwellings, including Cliff Palace and Balcony House. Be sure, however, to stop at the Far View Visitor Center (located within the park, 15 miles from the entry gate) to pick up your entry ticket, or you won't be allowed to enter the ruins. Obtain a map here, too, so that you can plan your exploration.

Cliff Palace, the largest cliff dwelling in the world, is reached via a ½-mile hike. Balcony House requires a bit of determination to reach, as it is located high up in the cliff. To explore this ruin you must climb 20-foot ladders and crawl through a small tunnel to gain access. Take heart, though. If you aren't into strenuous exercise, or if you have small children who can't maneuver ladders and rough trails, you can visit the many surface ruins or take the short walk that leads from the museum at Chapin Mesa Cliff Dwellings and Park Headquarters to Spruce Tree House in the canyon below. Here you can enter an excavated kiva to imagine the religious ceremonies that once took place inside this structure.

There are many possible routes to take throughout the park and numerous dwellings to explore, some with multiple rooms and chambers. Allow plenty of time for this adventure. There is so much to see here. Kids 4 to 12 years old can participate in the Junior Ranger Program. Details available at the Visitor Center.

Ute Mountain Ute Tribal Park (ages 6 and up)

On US 160/666, 20 miles south of Cortez; (970) 565-3751 ext. 282 or (800) 847-5485; Visitor Center (970) 749-1452; www.utemountainute.com. Tours offered Apr through Oct, weather permitting; reservations required. $$$$.

The Ute Mountain Tribal Park encompasses approximately 125,000 acres and is part of the Ute Mountain Ute Indian Reservation. The tribe has set aside an area on their reserve for the preservation of the Ancestral Puebloan culture. Hundreds of cliff dwellings and surface ruins plus historic Ute wall paintings and ancient petroglyphs exist here. Many of the dwellings compare in size and complexity with those in Mesa Verde, and a select number of these have been stabilized for visitation. In order to protect this fragile environment, the park is accessible by guided tour only.

The park is operated as a primitive area, so there are no food, lodging, or other services available. Full- and half-day tours begin at Tribal Park Headquarters. One- to four-day mountain bike and backpacking trips also can be arranged.

This attraction is best suited for families with older children because the park can be a physically challenging experience, with several long ladders to descend and vigorous climbs necessary to reach some of the ruins. You may use your own car for transportation or pay an extra $5 per person for transport via van. Be sure the gas tank is full, because the main ruins are 40 miles off the paved roads. Tours are to remote areas, so bring adequate water, food, and comfortable clothing.

Cortez Cultural Center & Museum   (all ages)
25 North Market St.; (970) 565-1151; www.cortezculturalcenter.org. Center open year-round; dances daily (rain or shine), Memorial Day to Labor Day, 7:30 p.m.; cultural program at 8:30 p.m. Free.

On summer evenings in Cortez, the pulsating beat of Native American drums draws tourists to the dance ring a block north of downtown. Native American families in handmade dance regalia share their heritage, traditions, and stories. Your family can join travelers from around the world in the Friendship Dance.

After the dances, move inside for storytelling or demonstrations by sand painters, pottery artists, code talkers, and flute players. If you arrive a little early, walk through the museum and exhibits. The gift shop here has items affordable to youngsters' allowances.

Notah Dineh Trading Company and Museum   (ages 6 and up)
345 West Main St.; (970) 565-9607 or (800) 444-2024; www.notahdineh.com. Open year-round, Mon through Sat 9 a.m. to 6:30 p.m. Free **admission.**

An excellent selection of authentic Native American jewelry, pottery, and Navajo rugs is featured in this spacious gallery. Shelves encircling the sales floor hold an outstanding beaded-basket collection. (Items are very expensive, so you might want to have that "don't touch" discussion before entering the store.) Downstairs, the highlight of the museum is a 12-by-18-foot rug, one of the largest known Two Grey Hill weavings. More interesting to youngsters is the depiction of an early trading post with lots of artifacts to identify.

A Goat's **Tale**

Set in the Southwest, this delightful story explains the process of rug making to children. Geraldine the Goat tells her own tale in *The Goat in the Rug,* by Geraldine (as told to Charles Blood and Martin Link).

Four Corners **Monument**

Tourists drive 40 miles into the high desert just to take a photo at this location. Here is the only place in America where four states—Colorado, Utah, Arizona, and New Mexico—meet. Watching as photographers arrange their family in all four states can be pretty entertaining. Native Americans from the area sell souvenirs, art, and snacks.

Anasazi Heritage Center (ages 6 and up)

On CO 184, 10 miles north of Cortez and 3 miles west of the town of Dolores; (970) 882-5600; www.co.blm.gov/ahc/hmepge.htm. Open daily year-round, 9 a.m. to 5 p.m. Mar through Oct, and 10 a.m. to 4 p.m. Nov through Feb. $.

Here, history dates back to about a.d. 600. The center contains one of the world's major collections of artifacts that once belonged to the Ancestral Puebloans. Set into the hillside near the 12th-century Dominguez and Escalante ruins, the facility includes a large exhibit hall, a 104-seat theater, a gift shop, and a gallery for temporary exhibits. Area archaeologists suggest that an introductory visit here will enrich your Mesa Verde experience.

View an entertaining orientation film, then head to the interactive exhibits. Use a floor weaving loom, microscopes, and computer stations. Make new discoveries at the Discovery Drawers. Grind just a handful of corn with a metate to understand the effort required to feed a family. Try your skill at tree-ring dating or microanalysis of pottery shards.

A ½-mile walk takes you up the hill to the Dominguez and Escalante ruins. The paved path is wheelchair accessible, but assistance is advised due to the trail's steepness. Along the way, signs identify native plants and their uses. A self-guiding booklet is available. Shaded tables make this a good picnic spot. The Anasazi Heritage Center also serves as headquarters for Canyons of the Ancients National Monument. Information available at the front desk.

Lowry Pueblo Ruins (all ages)

From US 666 at Pleasant View (20 miles north of Cortez), follow signs 9 miles west. (970) 882-5600; www.blm.gov/co/st/en/fo/ahc/archaeological_sites/lowry_pueblo.html. Open daily, weather permitting. Free.

A country road, passing hay fields, and row upon row of pinto beans growing in the rich red earth, leads away from crowds and organized tours to ruins in a different setting. There are no cliffs here. Structures sit atop a knoll with views extending into neighboring states. Inhabitants grew crops of corn, beans, squash, and tobacco; hunted small game; and made tools from animal bones. Skilled stoneworkers built a community of forty rooms and eight kivas (ceremonial chambers). The Great Kiva is one of the largest ever discovered. In the Painted Kiva you'll find ancient plastered walls decorated in bold designs. There is no museum or rangers on site; self-guiding booklets are available near the ruins. Facilities include picnic tables, fire pits, and latrines.

"Archaeology Detour" (ages 10 and up)

Crow Canyon Archaeological Center, 23390 Road K; (970) 565-8975 or (800) 422-8975; www .crowcanyon.org. All-day program offered June through Aug, Wed and Thurs, while other more extensive programs are offered year-round. Advance registration required. $$$$.

Come here first, then go to Mesa Verde. In this one-day workshop for families, you'll learn about the Ancestral Puebloans who lived in this area hundreds of years ago. Spend a half day at an active excavation, learning by walking through the site and talking to archaeologists. You'll be ready for the great lunch waiting back at Crow Canyon Center. In the afternoon you'll learn how to think like an archaeologist through hands-on activities. Then tour their lab and visit the Curation Room to see artifacts previously excavated by Crow Canyon staff. When the day is done, you'll agree with them, "It's not what you find, it's what you find out."

Crow Canyon Archaeology Center is a nonprofit organization dedicated to research and education. They also offer weeklong Family Archaeology Adventures for moms and dads with teens. In addition, their staff leads Family Travel Adventures in the Four Corners region, and they operate a very popular program for school groups.

Where to Eat

Francisca's, 125 East Main St.; (970) 565-4093; www.franciscasrestaurantinc.com. Open Mon through Fri 11 a.m. to 10 p.m. Features northern New Mexican-style dishes freshly prepared. Try the sopapillas served with local honey. $–$$

Main Street Brewery & Restaurant, 21 East Main St.; (970) 564-9112. Open daily for dinner. A relaxed western atmosphere, family-size booths, good service, and a game room for kids accompanied by an adult. A wide-ranging menu offers items from traditional sandwiches to bratwurst burritos. Warm apple strudel salutes the owner's German heritage. $

Nero's, 303 West Main St.; (970) 565-7366; www.subee.com/neros/home.html. Open daily for dinner. Full Italian menu with nightly specials. Enjoy summertime covered-patio dining. $–$$$

Where to Stay

Lebanon Schoolhouse B&B, 24925 County Rd. T, Dolores, 7 miles north of Cortez; (970) 882-4461 or (877) 882-4461; www .lebanonschoolhouse.com. This fully restored 1907 schoolhouse makes a great base for family adventure in the Four Corners area. Children especially enjoy the bedroom with its sleeping loft. Common areas include games, puzzles, a large selection of reference material about the area, television, and an antique pool table. Guests have kitchen privileges, and a full breakfast is included. Outside, the original schoolyard merry-go-round awaits a spin from energetic youngsters. You can walk to the nearby llama ranch. $$–$$$

For More Information

Cortez Area Chamber of Commerce, 928 East Main St.; (970) 565-3414; www.cortez chamber.com. The center is open daily, May through Sept, 8 a.m. to 6 p.m.; Oct through Apr, 8 a.m. to noon and 1 to 5 p.m.

Mesa Verde Country Visitor Information Bureau, (800) 253-1616; www.swcolo .org.

Bayfield

Heading east from Durango, US 160 leads to the small community of Bayfield.

Vallecito Lake (all ages)

15 miles north of Bayfield on County Road 501, off US 160; (970) 247-1573; www.vallecito lakechamber.com.

If you ask Coloradans where Vallecito Lake is, more than a few would have to admit that they don't know. Yet this beautiful mountain lake is easily accessed. With snow-capped mountains in the distance and surrounded by forests, dude ranches, lodges, and camp-grounds, the secluded lake and valley offer an abundance of outdoor enjoyment: hiking, boating, four-wheeling, horseback riding, and just plain relaxing. As for fishing, Vallecito Lake holds the state record for northern pike—thirty pounds, one ounce, 48¼ inches. It formerly held the state record for German brown trout—twenty-four pounds, ten ounces, and 37½ inches. Full-service marinas can provide you with boats, motors, and bait.

Chimney Rock

Chimney Rock is located on US 160, 16 miles east of Bayfield and 17 miles west of Pagosa Springs.

Chimney Rock Archaeological Area (ages 6 and up)

All tours originate at the entrance cabin located 5 miles east of Chimney Rock on US 160, then 3 miles south on CO 151; (970) 883-5359; www.chimneyrockco.org. Open mid-May through Sept. Tours depart at 9:30 and 10:30 a.m. and 1 and 2 p.m. $–$$.

The mystical Chimney Rock Archaeological Area has long served as a landmark—first to missionaries, conquistadores, and prospectors and now to those seeking to view the ruins left by the Ancestral Puebloan and Chacoan residents who are thought to have lived here in the 11th century. The high mesa site includes sixteen excavated areas. The High Mesa Village and the pueblo encompass structures that have been completely excavated and others whose treasures have only been partially unearthed. Some 200 other ruins exist throughout the 6 square miles of the Archaeological Area.

Chimney Rock tours are open for guided ventures only. They are led by members of the San Juan Mountains Association, Pagosa Chapter, a nonprofit volunteer group dedicated to promoting the interpretation and protection of priceless natural and cultural resources. No reservations are required for the daytime visits.

Monte Vista

Monte Vista lies along US 160 at the intersection of CO 15.

Where to Stay

Best Western Movie Manor Motor Inn, 2830 West US 160 (2½ miles west of Monte Vista); (719) 852-5921 or (800) 771-9468; www.coloradovacation.com/motel/movie. Open year-round, but movies are shown only from mid-May to mid-Sept. If you are traveling between Chimney Rock and Alamosa, plan to spend the night in the world's only movie motel. Most of the guest rooms have picture windows that face a giant outdoor movie screen. While a few dedicated drive-in moviegoers insist on watching the film from their cars, you can stock up on popcorn from the snack bar, return to your room, prop yourselves up on bed pillows, turn up the sound on the built-in speakers, and watch the latest release. Kids bathed and already in their pajamas can nod off to sleep whenever they are ready. Only G, PG, and PG13 movies are shown. If the movie playing doesn't happen to be suitable for your children, just pull your drapes and turn on the TV. $–$$

Alamosa

US 160 joins US 285 at Monte Vista and leads east to Alamosa.

Splashland Hot Springs (all ages)

1 mile north of Alamosa on CO 17; (719) 589-6307. Open mid-May through Sept, Mon, Thurs, Fri, and Sat 9 a.m. to 9 p.m.; Tues 9 a.m. to 7 p.m.; Sun noon to 6 p.m. $.

This fun-filled complex features a geothermal-water outdoor swimming pool, a diving area, and a wading pool for toddlers. A concession stand sells snacks and beverages, and you can rent swimsuits and towels if you didn't bring them along or if you don't want to pack wet suits and towels back into the car.

Alamosa/Monte Vista National Wildlife Refuge (all ages)

4 miles east of Alamosa on US 160 and then 2 miles south to El Rancho Lane; (719) 589-4021; www.fws.gov/alamosa/index.html. Visitor Center, 9383 El Rancho Lane, Alamosa. Open occasionally Mar through Oct; closed Nov through Feb. Call ahead for schedule. Refuge is open daily year-round, sunrise to sunset. Free.

The Bluff Overlook is open to the public and offers outstanding wildlife and wildlands viewing. Here you might see raptors, waterfowl, wading birds and shorebirds, sandhill and whooping cranes, and deer and elk. Early spring (mid-Feb to the end of Mar) would be the best time to view cranes and waterfowl, late Apr through summer to see wading birds and shorebirds, late Sept to hit the fall crane and waterfowl migration, and winter (Nov through Feb) to witness eagles.

Colorado Alligator Farm (all ages)

9162 County Rd. 9 (17 miles north of Alamosa on CO 17), Mosca; (719) 378-2612; www .gatorfarm.com. Open daily 9 a.m. to 5 p.m. $–$$$, children 5 and younger free.

Alligators in Colorado, at 7,600 feet above sea level, in one of the coldest regions of the state? You bet. More than eighty alligators and millions of fish live at the Colorado

Alligator Farm in southwestern Colorado's San Luis Valley. Ah, but you don't have to worry about these gators. They truly have it made. They lounge in an outdoor pen with a geothermally heated pool kept at eighty-seven degrees, which makes it possible for the alligators to survive the cold winters. They gorge themselves on 300 to 400 pounds of fish parts each day. Happier alligators would be hard to find.

Brought to Colorado as 1-foot-long babies more than ten years ago, the gators were the ingenious idea of Erwin Young, owner of a fish-processing plant. He hoped they would be the answer to the disposal of tons of fish heads, bones, and by-products left over from his fish farm—and he was right.

Approximately 30,000 visitors tour the farm each year. Whole busloads of school kids come from several surrounding states to see the critters.

Besides alligators you will see thousands of Rocky Mountain white tilapia (a hybrid tropical perch), catfish, bass, and other species swimming in indoor and outdoor ponds. The gator farm has become a sanctuary for exotic pets such as pythons, iguanas, and tortoises. Plan to stay for several hours when you visit. You can enjoy warm-water fishing for largemouth bass, catfish, and tilapia, a picnic area, a gift shop, and several nature trails.

Great Sand Dunes National Park (all ages)

38 miles northeast of Alamosa on CO 150; (719) 378-6399; www.nps.gov/grsa. The sand dunes are accessible year-round, 24 hours a day. The visitor center's hours vary. It is usually open from 9 a.m. to 5 p.m. daily. Camping available year-round ($). Access to the national park is free for those age 15 or younger. $.

"How far away is the beach?" is the question frequently asked of attendants at the National Park Service visitor center at the Great Sand Dunes National Park. No, there's no surf for swimming near these windswept masses that sometimes rise to heights of 750 feet, making them the tallest sand dunes in North America. And there isn't any snow, although often there are skiers at the sand dunes. Bring your old (very old) skis, join the hearty individuals who don't mind sand in their hair and down their necks when they lose their balance, and glide down the surface of dunes several hundred feet high. Keep in mind that it takes a lot of effort to ascend this "mountain." There are no lifts, and for every step you take, you seem to slide two steps backward on the soft sand. Don't have any old skis that you want sandpapered by this shifting "surf"? Not to worry. Stop at a grocery store in Alamosa and pick up some large boxes to construct makeshift sleds. Hang on tight to the edges of your cardboard sled and scoot down the dunes. Your kids will love this unique experience. Or just let them run, jump, roll, and slide on these ever-changing sand sculptures.

Stop at the visitor center for information on the dunes and other park features. You can obtain brochures, books, and maps here, and rangers will help you plan your visit. If you don't have much time, you can take a short hike along the Montvill Nature Trail or the Wellington Ditch Trail or have a picnic in the picnic area. If you have two to three hours, you might want to try hiking to the top of the highest dune, splash in Medano Creek, or take a ranger-guided hike. You can even spend the night on the dunes if you first obtain a free permit from the visitor center. Those intending to camp should be advised that the eighty-eight sites are first-come, first-served. They have drinking water and flush toilets but no shower facilities. Firewood is for sale at the visitor center. Kids age 3 to 12 can participate in the Junior Ranger program and utilize the interactive exhibits at the visitor center.

For More Information

Alamosa Convention and Visitors Bureau, 610 State St., Alamosa; (800) 258-7597; www.alamosa.org.

Antonito

If you head south from Alamosa on US 285, almost to the Colorado and New Mexico border, you will reach the small town of Antonito.

Cumbres & Toltec Scenic Railroad (all ages)

(888) 286-2737; www.cumbrestoltec.com. Open daily Memorial Day through mid-Oct, with varying departure times. $$$$.

This historic excursion train travels from Antonito to Chama, New Mexico, and back. A Registered National Historic Site, the coal-fired, steam-powered train zigzags back and forth across the Colorado and New Mexico border, taking passengers over 10,015-foot Cumbres Pass, through two tunnels, and along the Toltec Gorge, which plunges 600 feet to the Los Pinos River. The Cumbres & Toltec operates the longest and highest narrow-gauge steam railroad excursion in the United States. It runs on a 64-mile segment of track built by the Denver & Rio Grande Railroad from 1875 to 1883. The line's original purpose was to carry passengers and mining supplies into the Silverton area and to bring the silver and gold out. It also carried lumber, livestock, and agricultural products originating at different points along the right-of-way.

Passengers are taken aboard at either Antonito or Chama to ride to Osier, Colorado, for lunch. They then return to their departure points by train, or they can take the complete trip between Antonito and Chama (or vice versa) and return to their starting point via air-conditioned bus. Phone for a brochure listing a timetable, ride options, and current fares. Reservations are recommended.

Where to Stay

Conejos River Ranch, 14 miles west of Antonito on CO 17; P.O. Box 175, Conejos, CO 81129; (719) 376-2464; www.conejos ranch.com. The perfect home base for those wanting to ride the Cumbres & Toltec train, the ranch consists of eight bed-and-breakfast rooms in the main lodge and eight one-, two-, and three-bedroom housekeeping cabins. The Conejos River runs through the property, and the Rio Grande National Forest surrounds it. Nearby activities include hiking, horseback riding, wildlife viewing, snowmobiling,

La Mesa de la Piedad y de la Misericordia
(Hill of Piety and Mercy)

Located on top of a mesa in San Luis is a series of stations of the cross depicting the last hours of Christ's life. Also included is a fifteenth station, representing the resurrection. The dramatic bronze sculptures found at each station were created by area resident Huberto Maestas, who has a studio in nearby San Pablo. **Free.**

cross-country skiing, and, of course, the narrow-gauge train ride. Kids delight in fishing from the stocked children's pond and feeding the ranch goats, sheep, donkeys, and horses. Ranch manager, Ms. "Shorty" Fry, shares the story about one little girl who began to cry the night before her family was to depart the ranch. When asked what was the matter, the little girl replied, "Tomorrow we have to leave here and go to Disney World." How's that for a testimonial? Open from May through Nov. A two-night minimum stay is required. The restaurant serves dinner seven nights a week at a reasonable cost. Bed-and-breakfast accommodations, including breakfast, $$–$$$; cabins, $$$–$$$$

San Luis

The small town of San Luis is accessible from Antonito by traveling north on US 285 and then turning east onto CO 142, which ends in San Luis. From Alamosa head east on US 160 and then turn south at Fort Garland onto CO 159 and continue for about 16 miles.

Established in 1851, the small village of San Luis is said to be Colorado's oldest town. Centered around the beautiful Sangre de Cristo Parish Church, the community reflects a quiet, peaceful way of life.

Where to Eat

Fabian's Cafe and Deli, on Main Street, 3 blocks from Casa de Salazar; (719) 672-0322. Breakfast and lunch served until 3 p.m. For wonderful Mexican food served in a relaxed atmosphere, stop by this family-owned restaurant. The friendly, spotlessly clean cafe serves a terrific breakfast burrito with homemade, full-flavored, but not too hot, green chili. $

Where to Stay

El Convento Bed & Breakfast, 512 Church Place; (719) 672-4223. Open year-round. This bed-and-breakfast has four guest rooms, two with kiva fireplaces, and all with private baths. $$

Annual Events

JUNE

Fat Tire Bike Week, (970) 349-6438; late June. During this festive celebration, Crested Butte hosts NORBA-sanctioned races, clinics, daily backcountry tours, bike polo, bicycle rodeo, and much more.

JULY

Cattlemen's Days, (970) 641-1501; www .gunnisonchamber.com; mid-July. Gunnison's annual Cattlemen's Days festival is said to be the oldest rodeo in the state. From horse, cattle, sheep, and swine shows to rodeos, a parade, a carnival, barbecues, and a hamburger fry, the activities are nonstop for the ten-day celebration.

Montezuma County Fair, Montezuma County Fairgrounds, Cortez, late-July–early-Aug. Exhibits, events, and judging. Phone for exact dates (970) 565-3123.

AUGUST

Escalante Days, Finders Park, Dolores. Barbecue, games, duck races, chain saw competition, mountain bike race, arts and crafts, parades. Early Aug; call for information; (970) 882-4018.

Index

Travel Like a Pro

The Cheap Bastard's Guide to
NEW YORK CITY
MORE THAN 1,000 FREE LISTINGS

100 BEST
Resorts of the Caribbean

OFF THE BEATEN PATH
VIRGINIA A GUIDE TO UNIQUE PLACES

The Luxury Guide to
Walt Disney World Resort Second Edition
How to Get the Most Out of the
Best Disney Has to Offer

shifra stein's
day trips
from kansas city
fifteenth edition

NINTH EDITION
JOHN HOWELL S III
CHOOSE COSTA RICA
FOR RETIREMENT

FUN WITH THE FAMILY
Hundreds of Ideas for Day Trips with the Kids
Connecticut

INSIDERS' GUIDE
Florida Keys
and Key West

SCENIC DRIVING
COLORADO
STEWART M. GREEN